Hegel's Philosophy of Right

Hegel's Philosophy of Right

Edited by Thom Brooks

WILEY-BLACKWELL

A John Wiley & Sons, Ltd., Publication

This edition first published 2012
© 2012 Blackwell Publishing Ltd

Blackwell Publishing was acquired by John Wiley & Sons in February 2007. Blackwell's publishing program has been merged with Wiley's global Scientific, Technical, and Medical business to form Wiley-Blackwell.

Registered Office
John Wiley & Sons Ltd, The Atrium, Southern Gate, Chichester, West Sussex, PO19 8SQ, United Kingdom

Editorial Offices
350 Main Street, Malden, MA 02148-5020, USA
9600 Garsington Road, Oxford, OX4 2DQ, UK
The Atrium, Southern Gate, Chichester, West Sussex, PO19 8SQ, UK

For details of our global editorial offices, for customer services, and for information about how to apply for permission to reuse the copyright material in this book please see our website at www.wiley.com/wiley-blackwell.

The right of Thom Brooks to be identified as the editor of the editorial material in this work has been asserted in accordance with the UK Copyright, Designs and Patents Act 1988.

Library of Congress Cataloging-in-Publication Data
Hegel's Philosophy of right / edited by Thom Brooks.
     p. cm.
   Includes bibliographical references and index.
   ISBN 978-1-4051-8813-5 (hardcover : alk. paper)
   1. Hegel, Georg Wilhelm Friedrich, 1770-1831. 2. Hegel, Georg Wilhelm Friedrich, 1770-1831. Grundlinien der Philosophie des Rechts. 3. Law–Philosophy. 4. Natural law. 5. State, The. 6. Ethics. 7. Political science. I. Brooks, Thom.
   K230.H43.A647 2012
   340'.1–dc23
                                                                                        2011024993

A catalogue record for this book is available from the British Library.

This book is published in the following electronic formats: ePDFs 9781444354225; Wiley Online Library 9781444354256; ePub 9781444354232; Mobi 9781444354249

Set in 10.5/13pt Minion Thomson Digital, Noida, India
Printed in Singapore by Ho Printing Singapore Pte Ltd

1   2012

Contents

Notes on Contributors   vii
Acknowledgments   ix

Introduction   1
 Thom Brooks

Part I Ethics   7

1 Consequentialism and Deontology in the Philosophy of Right   9
   Dean Moyar

2 The Empty Formalism Objection Revisited: §135R
   and Recent Kantian Responses   43
   Fabian Freyenhagen

3 On Hegel's Critique of Kant's Ethics: Beyond the
   Empty Formalism Objection   73
   Robert Stern

Part II Politics   101

4 Hegel and the Unified Theory of Punishment   103
   Thom Brooks

5 Hard Work: Hegel and the Meaning of the
   State in his Philosophy of Right   124
   Kimberly Hutchings

6 Gender, the Family, and the Organic State in
   Hegel's Political Thought   143
   Alison Stone

Part III Law   **165**

7 Natural Law Internalism   167
Thom Brooks

8 Hegel on the Relation between Law and Justice   180
Alan Brudner

Index   209

Notes on Contributors

Thom Brooks is Reader in Political and Legal Philosophy at Newcastle University. He is editor and founder of the *Journal of Moral Philosophy*. His research interests are in British and German Idealism, democratic theory, global justice, punishment, and theories of justice. He is the author of *Hegel's Political Philosophy: A Systematic Reading of the Philosophy of Right* (2007) and *Punishment* (2012) and editor of several books, including *Rousseau and Law* (2005), *The Global Justice Reader* (2008), *The Right to a Fair Trial* (2009), *New Waves in Ethics* (2011), and *Punishment* (forthcoming). He is currently editing a collection, *Rawls's Political Liberalism*, with Martha C. Nussbaum.

Alan Brudner is Albert Abel Professor of Law and Professor of Political Science at the University of Toronto. He is the author of *Punishment and Freedom* (2009), *Constitutional Goods* (2004), and *The Unity of the Common Law: Studies in Hegelian Jurisprudence* (1995), as well as articles on a variety of topics in legal and political theory.

Fabian Freyenhagen is Lecturer in Philosophy at the University of Essex. His research interests are in moral and political philosophy as well as in modern European philosophy (especially Kant and Adorno). He is co-investigator in the AHRC-funded Essex Autonomy Project and has published in journals such as *Kantian Review* and *Inquiry*.

Kimberly Hutchings is Professor of International Relations at the London School of Economics. She is the author of *Kant, Critique and Politics* (1996), *International Political Theory: Re-thinking Ethics in a Global Era* (1999), *Hegel and Feminist Philosophy* (2003), *Time and World Politics: Thinking the Present* (2008), and *Global Ethics: An Introduction* (2010). She is also the co-editor, with Tuija Pulkkinen, of *Hegel and Feminist Thought: Beyond*

Antigone? (2010). Her interests include the work of Kant and Hegel; international, feminist, and postcolonial ethical and political theory; and politics and violence. She is currently working on a series of co-written papers (with Elizabeth Frazer) on conceptions of the relation between politics and violence in the western tradition of political thought.

Dean Moyar is Associate Professor in the Department of Philosophy at Johns Hopkins University. He received his B.S. from Duke University and his Ph.D. from the University of Chicago. His essays have appeared in the *Journal of Moral Philosophy* and *Hegel-Studien*, among other journals. He is the co-editor (with Michael Quante) of *Hegel's Phenomenology of Spirit: A Critical Guide* (2007), the editor of *The Routledge Companion to Nineteenth Century Philosophy* (2010), and the author of *Hegel's Conscience* (2011).

Robert Stern is Professor of Philosophy at the University of Sheffield. He is the author of *Hegel, Kant, and the Structure of the Object* (1990) and *Hegel and the "Phenomenology of Spirit"* (2002), as well as of numerous papers, many of which appear in his collection *Hegelian Metaphysics* (2009).

Alison Stone is Senior Lecturer in Philosophy at Lancaster University and is the author of *Petrified Intelligence: Nature in Hegel's Philosophy* (2004), *Luce Irigaray and the Philosophy of Sexual Difference* (2006) and *An Introduction to Feminist Philosophy* (2007). She is currently working on a book on *Feminism, Psychoanalysis, and Maternal Subjectivity*, which is forthcoming.

Acknowledgments

There are several debts accumulated in the production of this collection of essays that must be recorded. First of all, my most sincere thanks must go to Nick Bellorini for his strong support of the project since the beginning, which has been crucial, as well as for his excellent advice. I must also express my special thanks to Jeff Dean and Tiffany Mok for their help at several points and, most especially, for their patience as this collection came together. My largest thanks must go to the contributors to this important volume for what are, in my view, genuinely outstanding essays that deepen and broaden our knowledge of one of philosophy's most important texts. This volume is dedicated to them – Alan, Alison, Dean, Fabian, Kimberly, and Robert – for making it all that it is. Finally, I must note that research on this book benefited from my term of research leave at both Newcastle University and the University of Oxford.

Thom Brooks
Oxford

Introduction

Thom Brooks

G. W. F. Hegel's *Philosophy of Right* is widely acknowledged as one of the most important texts in the history of moral and political philosophy. It has exercised a direct influence on several philosophical movements, such as British Idealism, communitarianism, critical theory, and Marxism. Its influence continues today through the work of several leading figures, such as Axel Honneth, John Rawls, and Charles Taylor. *Hegel's Philosophy of Right* aspires to provide the most significant collection of essays in recent years on this important text, breaking new ground across the areas of ethics, politics, and law from both historical and contemporary perspectives. This introduction will discuss the background to this project, the general arguments of Hegel's *Philosophy of Right*, and the essays included in the volume.

1 Background

Hegel's *Philosophy of Right* has received significant attention in previous important work. Perhaps the leading classic collection of essays on the *Philosophy of Right* was edited by Z. A. Pelczynski in his *Hegel's Political Philosophy: Problems and Perspectives* (1971a). This collection contained now classic essays exploring Hegel's views on ethics, punishment, the state, war, and much more (see Cooper 1971; Ilting 1971; Pelczynski 1971a, 1971b, 1971c; Shklar 1971; Verene 1971). Moreover, wide-ranging work set a clear bar for all work following afterward.

Hegel's Philosophy of Right: Essays on Ethics, Politics, and Law, First Edition.
Edited by Thom Brooks.
© 2012 Blackwell Publishing Ltd. Published 2012 by Blackwell Publishing Ltd.

There has been excellent work since Pelczynski's collections which I do not have the space to survey here, although work since has tended to have a more narrow focus whether it is on Hegel's ethics, politics, or law. The present book is the first to speak substantively to these three areas in its pages and for good reason. The *Philosophy of Right* is not merely a book that addresses ethics, politics, and law, but whose analysis is deeply interwoven with elements of each area that speak to other areas. It is therefore difficult to substantively address even the majority of the *Philosophy of Right* and its rich array of arguments by only focusing on one particular area to the exclusion of others. While this book may not address all topics, it does seek to speak across a wide range of areas concerning Hegel's *Philosophy of Right* and to cover new ground.

2 The *Philosophy of Right*: New Essays, New Insights

The full title of Hegel's text is *Groundwork of the Philosophy of Right or Natural Law and Political Science in Outline* (*Grundlinien der Philosophie des Rechts oder Naturrecht und Staatswissenschaft im Grundrisse*). This title illustrates the nature of this text: the *Philosophy of Right* is composed of outlines to Hegel's lectures for use by his students. His first lectures on ethics and politics took place during his time in Heidelberg in 1817–1818. Hegel then moved to Berlin where he lectured on these topics again in the 1818/1819 and 1819/1820 academic years before publishing his lecture outlines in 1821. It was published during a turbulent time where there was academic suppression by the then Prussian authorities, for which some contemporaries wrongly accused Hegel of supporting.[1]

The essays in this volume are divided into three sections: ethics, politics, and law. The idea is that the collection will have significant, but also provide sufficient, breadth in the range of topics treated covering a wide variety of the *Philosophy of Right*'s contents. These new essays each offer us new insights into this important work in particular and philosophical discussions more generally.

The first section focuses on ethics with contributions by Dean Moyar, Fabian Freyenhagen, and Robert Stern. Moyar addresses the relationship of Hegelian ethics with contemporary debates in value theory such as that between deontologists and consequentialists. He argues that Hegel's *Philosophy of Right* has much in common with the latter over the former (although this is not to deny several deontological "side constraints" that are also present). In fact, Hegel's value theory is both consequentialist and deontological even if consequentialist considerations may hold a certain priority.

Both Freyenhagen and Stern address the so-called "empty formalism" objection that Hegel directs at Immanuel Kant's moral philosophy. This is perhaps the most well-known criticism of Kant and the essays included here attempt to move the debate in new directions. Freyenhagen claims that the debate has thus far ended in a stalemate. He envisages several Kantian reply strategies to Hegel's criticism in a philosophical boxing match where Hegelians win a split decision on points. Stern argues that, in fact, it might be possible to bring peace to both sides in a perhaps uneasy truce. Thus, Kant's position may be made more compatible with the form of intuitionism favored by Hegel and, if so, resolve hostilities in a possible reconciliation between them.

The second section focuses on politics, with contributions by Thom Brooks, Kimberly Hutchings, and Alison Stone. Brooks argues not simply that past interpreters of Hegel's theory of punishment have mischaracterized it, but that Hegel offers a new and compelling theory called the unified theory of punishment (see Brooks 2010; forthcoming). Interpreters have previously believed that Hegel offers a retributivist theory of punishment. This view fails to consider the multifaceted nature of Hegel's penal theory. He does not merely claim that punishment should be meted only on the deserving in proportion to their wrong, not unlike many retributivist accounts, but he also claims that punishment can incorporate deterrent, rehabilitative, and expressivist elements in a unified account. This fact was not lost on British Idealists who tried to develop the unified theory of punishment further in the late nineteenth century. This view of punishment is compelling because it helps us better understand how we might provide a theory of punishment that can contain different principles of punishing within a new and coherent framework. There is a need for such a coherent theory in light of the Model Penal Code. This Code is widely influential in helping judges determine sentences, but it has often been criticized for lacking a coherent theory of how its different principles may be brought safely together. Hegel's unified theory of punishment is a welcome step in the right direction by offering just such a useful account.

Hutchings focuses on the different dimensions of ethical life present in Hegel's *Philosophy of Right*. These dimensions are explored with a view to interrelationship of logic, history, and practice in his political thought. She argues that we should take Hegel's historicism seriously in the interpretation of his work. This permits us to best assess how Hegel's work speaks to many of our contemporary dilemmas concerning political organization and the hard work of freedom in a fruitful and revealing way.

Stone considers Hegel's understanding of the family, an area of his work that has gone less explored. She notes a clear tension in Hegel's treatment. On the one hand, Hegel posits that all citizens should have opportunities for full participation in their political communities. On the other hand, this participatory sphere appears reserved for men alone. Stone argues that this latter denial of full opportunities to women is not an accident, but follows from core elements in Hegel's political philosophy. This need not mean that his philosophy is irredeemably sexist, but rather points toward the need to imagine anew his organic conception of the state in order to best spell out its egalitarian elements. Hegel's philosophy can address this problem after all, but only if we focus more clearly on the relationship between his political philosophy and his work on the philosophy of nature concerning organicism.

The third and final section focuses on law, with contributions by Thom Brooks and Alan Brudner. Brooks's essay concerns Hegel's philosophy of law. While many commentators agree that Hegel's legal philosophy was a form of natural law, they have largely failed to recognize the significant differences that Hegel introduces. Natural lawyers claim that some laws may be understood as better (or more "true") than others in relation to how well they cohere with a standard of justice. Of course, there is deep disagreement on how we determine the standard of justice. Nevertheless, all determine this standard and then apply it to help us analyze law. Hegel accepts that some laws and legal systems may be better than others according to a standard of justice. The crucial difference is that his natural law is internalist while the natural law of others is externalist. Others have a natural law externalist theory because they apply a standard of justice whose origins are external to the law. Hegel's natural law internalism is different in that the standard of justice employed is internal to law. Brooks then considers the many merits of this novel understanding of law before bowing before its demerits. The chief demerit is that it is unclear whether Hegel's natural law internalism can determine internal standards of justice with safety without spelling these standards out in advance: how can we be sure we do not find what we are looking for?

This ambiguity in Hegel's work about the relation between law and justice concerns Brudner as well. Brudner turns his attention to the question of whether Hegel systematically addresses the question of whether the concept of law does (or does not) entail the justice of law. While Hegel may appear to give several contradictory answers, we can make good progress. Brudner highlights the importance of mutual recognition and its development. Legal authority has its roots in the idea of mutual recognition: authority gains its existence from the character of recognition subjects voluntarily agree to offer. *De facto* authority is a worse form of authority because it fails to attract the voluntary mutual recognition as an authority from its subjects. The possibility of mutual recognition speaks to the importance of several different procedural elements of legality, such as generality, publicity, and clarity, that help secure recognition. There is then a different kind of inner morality from that of Lon Fuller (1969). Brudner argues that Hegel's legal thought contains resources within itself to critique authority's jurisprudential authority without the need to invoke an external standard of justice, in contrast to most other accounts of natural law. Ultimately, Hegel's legal thought positions itself in a space between that occupied by many natural lawyers and legal positivists offering an attractive picture of how we may better understand legal authority.

Together, these essays aspire to improve our understanding of Hegel's seminal *Philosophy of Right* across a broad range of topics to a new standard. Each is written for advanced students and scholars of Hegel's philosophy largely (but not exclusively) focusing on the Anglophone literature on Hegelian philosophy.

Note

1. Such accusations were levied by contemporaries such as Jakob Friedrich Fries and much criticism centered on Hegel's well-known saying, "What is rational is actual; and what is actual is rational" (*PR* 20). For helpful analyses of this saying, see *EL* and Stern 2006. For a useful discussion of the relevant historical context, see Pinkard 2001.

Abbreviations

EL   G. W. F. Hegel, *Elements of the Philosophy of Right*, ed. Allen W. Wood, trans. H. B. Nisbet. Cambridge: Cambridge University Press, 1991.

PR   G. W. F. Hegel, *The Encyclopaedia Logic: Part I of the Encyclopaedia of Philosophical Sciences with the Zusätze*, trans. T. F. Geraets, W. A. Suchting, and H. S. Harris. Indianapolis: Hackett, 1991.

Thom Brooks

References

Brooks, Thom (2010) "Punishment and British Idealism." In Jesper Rybergand J. Angelo Corlett, eds., *Punishment and Ethics: New Perspectives.* Basingstoke: Palgrave Macmillan, pp. 16–32.

Cooper, David E. (1971) "Hegel's Theory of Punishment." In Z. A. Pelczynski, ed., *Hegel's Political Philosophy: Problems and Perspectives.* Cambridge: Cambridge University Press, pp. 151–167.

Fuller, Lon L. (1969) *The Morality of Law,* rev. edn. New Haven: Yale University Press.

Ilting, K.-H. (1971) "The Structure of Hegel's *Philosophy of Right.*" In Z. A. Pelczynski, ed., *Hegel's Political Philosophy: Problems and Perspectives.* Cambridge: Cambridge University Press, pp. 90–110.

Pelczynski, Z. A., ed. (1971a) *Hegel's Political Philosophy: Problems and Perspectives.* Cambridge: Cambridge University Press.

Pelczynski, Z. A. (1971b) "The Hegelian Conception of the State." In Pelczynski 1971a: 1–29.

Pelczynski, Z. A. (1971c) "Hegel's Political Philosophy: Some Thoughts on its Contemporary Relevance." In Pelczynski 1971a: 230–241.

Pinkard, Terry (2001) *Hegel: A Biography.* Cambridge: Cambridge University Press.

Shklar, Judith N. (1971) "Hegel's *Phenomenology*: An Elegy for Hellas." In Pelczynski 1971a: 73–89.

Stern, Robert (2006) "Hegel's Doppelsatz: A Neutral Reading." *Journal of the History of Philosophy* 44: 235–266.

Verene, D. P. (1971) "Hegel's Account of War." In Pelczynski 1971a: 168–180.

Part I
Ethics

1

Consequentialism and Deontology in the *Philosophy of Right*

Dean Moyar

1

Hegel's philosophy resists our familiar ways of categorizing theories. This resistance presents a challenge for viewing Hegel through a contemporary lens, but it hardly prevents us from asking where his views fit within contemporary debates. Since conceptual distinctions are the way in which we understand the meaning of a position, a theory in which no distinctions could get a grip would be uninteresting and perhaps even unintelligible. Hegel himself appreciates this point very well, and he is among the tradition's most strident critics of the kind of philosophy of identity in which distinctions and oppositions are completely washed out. Though his conceptions of the Absolute Idea and Absolute Spirit do incorporate and thus *in some sense* overcome fundamental oppositions, Hegel has a place for many of our familiar philosophical distinctions within (and indeed as constitutive of the boundary between) the conceptual levels that characterize each part of his overall system.

In the *Philosophy of Right* two levels, "Abstract Right" and "Morality," can be roughly aligned with deontological and consequentialist types of ethical theory. These types line up with central concepts of Hegel's two levels, namely the rights of the person and the idea of the Good. Though in his ultimate view of Ethical Life Hegel does think that the two sides can be integrated, that integration is fully intelligible only once we have appreciated the distinctions that have been drawn earlier in the conceptual development.

Hegel's Philosophy of Right: Essays on Ethics, Politics, and Law, First Edition.
Edited by Thom Brooks.
© 2012 Blackwell Publishing Ltd. Published 2012 by Blackwell Publishing Ltd.

Dean Moyar

Besides illuminating some of the architectonic issues in the *Philosophy of Right*, this essay has three main goals. First, I develop an account of Hegel's conception of ethical value and its realization. Such an account is needed because, although he occasionally uses the term "value" (*Wert*) and its cognates, it is quite hard to see how to match up his discussions with the types of "value theory" discussed today. Second, I propose a way to understand Hegel's transitions in the *Philosophy of Right* in more accessible terms than we get simply by relying on his appeals to his logic and on the (often very sketchy) discussions of practical phenomena. Third, I build toward an account of individual and institutional action that sheds light on Hegel's motivations for structuring Ethical Life in the way that he does. His split between these two types of action preserves a contrast between the deontological and consequentialist approaches, even while highlighting their interdependence and showing why neither approach is adequate on its own.

In its most familiar form, the consequentialist/deontological distinction is a distinction between two ways of assessing actions. On the consequentialist model, actions are assessed in terms of the overall value that is achieved through the action. Typically the criterion is one of *maximizing* value. The value to be maximized can be conceived as a single metric, such as pleasure, or in pluralistic terms to include many different values. In either case an account of value, or a conception of the Good, is defined first, and the question of which action is right (permissible or impermissible) is answered based on which action maximizes that Good. By contrast, deontological theories aim first and foremost to specify normative principles of permissibility or impermissibility, and do not take achieving value, or bringing about certain states of affairs, as their central concern. Perhaps the most familiar deontological model is a test of the universalization of one's action (or maxim of action) to determine its rightness or wrongness. Another model is a contractualist account of principles that reasonable individuals would agree to, or not reject, in a suitably ideal contractual situation. Such theories can include an account of the Good, and can even require that individuals adopt certain ends, but typically there will be some conception of the right that serves as a constraint on action apart from the calculation of consequences.[1]

Kant's moral theory is often taken to be the main representative of deontology in the history of ethics.[2] Given how deeply Hegel's ethics is informed by his engagement with Kant, it is not surprising that Hegel should have something to say on the nature of the deontology/consequentialism split. The prima facie argument for taking Hegel to be a consequentialist is his constant emphasis on *Verwirklichung*, actualization. Some of his best-known claims in ethics are directed against conceptions of ethics that are focused on upholding a pure abstract standard of what is right against the messy realization of the Good. The pervasive role of teleology in Hegel's accounts of practical rationality would itself seem to make the case that he is a consequentialist. Yet even a cursory look at the structure of the *Philosophy of Right* suggests otherwise. The strict universality of Abstract Right comes first, while the Good comes later, and there is little to no mention of calculating or maximizing value. Given that deontologists can also require that one act to realize valuable purposes, and so can share a concern for "actualization," there is a plausible way to interpret Hegel's ethical thought as fundamentally deontological.

A few words on the common criticisms of the two types of theory will help bring out what is distinctive in the positions, and help clarify the stakes in locating Hegel's thought in reference to these positions. Consequentialists are often accused of not respecting the distinctness of persons. This leads, so the accusation goes, to the willingness of consequentialism to justify unacceptable "means" by invoking the end of maximizing overall value. Consequentialism has a hard time ruling out harming individuals for the sake of the many because it forces us to think of individual rights and moral claims as items that can be traded off against other value considerations. A similar intuition guides the famous attack by Bernard Williams that has come to be known as the "integrity objection" to utilitarianism. Williams stresses the first-personal character of agency, ridiculing the idea that our actions are somehow supposed to channel a system of value that would automatically trump the projects with which we identify in living our individual lives. The objection is that it would be deeply alienating to be forced to obey "when the sums come in from the utility network," for "we are not agents of the universal satisfaction system, we are not primarily janitors of any system of values" (Smart and Williams 1973: 116, 118). The charges are that in ignoring the separateness of persons, the consequentialist adopts an implausible moral psychology and risks real harm to our sense of agency.

For the consequentialist, one trouble with deontology is that it has to presuppose an account of value in order to secure any real *determinacy* in its demands. Far from being able to specify rightness independently of value, deontologists must bring in value considerations if their tests of univer-salization or reasonableness are to produce actual results.[3] They cannot simply *avoid* questions of value, and this leads into a second objection. To distinguish itself from consequentialism, deontology seems to require actions that *decrease the overall amount of good in the world*. Some distinctive deontological actions make the world a worse place compared to other alternatives, and a requirement to make the world worse seems at least very odd, if not downright irrational. The deontologist has to say that following some rules of right action is simply right, regardless of the consequences, and this does produce some intuitively unwelcome results. A related worry is that such theories can be *too* agent-oriented, and thus not concerned enough about the world of value beyond the issues that involve the agent's own integrity. The consequentialist will say that too much focus on integrity can lead to moral narcissism, allowing the individual to care about himself, to keep his hands clean, at the expense of other agents. The agent is in effect maximizing consequences for himself alone, for he has put undue weight on his own moral cleanliness.

To better fix the distinction, I will wrap up this section by formulating the differences between the types of theory through their views on two main issues and through their contrasting pairs of intuitions. For the first main issue, I will assume that deontological theories can be expressed in terms of value (even though the Good is not given *priority* over the Right on such accounts). What then distinguishes the two is that while the deontologist thinks of the agent as *honoring* or *instantiating* the value, the consequentialist thinks of the agent as *promoting* the value.[4] This contrast comes out most clearly when we think of a short-term violation of a value in order to promote its long-term flourishing. The deontologist might say that we should always honor the right to free speech, whereas the consequentialist might say that it is good to deny the right in the case of neo-Nazis or other groups whose program is to eliminate the right altogether. Sometimes a consequentialist is willing to "dishonor" the value in the short term in order to promote the value in the long term. The consequentialist will be focused on *promoting* value, while the deontologist on the contrary will stress *honoring* value and will not be willing to break moral rules, violate moral rights, in order to promote value. Essential to the deontological view is what I call the *sufficiency of honoring value* thesis, which says that it is always enough for an individual to honor values, and almost never permissible to dishonor the value (or violate the norm) in order to promote that value in the long run. Endorsed by the deontologist, this *sufficiency of honoring value* thesis is rejected by the consequentialist.

The second issue is trickier, and turns on how we think of value and its optimization as determining what we ought to do. The deontologist (consonant with an integrity theorist like Williams) will find repugnant all talk of objective value determining the status of actions, or of a "value network" (changing only slightly Williams's "utility network") generating obligation. Taking the first-person stance as central and irreducible, they hold that statements of obligations must be addressed to individual agents and conceived in terms of the free will of individual agents. I call this the *agential self-sufficiency* claim. Of course it does allow for universal demands to be placed on the individual will, but typically there is a voluntary dimension to taking up or endorsing or legislating those demands such that they are not imposed "from the outside." Note that *on this issue* I am not assuming that the deontologist endorses a substantive value theory, for when deontologists stress agential self-sufficiency they often bracket or exclude questions of value. In one way or another consequentialists must reject agential self-sufficiency, and hold that a system or network of value does indeed determine obligation. Some consequentialists prefer to distinguish their position by stressing the agent-neutral quality of the value to be promoted, but given the complexities of the agent-neutral/agent-relative distinction,[5] and given that it is entirely possible to be a consequentialist while endorsing agent-relative value, I find that (even despite its vagueness) the agential self-sufficiency formulation is superior.

For each side there are two main intuitions driving the adoption of the position. On the consequentialist side, there is (1) the intuition that ethical action must serve *greater overall value*, where "overall" does extend to some degree into the future, and (2) *value* has objective standing and the world of value can be ordered so that in any case of action there will be some option that is determined as better, objectively, as a function of value. On the deontologist's side, there is (1) the intuition that objective value is too theoretical, too metaphysical even, to guide an agent's willing, and (2) that consequences cannot make an intrinsically wrong action right.

These intuitions can be fit into a single picture by distinguishing between levels, and indeed I will argue that Hegel does so. It is thus worthwhile to sketch here a more familiar attempt to get the intuitions into a single picture, namely *rule consequentialism*. This theory asserts that individuals should act primarily according to moral rules rather than in order to maximize value, but it also holds that the rules themselves are validated because they maximize consequences. The rule consequentialist can affirm that wrong actions are wrong because of rules, and that an individual's actions are not determined by calculating consequences but by endorsing moral rules. On the other side, the intuitions of the consequentialist are borne out in that the rules are justified by objective value and in that at the overall level consequences have the final say. I will return to rule consequentialism in my closing assessment, and will only note here that there is a strong internal tension in this theory. Agents are supposed to act for rule-based reasons, but those reasons (rules) are supported by other considerations that are not supposed to enter into the agent's deliberation. There are strong intuitions behind the thesis that an ethical agent performs an action for the reason that (ultimately) makes the action right, but this thesis is denied by rule consequentialism. This tension is closely related to a tension in the status of the rules themselves. It seems that a rule must change in response to particular cases in which consequentialist considerations count against the rule in its current form. If so, the split between the two levels will collapse because simply following a rule in its current form will not suffice, and the individual will also take overall consequences into account in her deliberations. If not, rule consequentialism can become a kind of "rule-worship"[6] because obeying a rule is given undue value. So either rule consequentialism collapses into act consequentialism, or we are left with individuals acting on rules for a different set of reasons than the reasons that make the rules right. I will return to these worries in my closing assessment of Hegel's own position.

2

In this section I set out a way to understand the *Philosophy of Right* as expounding a value theory of a sort that at least *could* be consequentialist. The first task of such a reading is to interpret Hegel's claims about the free, rational will as claims about value. It is relatively uncontroversial that *freedom* is the master value in Hegel's ethics, but beyond that general claim it has proven quite hard to give a theory of value that applies to all the different levels of the *Philosophy of Right*.[7] Part of the trouble here is that Hegel is so focused on freedom as an *activity*. Because of this orientation of his basic conceptual apparatus, it is difficult to think of freedom along consequentialist lines as a property or as a quantifiable measure. Hegel begins in the Introduction by describing the activity of the free will in the abstract terms of the Concept. The account of the free will then becomes an account of the practical norms, and ultimately the institutions, that individuals inhabit in living free lives. At many points in this account it is unclear whether the agent is required either to honor or to promote a single value called freedom. When the *value* of freedom does come into sight directly, as in the account of the Good as "realized freedom" (*PR* §128),[8] it quickly falls out once again as a direct purpose of action (I discuss this in section 5), making it hard to decipher just how the agent relates to the overall value in different states of affairs. But Hegel's account of the rationality and freedom of the will that develops in the different stages of right *can* be identified with a certain structure of valuing. Or so I shall argue in this section.

The second problem, which I take up in subsequent sections, concerns the relationship between the teleological development of the different stages of right, on the one hand, and the teleology of individual actions that is the typical focus of contemporary ethical debates, on the other. Is the model of activity that drives the dialectic the same as the activity of the ethical individual? I will argue that their underlying conceptual structures are the same. The *development* occurs at points of normative instability involved in conceptual shifts, whereas the action of the individual rational will assumes a relatively stable normative landscape. While my account will emphasize the consequentialist element in the conceptual development and in individual action, there is also in every phase of the development a deontological element as well. Carefully unpacked, the contrast between the consequentialist and deontological dimensions in both individual action and the dialectical development opens a new window into understanding the dialectic of right.

The first step in establishing a value reading is to consult the end of the *Encyclopedia* account of Subjective Spirit in order to understand that Hegel is beginning from a claim about the value of the individual human being. At the close of his account of the individual capacities of mind that he labels "Psychology," Hegel introduces "the free spirit." He states (in a claim I explore below) that the free spirit takes the will itself as its "object and purpose" (1971: §481), and he also links the free Spirit to the basic concepts of Christianity. According to Hegel's interpretation of Christianity, its leading ethical idea is that "the individual *as such* has an *infinite* value" (1971: §482). Appreciating this value claim allows us to see that for Hegel the value of free individuality is the core value that is realized in the realm of Objective Spirit, and indeed that the latter just is the system of the realization of that value.

While this claim opens up a value reading, it also presents an immediate problem with executing such a reading. The problem is how to understand the conception of "infinite value" in a way that lends itself to *determinate expressions* of value. It could be seen as a devastating objection to a consequentialist reading of Hegel that he values individuals in a way that does not allow them (or their claims) to be traded off against each other, calculated or weighed. Yet Hegel does *not* of course shy away from endorsing claims that subordinate individuals to social processes, and that even allow for diverse forms of inequality between persons. How then are we to understand the relation of the individual's infinite value to the finite conditions of Objective Spirit?

The three-moment structure of the Concept is the key to just about everything in Hegel, and it is his discussion of the Concept and the will in *Philosophy of Right* §§5–7 that must serve as our starting point for thinking about value. The first moment – the abstract universality of the I – looks very much like the core of the deontological standpoint. The canonical example is the abstract universality of the principle underlying the French Revolution: roughly, "everyone is equal and should be treated equally." It seems that there is no weighing of consequences that could count against this principle, for as a pure standard of justice it cannot be overridden.

The insufficiency of abstract or formal universality can be clarified through Robert Brandom's recent discussion of material inferences. Brandom develops a point about inference and meaning from Wilfrid Sellars. The point concerns how to think of *good* inferences. For an inference to be good, must it have at least implicitly the full logical form of a valid inference? The familiar example is "It is raining, therefore the streets will be wet." Where is the major premise that would allow it to become a *logically* valid inference? Sellars and Brandom claim that we do not need to insert an implicit premise, "Every time it rains the streets get wet," before we can say that the basic inference is valid. As Brandom puts the point, "Why should all goodness of inference be seen as logical goodness, even at the cost of postulating 'implicit' premises involving logical concepts?" (1994: 101). One of the problems here is that if inferential goodness has its source solely in logical form, that goodness will be separate from the particular content of the specific inference that is being made. In their contrasting account, Sellars and Brandom hold that the meaning of concepts consists in their use as premises and conclusions in successful material inferences. A language that had only logical inferences would be one devoid of any meaning beyond that given in the (relatively empty) logical rules themselves.

The relevance of this account of inference to Hegel's account of the will and value begins to come out when we align value with meaning.[9] Taking value as the practical counterpart to meaning, we can ask how we should think of formal versus material *practical* inferences in relation to ethical value. There are practical inferences characteristic of the abstract universality of the first moment of the will, and our first move is to identify these with the abstract deductive forms of inference. Hegel's criticism of abstract universality then lines up with the criticism of formal inference sketched above. The universal practical inference that aligns with standard logically valid inference would be something like the following:

> Every person must be treated according to our equal capacity for valuing.
> Here is a person X.
> I will to treat person X equally, according to our equal capacity for valuing.

There is an act of willing in the conclusion, and the question is how to conceive of the value of that willing. In Hegel's treatment, the value comes from the ability of the subject to abstract from all merely given determinations and to act from pure subjectivity. That is a capacity, common to all individuals, which renders our actions free and is thereby a source of value. By valuing that same capacity in others, I realize in action the value of my own capacity for action.

On the other hand, it is not at all clear what value is expressed in this formal inference, for we do not actually know what specific action is willed. There is a commitment to equal treatment and thus to infinite value, but that leaves out the value of the actual action with its specific purpose. For this reason, Hegel thinks that what really comes to the fore in this moment of the will is the following inference:

> Every person must be treated according to our equal capacity for valuing.
> Here is a person X who is not being treated equally.
> I will to eliminate the conditions responsible for X not being treated equally.

Call this Robespierre's Inference, for it encapsulates the "fury of destruction" that Hegel associates with making abstract universality the sole basis of practical inferences.

Turning now to the moment of particularity, the second moment of the Concept, we can see Hegel as stressing the *material* side of the material practical inference. Hegel writes that this moment represents the specific, limited purpose of willing. We can think of the distinctive practical inference of this moment along the lines of "It is raining, therefore the streets will be wet." In the practical case the statement of fact is replaced by a description of a situation calling for action on ethical value. For example:

My friend needs someone to watch her child for an hour while she goes to a meeting, therefore I will watch her child for an hour. I do it without explicitly intending to realize the value of friendship, without thinking "Being a friend requires that I help a friend when she is in need." In the material practical inference there is no need to bring in the major premise. An inference from seeing a value to be realized and acting to realize the value is perfectly intelligible, and in this case we know the value of the willing by knowing the specific value realized in the action. We do not take the extra step of adding the major premise – it does not enter into our reasoning.

There is obviously something missing with the simple practical material inference. It contains no mention of freedom, no mention of the abstract capacity for valuing. Without such an element, though we might say that *first-order* value is realized, the form of responsibility for one's action is left open. This is why Hegel writes, "This content may further be given by nature, or generated by the concept of spirit" (*PR* §6). If people act under compulsion or for lack of the ability to imagine any alternative they may very well realize value, but we would in many cases say the action is less than fully free and that the full value of the action is compromised.

Though Hegel's presentation in the *Philosophy of Right*, with universality preceding determinacy, makes the point hard to see, determinacy and abstract universality roughly correspond to first-order and second-order value/valuing. Determinacy or material inference represents first-order value, whereas universality is the moment of *second-order value*, the reflexive valuing of the capacity for valuing in oneself and in others. It makes sense to think of *adding* first-order value, but we should think of second-order value primarily as a *multiplier*.[10] If there is no realization of first-order value then there is no value at all (because one is multiplying by a zero). But first-order valuing itself is often quite limited without the multiplying effect of the capacity for freedom that is expressed (if not usually explicitly thematized) in the action.

Hegel brings out this integrated valuing within the full structure of the Concept contained in *individuality*. This is still a model of material inference, but one that also involves the regulating powers of self-consciousness and the second-order valuing of universality.[11] I thus call the full model one of *free material inference*. Abstract universality taken by itself could recognize violations of freedom but could not account for determinate realizations of value. With particularity, determinate value comes into view but the subject's relation to the content could simply be given. By contrast with the one-sided moments, we can state the inference of individuality in the following way:

> In action X I would realize a determinate value through exercising my universal capacities.
> I will action X as an expression of my universal capacities.

In this individuality, which Hegel calls "being with oneself in otherness," I am committed to something limited, but I am not so immersed in that content that I have lost my capacity to be a subject in the universal sense. Hegel's oft-discussed example of this structure is in fact friendship. In friendship I have bound myself to another particular person, and I do often directly infer from "My friend needs me to X" to "I will do X." But it is essential to genuine friendship that my higher-order capacities are engaged, even though I do not reason from the major premise "I should always exercise universal capacities to realize determinate value." My capacity for universality is important in regulating my actions as a friend so as to limit, for instance, my willingness to transgress other duties in order to help that friend. That friendship presupposes this capacity on the part of each also expresses the independence of friends.[12] Friendships are more valuable in that each agent acts with such a set of universal capacities and in that this set itself is valued by each as a kind of background condition of the friendship. I value being a friend as an expression of my freedom and my friend's freedom, rather than simply as a matter of sheer attachment.

Reading the free will as a structure of free material inferences enables us to shed some light on his definition of *right* and how right can be linked to value. Hegel gives a very brief definition, "*Right* is any existence [*Dasein*] in general which is the *existence* of the *free will*" (*PR* §29). It must be said that this definition is not by itself very informative. He follows up only by an attack on Kant's definition of right, and on all individualistic definitions of right, that negatively indicate a limiting factor on the arbitrary will, and that positively rely on an abstract formal identity of universality. He ends the remark with an allusion once more to the French Revolution and to the "terrifying nature" of the deeds produced by this abstract universality. The only elaboration of his own definition is a hint at an "immanent rationality" that is ruled out by the formalism of Kantian right. This is clearly the same terrain covered in his discussion of the three moments of the free will in §§5–7, and it can seem that his sole intent in giving the definition is to rule out the formal inference as the exclusive model of right. But the opposition to formality suggests that we read the definition of right itself in terms of the free material inference of individuality. If the free will is the activity of drawing material practical inferences with implicit universality, we can say that right, as the *Dasein* of the free will, represents the *generalized success conditions* of such free material practical inferences in the public sphere of human interaction. What I mean here with generalized success conditions is that right provides a stable set of value structures within which individuals can draw practical inferences that other individuals will recognize as valid (and that thus will be successful). The normative framework does not float free from the interactions, but rather the framework is just an authoritative expression of the conditions under which practical inferences are successful. The overall rationality of this success is found in the whole system of Objective Spirit, with its complex of interrelated practical inferences.

How does this help us with the question of value and the relative importance of the consequentialist and deontological strands in the *Philosophy of Right*? The first thing we can say is that in every stage of right, even in Abstract Right, some first-order value is realized. Without the first-order value, the inference would not be a material inference of individuality. Hegel stresses the *Dasein* of the free will in his definition to bring out the determinacy of right as the willing of a first-order value. A concept of right is valuable insofar as it enables successful free material inference.

Every stage of right also involves certain universal capacities, and these do introduce deontological "side constraints" into the picture. The first stage of right, the right of the person, seems to put a strict constraint on treating persons in ways that are incompatible with their status as free. None of these side constraints is absolute, however, for each is limited in its incorporation into concrete practice. There is a question of whether we should think of these deontological norms as *side* constraints on first-order valuing at all. As we have seen, the trouble with the purely universal capacities and norms is that they seem to take no definite object. But Hegel does in fact conceptualize the abstract norms themselves as objects of the will, and he does so precisely in the service of making a transition to a more determinate sphere (a dynamic that I spell out in section 4).

Once we read right as a category implicated in what we think of as value, Hegel's claims about the development of Right through the Concept, and the possible collisions between the levels, become more tractable. In a key section of the Introduction to the *Philosophy of Right*, Hegel writes, "Right is something *utterly sacred*, for the simple reason that it is the existence [*Dasein*] of the absolute concept, of self-conscious freedom" (*PR* §30). To some critics, this claim rings hollow given Hegel's willingness to place the right of the state higher than the personal right of individuals. Hegel goes on to distinguish Abstract Right from later stages, presumably meaning the level of Ethical Life, which "possesses a higher right, for it is the *more concrete* sphere, richer within itself and more truly universal" (*PR* §30). The stages of the account go from the abstract to the richer, and the worry has frequently been raised that Hegel seems with his reference to a "higher right" to countenance the violation of abstract rights in the name of the state. If Abstract Right is taken as a set of strict side constraints, this talk of higher or richer levels seems to simply contradict or violate the claims of Abstract Right. But if we read right in terms of material inferences in which value is realized, references to higher right and richer content are relatively un-problematic. We can think of the earlier stages as working with abstract descriptions of first-order value (property, welfare) in order to develop a basic framework for practical inference, and later stages as taking the framework for granted while setting out a more determinate structure of first-order value. So while there is no supremely overriding appeal to sheer formality, to the abstract framework floating free of the determinate practice, the richer forms of right build upon the abstract framework. There are collisions between the various possible premises of the inferences, but only insofar as those premises are in play as valuable components of a social order. The question of Hegel's consequentialism, then, is whether or not the outcomes of those collisions are decided by an appeal to the overall value of the consequences.

3

Some readers will object at this point that it is a mistake to read Hegel as a value theorist in the way just proposed because his fundamental conception of *mutual recognition* adumbrates a thoroughly deontological approach to normativity. Originating in Fichte's *Doctrine of Right*, mutual recognition was a central concept for Hegel in his Jena period, and many recent commentators have stressed the continued importance of the theme in the *Encyclopedia* and *Philosophy of Right*.[13] On this view the key to Hegel's ethics is *treating each other as free*, or according each other a certain "deontic status."[14] At best it would be misleading to take realizing value as Hegel's central concern in developing the account of right or in characterizing ethical action. At worst, reading Hegel as a value theorist clouds in obscurity the intersubjective character of Hegel's ethics and its grounding in free human activity. As the example of friendship shows, the individuality of the free will can itself be explicated in terms of intersubjective relations rather than in terms of value.

The case for mutual recognition in the sense opposed to value is strongest when focusing on Abstract Right and its account of the person and personality. Hegel calls personality "the capacity for right" and gives as the "commandment of right" the formula "*be a person and respect others as persons*" (*PR* §36). The decisive claim comes in the transition from property to contract, where Hegel writes:

> But as the existence [*Dasein*] of the *will*, property is for another only as *for the will* of another person. This relation of will to will is the true distinctive ground in which freedom has its *existence* [*Dasein*]. . . . since it is a relationship of objective spirit, the moment of recognition is already contained and presupposed within it. (*PR* §71; translation altered)

The fundamental claim about right as the existence of the free will is explicated here as an intersubjective relationship. This suggests that right itself is an intersubjective category, a way of treating each other. Yet the claim that intersubjectivity is "the true distinctive ground" is compatible with right being a value term. We could say that right is a structure of value exists insofar as through it individuals recognize each other as free. One thing that certainly is clear from this passage is that recognition is a fundamental concept for the *Philosophy of Right*, and must be integrated into any full account of his ethics. Hegel explains the relative lack of discussion of intersubjectivity in the *Philosophy of Right* by reference to the overall framework of Objective Spirit, which has the moment of recognition built into it, so that recognition does not need to be thematized.

There is a prima facie plausible argument that deontic recognition only characterizes Abstract Right, and that it is the deontic status aspect of recognition that is overcome in the subsequent spheres of right. Yet Hegel seems to deny just this claim in a comment on his discussion of recognition in the *Encyclopedia*, where he writes:

> Each is thus universal self-consciousness and objective; each has real universality in the shape of reciprocity [*Gegenseitigkeit*], in so far as each knows itself recognized in the other free self, and is aware of this in so far as it recognizes the other and knows him to be free.

> This ... is the form of consciousness of the *substance* of each essential
> spirituality – of the family, fatherland, state, and of all the virtues, love,
> friendship, valor, honor, fame. (1971: §436)

The agent's freedom is objective "in the shape of reciprocity" because he is
recognized by another whom he recognizes as free. Hegel emphatically
connects this mutual recognition to the main institutions of Ethical Life and
to the virtues, thus ruling out a restriction of the recognition relationship to
Abstract Right. This is a way of treating each other, and seems to place Hegel
firmly in the deontologist's camp.

But before we think that recognition rules out a consequentialist-leaning
value reading of Hegel's ethics, we need to consider a distinction between
direct and indirect recognition.[15] Recognition is direct in that individuals
take other individuals as their explicit objects of concern when they are
formulating their intentions to act. But we can also think of recognition as
indirect, where the mediating element that makes it indirect is action on
objective value. In that *action* is valuable to others, those others indirectly
recognize me when I act on value (i.e., on what others will recognize as
valuable), and are indirectly recognized by me in my respect for what Hegel
calls the right of objectivity. This point finds support in what Hegel actually
says in the passage above, namely that this reciprocity is "the form of
consciousness of the *substance*" of the ethical determinations.[16] If we
substitute "value" for "substance" here,[17] we can read Hegel as saying that
when we reflect explicitly on "each essential spirituality" and consider why it
is valuable, then we understand that it is valuable because within it our
freedom is objective in the shape of reciprocity. But when we act within the
family or within the state, we are not explicitly seeking that recognition by
others (except in a limited class of cases). Rather, we act on purposes that are
objectively valuable and our action is recognized because it expresses or
achieves that value.

The contrast between direct and indirect recognition parallels the contrast
between the formal and material practical inference. The formal/universal
inference, as in the example from the French Revolution, typically takes
another agent's *status* as the object (i.e., the goal) of action. All there really is in
the world of abstract universality is other abstract persons or subjects, for
even property counts as valuable only as a direct extension of the abstract
person with property rights. The trouble is just that there is no determinate
way to engage abstract persons or radically equal subjects and citizens
because determinate engagement would mean differential recognition,

which is ruled out by strict direct mutuality.[18] In the successful free material practical inference there is indirect recognition because the action realizes first-order value, and the practical inference is successful in that the action is *recognized* as valuable by others. The generalized success conditions of the free material inference are conditions of mutual recognition, but the moment of universality characteristic of abstract recognition typically remains in the background. If we do not put indirect recognition at the forefront, we will end up back in the problems that Hegel analyzed with formal inference.

4

In Hegel's general descriptions of Objective Spirit the foremost idea is that freedom takes the shape of a "world." This means enriching the possibilities of mutual recognition by giving an account of the social practices in which freedom finds determinate expression. In the terms that I have been developing, this process involves giving further texture and definition to the success conditions of material inference, to the contexts in which agents actualize their capacities for freedom. Because successful practical inference depends on mutual recognition, the same developmental process simultaneously sets out forms of recognition and possibilities of material inference. The norms laid out in the *Philosophy of Right* have an "immanent rationality" because of the transitions that lead from one to another in a chain of dialectical necessity, a chain that eventuates in a systematic whole.

It might seem that the dialectical transitions raise a different set of issues than those of action assessment involved in the consequentialism debate. Yet it is hard to see how there could be a sharp difference here. The guiding dynamics of the Concept apply to both dimensions, and this means that both dimensions have an inferential structure. Because the justification of the account is holistic, understanding the transitions is key to understanding the status of the rights in subsequent stages of right. In this section I argue that there is a sense in which the higher stages are designed to *promote* the value of freedom, and that the activity of the dialectic through which the content of right develops can thus be understood in consequentialist terms.

Philip Pettit's characterization of the contrast between *honoring* and *promoting* value connects usefully with the issues of recognition and material inference. Pettit claims that in an ideal world, honoring and promoting a value would be the same thing. As he puts it, "To instantiate a value is to behave in the way that would promote the value in a world, roughly, where others were equally compliant. . . . to behave in a way that would promote it in a suitably compliant context, even if it does not promote it in the actual, imperfect world" (Baron et al. 1997: 127). He also writes of honoring/instantiating that "with an appropriate value it means acting in the way that would promote the value in a suitably compliant world, even if that mode of action does not promote it in the actual world" (Baron et al. 1997: 261). One part of this idea is that the distinction between promoting and honoring/instantiating disappears under conditions of suitable compliance, in a "world" in which there are no threats to the value that could seriously undermine it. The other part is the claim that given that we live in "the actual, imperfect world," it makes more sense to subscribe to a view (consequentialism) that requires promotion of the value than to one that simply seeks to honor value. As in the case of free speech and the speech of illiberal groups, we need to act in ways that preserve our values against the non-compliant rather than in ways that just instantiate the values for ourselves.

This contrast between honoring and promoting has a clear connection to the issues of recognition and actualization, and it is for that reason a useful tool for thinking through Hegel's transitions from one stage of right to another. Pettit's "suitably compliant context" is just a world in which agents mutually recognize one another's claims and do not threaten to undermine one another's values. In the conceptual moves that for Hegel lead to a dialectical transition, the practical inferences that instantiate a given value become unstable. In the process of the breakdown of a given stage of right there arises a context of non-compliance, a failure of mutual recognition. The breakdown of each stage is a move toward a transitional, non-compliant context in which it becomes necessary to *promote* the relevant values rather than simply to honor the current norms. Such promotion looks at first like a violation of right, but the subsequent stage of right promotes the earlier values in a way that does not require the violation of the previous right. The new stage of right establishes new conditions that integrate the element(s) that caused the disruption in the previous stage. The new stage restores the compliance condition and thus a condition in which the normal activity of honoring/ instantiating the values is sufficient. In the transition the subsequent shape of right integrates the shortcomings of the previous shape to reach a condition of mutual recognition that is more comprehensive and more stable.

This account can be said to have consequentialist underpinnings because the turn in the dialectic toward promotion, namely the need to violate the right in the service of the value behind the right, has the same structure as the consequentialist claim. The tricky part in Hegel is that the *legitimate* promoting activity full emerges only in the new stage of right. Only once we have moved to a new shape does the value configuration that disrupted the first shape get promoted, and by that point the earlier claim has become almost unrecognizable. In moving to the subsequent shape, the new element behind the claim for recognition is converted into a new right and a new shape of value that can be honored in normal action-recognition contexts. The goal of this dialectic is a comprehensive context in which every essential value claim is recognized. The endpoint or completion of the account comes when the maximally complete set of success conditions for individual valuing have been realized. At the level of the whole system, honoring will be enough for the individual.

The transition from Abstract Right to Morality illustrates well the dynamics I have just sketched. The transition begins with the excess abstractness of property and contract claims. This deficiency goes back to Hegel's claim early in Abstract Right that the "*particularity* of the will . . . is not yet contained in the abstract personality as such" (*PR* §37). Particularity gets into the picture through the phenomena of crime and avenging justice that conclude "Abstract Right." Crime appears as a reflection of the inadequacy of abstractly universal norms to meet the demands of concrete individuals in the actual world. The act of the criminal is in a sense a recoil from the overly abstract recognition at the level of merely formal right.[19] Hegel thinks of crime as a failure of recognition, and though he is not sympathetic to the criminal, he clearly thinks that crime arises as a necessary moment in the development of right. The practice of honoring the value of the sheer person has proven inadequate. What ensues upon this no longer "suitably compliant" context?

The first result is that the concept of punishment arises. Hegel insists both that my universal capacity for freedom is *respected* in punishment (it is acknowledged that in committing a crime my rational capacities were engaged), and that determinate harm must be done to me commensurate with the determinate harm that I have done to another. The need to arrive at what is commensurate or equivalent to a crime brings about the first long discussion of the *value* of an action (in *PR* §101). Value must be placed on the action itself in order for the retributive character of punishment to be fulfilled – in order to get beyond a strict (eye for an eye) equivalence of reaction to the action of the criminal. The determinacy or particularity of the crime has to be transformed into a *general measure* of value so that retribution can function (as it typically does) through fines and imprisonment. Value is "the *inner quality* of things" (*PR* §101), the universality of the particular acts that allows two particulars (the crime and the punishment) to be equated.

The next stage of the transition is the first reaction to the crime, namely *revenge* (*PR* §102). This is itself another infringement of right, an "*avenging justice*" (*PR* §103) that is the exercise of a particular will that wills a particular vengeance. We can see what is wrong with this avenging justice by asking whether the avenger promotes the right kind of value. In one sense, he can be seen as claiming *to violate right in order to promote that very same right*. This seems to be the classic distinguishing mark of the consequentialist, who is willing to dishonor value in the short term in order to promote value in the long term. But on the other hand, the avenging act cannot really do the work of promoting the value of freedom. If the right to be promoted is universal, it very much matters that the promoting activity aim at the universal and not simply at a particular act of vengeance. The criminal's capacity for freedom is not respected if the punishment is exercised simply as a particular harm. The right/value of personhood would not be genuinely promoted. Rather, as Hegel emphasizes, the wrong "becomes part of an infinite progression and is inherited indefinitely from generation to generation" (*PR* §102), which is the exact contrary of the consequentialist claim for long-term benefit.

The true shape of punishment is *punitive* rather than *avenging*, where that means that the aim or purpose of the will is the particularized universal (or the universalizing particular). The general description of the new concept is that it is a particular will that wills the universal. When Hegel says that now personality becomes the object (meaning the goal) of the will (*PR* §104), he is saying that we have shifted to a context of value promotion. In the development of the moral sphere the universal must be *promoted* because there is a real *difference* between the individual qua universal and qua particular (whereas these moments were in an immediate, abstract unity in abstract right). Morality will demand the promotion of universal value because each agent *starts from* an accepted claim for his own intrinsic value as a particular agent. In "Morality" the value of the individual's particularity, his subjective point of view, is recognized. Universality is promoted in a quasi-consequentialist sense because now, taking the particularity of the subjective will as an essential moment, the universality of personality is an aim or goal (the "object" of the will) for a subjective will attempting to determine itself to universality. As long as the moral sphere is one of suitable compliance, this new promotion takes the form of honoring the relevant values and moral individuals can recognize each other. But at two crucial moments within Morality, that recognition is disrupted and a new structure of value is introduced.

5

"Morality" arises from the need to bring particularity into the normative picture, to put our admittedly contingent particularity in the service of the value of freedom. The alternative is simply to remain in the abstract personality's opposition of formal right and the contingent particularity of individual human beings. I will argue that morality is in the end quite amenable to a consequentialist interpretation. Yet Hegel is very insistent on endorsing a claim that the agent's perspective is essential to moral action, which is a standard claim of deontology. The content of action is essentially tied to the agent's identification with the content, which Hegel calls "the *right of the subjective will*" (*PR* §107). The claim contained in this right is that "the will can *recognize* something or *be* something only in so far as that thing is *its own*, in so far as the will is present to itself in it as subjectivity" (*PR* §107; translation altered). This claim seems to affirm directly the *agential self-sufficiency* claim that I have identified with deontology's resistance to consequentialism. Yet this strong agent-centered claim stands in tension with the moment of universality that is also essential to "Morality." Hegel indicates that "Morality" is the realm of the "difference" (*PR* §108) between subjectivity and objectivity, and between the particular will and the universal concept of the will. Because of this difference, Morality is the domain of requirement and obligation, the domain of a contingent subjectivity that aims to realize necessary universality. We will see that this universality, as the demand to conceive of value in objective terms, ultimately leads in "Morality" to the *Aufhebung* of the *agential self-sufficiency* claim. In Ethical Life, then, the claim will remain in force within circumscribed contexts, but the contexts themselves will limit the reach of the claim.

The conceptions within "Morality" are especially unstable owing to the difference of the particular and universal, of the subjective and objective. The guiding value is at first subjective welfare, but quickly the objective Good comes to the fore; the agent-centered claim for the subjective right of satisfaction quickly becomes a form of self-denial in the service of objective duty. This instability is reflected in the instability of mutual recognition between moral agents (who are essential because of the development of subjectivity involves the will's relationship to the "will of others" (*PR* §112)). The trouble with recognition here is that there are no determinate external standards of compliance at this stage, but only general demands and particular purposes. In this situation, "suitable compliance" is not a workable criterion, and thus there is often no clear boundary between honoring and promoting value. Either one stipulates honoring through one's subjective perspective, or one claims to promote value in opposition to the hypocrisy of the particular will that only claims to be moral. Nonetheless, the agent does come to respect others not only in the sense that the individual can be held to standards of responsibility that others recognize, but also in the sense that individuals actually consider the well-being of others as a value that they should realize in their actions.

In the second stage of "Morality," "Intention and Welfare," Hegel thematizes the value of action for an individual. He writes in §122, "This particular aspect gives the action its subjective *value* and *interest* for me. In contrast with this end – i.e. *the intention from the point of view of its content* – the immediate character of the action in its further content is reduced to a means." There is nothing about this subjective value that excludes the action also having an objective value. Hegel emphasizes the subjective character of the content because that moment of particularity distinguishes this moment of (quasi inner) intention from the universal moment emphasized in Abstract Right. It is surely no coincidence that this subjective value and right of satisfaction look like the utilitarian's preference satisfaction. For Hegel this satisfaction is only a moment, but it is an indispensable one that gives a consequentialist turn to the theory of individual agency.

Hegel stresses that subjective and objective ends (content, value) are not mutually exclusive. We should not play them off against each other but rather seek to find the proper way to think through their intersection. After criticizing those who would impugn actions because the individual has some particular interest in it, Hegel writes:

> What the subject *is, is the series of its actions.* If these are a series of worthless [*wertloser,* "valueless"] productions, then the subjectivity of volition is likewise worthless [*wertlose*]; and conversely, if the series of the individual's deeds are of a substantial nature, then so also is his inner will. (*PR* §124)[20]

Hegel is primarily making the point here that value cannot be split between inner intention and outer realization. If it could be split, a will with valuable intentions could be valuable even if those intentions were never realized.

There is also a strong consequentialist thrust in this statement, given that it is the achieved value, the "productions," that determine the value of the volition. Hegel's focus in the long elaboration of §124 is on the valuing of particularity that is characteristic of modernity. Modernity has come to recognize the value of particularity, so that a successful romantic marriage and the successful pursuit of a private career are now valued alongside selfless universal ends. Because the ordinary particular actions are substantial, we have no excuse not to realize value in the series of our actions. While this discussion does not raise an honoring/promoting contrast, it does imply that the overall value of our willing is a function of a system of value that can be assessed by others.

The consequentialist structure that I have identified as the heart of the practical dialectic is evident in the transition from "welfare" (the individual's particular interests taken as a whole) to what he calls "the Good." The transition begins with a claim that seems to go directly against the consequentialist: "an intention to promote my welfare and that of others – and in the latter case in particular it is called a *moral intention* – cannot justify an *action which is wrong*" (PR §126).[21] Hegel seems to have in mind stealing to help the poor, and he is especially critical of the glorification of the robber's supposedly just motives against the injustice of society. Despite these reservations, Hegel does support the "right of necessity," the right to steal when one's own life is threatened. In that case there is a real collision between Abstract Right and Welfare, with the higher value of life/welfare taking precedence. In this case the value of life, all of one's freedom, takes precedence over the relative value of a property right. There is a failure of recognition in the standoff between the starving poor claiming the right to welfare and the rich demanding absolute property rights. This is also a right that *should not need to be exercised*, and the integration of the success conditions of Abstract Right and Welfare is the next move, designed to find a stable way to promote the previous rights.

The lesson that Hegel draws from the right of necessity is that we need to overcome "the finitude and hence the contingency of both right and welfare" (PR §128). If we think of right and welfare as corresponding to the key categories of deontology and the utilitarian version of consequentialism, respectively, the lesson in this transition is that both categories are insufficient as criteria for evaluating individual actions. Without some set of objective conditions in the world to secure the "suitable compliance," we are left with a right of necessity that is a violation of Abstract Right in the service of "personal existence as *life*" (*PR* §127). The consequentialist character of this comes out in that both rights are expressions of the value of freedom, so the right of necessity is a violation of freedom in the service of freedom. There is "an injury only to an individual and limited existence of freedom" (*PR* §127) in the service of preserving the very life of the particular free individual.

Hegel's conception of "the Good" sets a goal for the objective conditions of compliance. It is in effect a consequentialization of the previous moments of right, including them all in a kind of super-purpose that structures the ethical world. Hegel writes:

> The *Good* is the *Idea*, as the unity of the *Concept* of the will and the *particular will*, in which Abstract Right, welfare, the subjectivity of knowing, and the contingency of external existence, as *self-sufficient for themselves*, are superseded; but they are at the same time *essentially contained* and *preserved* within it. – [The Good is] *realized freedom, the absolute and ultimate end of the world.* (*PR* §129)

The moments of universality and particularity are integrated here as the complete or final purpose of the world. Initially this purpose is just an abstract demand for integration of the previous moments so that they do not stand in a contingent relation to each other, so that each is not promoted at the expense of the other. Hegel emphasizes the need to overcome the previous tension in writing, "welfare is not a good without *right*. Similarly, right is not the good without welfare (*fiat iustitia* should not have *pereat mundus* as its consequence)" (*PR* §130). The wording here – "right is not the good" – shows that Hegel holds that all rights, including those in Abstract Right, can be reformulated in terms of value.

We should ask at this point, does the Good as the final purpose of the world institute a criterion that says that an action is right if and only if it promotes the Good as much as or more than any other available option? The answer to this question is yes, but given the expansive and abstract account of the Good, it is not clear that the Good is a meaningful criterion for action that would let us claim that Hegel is a bona fide consequentialist. Some consequentialists, such as Pettit, believe that a theory is consequentialist only if it determines rightness as the promotion of *neutral* value. But it is hard to see Hegel, at least at this point, distinguishing sharply between neutral and relative value, given that he includes within the Good the moment of "the contingency of external existence" (*PR* §129). More generally, this conception of the Good does not give us a genuinely action-guiding criterion for determining which options are right in cases where values conflict. Hegel simply says that they do not conflict, or they should not conflict, but there is no clear weighting available for actually evaluating options. There is only the Good as a general purpose to stand as the major premise in the practical syllogism. Just which action falls in the minor premise as *the* good action is not something we can learn from the abstract formulation of the solution. Hegel is aware of these problems, and thus turns to the concept of conscience to examine the function of practical judgment in actualizing the Good.

6

The Good arises within Morality, and thus at the level of the subjective will. The will remains in the standpoint of "difference," so that the individual will is not necessarily identical with the Good, but *relates* to the Good through duty or ought. Hegel presents the abstractness of the Good as leaving the individual with simply two universal duties: "all that is available so far is this: to do *right*, and to promote *welfare*, one's own welfare and welfare in its universal determination, the welfare of others" (*PR* §134). In one sense this is just a repetition at a higher level of the split between deontological abstract right and utilitarian welfare. Hegel has now raised these categories to a universal and objective determination, so that they hold reciprocally between all agents and so that each individual must incorporate the right and welfare of all into her projects. But the main questions about how to reconcile the two types of claims, and how to specify them, appear to be left unanswered. Immediately following the statement of "all that is available" comes Hegel's rejection of the Kantian formula of universality as a possible criterion. He then introduces conscience as the moment of particularity, "the determining and decisive factor" (*PR* §136). Conscience and integrity are usually associated with deontology, but here Hegel seems to be turning away from Kantian deontology to give to conscience the role of assessing a particular action as the realization of the Good. Does *that* assessment or judgment determine an action as right through the expected consequences?

The *Philosophy of Right* does a very poor job of expressing Hegel's full view of conscience. The condensed presentation of the individual's deliberative activity and the misleading contrast of formal and true conscience (in *PR* §137) conceal the import and complexity of conscience's role. For a fuller view we need to look at the *Phenomenology* discussion of conscience.[22] In the presentation of the "Concept" of conscience in the *Phenomenology*, the shape of spirit defined by the community of conscientious individuals, Hegel stresses the *actuality* of this agency by contrast to the *emptiness* of the previous deontological shapes. He writes: "First as conscience does it [the self] have in its *self-certainty the content* for the previously empty duty, as also for the empty right and the empty universal will; and because this self-certainty is at the same time the *immediate*, it is the definite existence itself" (*PS* ¶633).[23]

The deontological "selves" that Hegel presented earlier in the "Spirit" chapter find the key condition of their realization in the individual of conscience. The agency of conscience integrates the particular and universal moments, so conscience does not sacrifice difference, or definite existence (*Dasein*), in determining what is right. By insisting on a standard of universality, or intrinsic rightness, at the expense of particularity or first-order value, the previous shapes had self-destructed. The agent of conscience achieves value by acting on a specific purpose with which he identifies in a distinctive first-person way. That identification itself has value as the formal expression of freedom (as a second-order value). Crucially, this expression is now compatible with particularity, or with determinate ethical purposes.

In the *Phenomenology* Hegel also writes that conscience, in contrast to the Kantian moral worldview, contains the moment of mutual recognition. This surprising assumption, along with the dialectic that ensues, casts a good deal of light on the transition from conscience to ethical life in the *Philosophy of Right*. The abstract recognition of the deontological selves can be aligned with a roughly deontological picture of intrinsic rightness as a mode of treating each other. But that is a picture of *direct* mutual recognition, while conscience involves a picture of *indirect* recognition that sees the value of one's actions as the medium through which recognition takes place. Hegel writes:

> The action is recognized and thereby made actual because the definitely existent [*daseiende*] actuality is immediately linked with the belief or with the knowledge; or, in other words, the knowing of one's purpose is immediately the element of definite existence, universal recognition. Because the essence of the action, the duty, consists in the *belief* of conscience that it is such; this belief is just the *in-itself* itself; it is the *in-itself universal* self-*consciousness*, or the *being recognized*, and hence actuality. (*PS* ¶640)[24]

The purpose is recognized because it expresses value that others will recognize, and in conscience I know that the action with which I identify is also the one that others will understand as best realizing the Good. I have internalized their perspective, so that my own belief in the rightness of my action will reflect the fact that objective value has been optimized.

Conscience, as the individual honoring value in determinate situations, functions well when we presuppose that there is agreement on what purposes are valuable. But when the terms of recognition or compliance become unstable (i.e., when we remove the presupposition) a normative burden is placed on the individual agent that he does not have the resources to bear. The problems that Hegel analyzes with conscience count against both deontological and consequentialist readings of the individual's authority, though the biggest target turns out to be the agential self-sufficiency claim.

In the passage that most directly calls to mind consequentialist considerations, Hegel writes that conscience cannot in fact claim to be acting on knowledge of a universal, for the reality known in action "is a plurality of circumstances which breaks up and spreads out endlessly in all directions, backwards into their conditions, sideways into their connections, forwards in their consequences" (*PS* ¶642). In order to act, the agent of conscience cuts off consideration of the consequences and *honors* value in the way it best sees fit. But to others the agent seems to be *promoting what he values* at the expense of honoring other values. Hegel thus writes of an example in which the individual increases his property out of a sense of duty, "what others call violence and wrongdoing, is the fulfillment of the individual's duty to maintain his independence in the face of others" (*PS* ¶644). The individual refers to his belief in the rightness of his deed, where this has to be seen as a strongly deontological claim of honoring value and claiming agential self-sufficiency. In one sense the individual's reliance on his belief is a necessary aspect of living a moral life, and given modern moral complexity an individual will often have to make what we refer to as "judgment calls." Yet without any reliable terms of compliance, other agents will not see that the right value is being honored, and they can make a good prima facie case that the individual should have acted differently. They may try to one-sidedly assert the universal common good *against* the individual's claim of conscience. In response, Hegel claims that the one-sided assertion of the universal *unproductively* dishonors the value of conscience itself.

In the full breakdown of compliance, of unanimity on what counts as honoring value, the agent of conscience comes to take his own particularity as the value to be promoted in action. This is the source of Hegel's complaints about the subjectivism of modern practical reason. These complaints count more against deontology than against consequentialism, given the classic deontologist's emphasis on the agent relative (rather than on the neutral value realized in action). But they also count against a conception of consequentialism that would put the responsibility for determining what is right entirely on the individual deliberator. Not only is calculating *all* the consequences too complex even if we agreed on the weighting given to different values, but that weighting itself is also a matter of reasonable disagreement. It is an illusion to think that an individual can establish a uniquely correct ordering of value in every situation.

The transition to Ethical Life reenacts the basic move from individual welfare to the Good. Ethical Life is "the living Good" in which the individual's conscience is incorporated into an objective structure of value. This move does not eliminate the need for individuals to deliberate for themselves, but it does transfer the burden of justification and value promotion from the moral individual to the ethical contexts of action. The dialectic of conscience essentially places a demand on ethical contexts such that the individual can honor what she takes to be right. The individual is not (normally) forced to choose between honoring accepted norms and promoting the value of freedom (through thematizing her own subjectivity) because there is a new kind of agency, institutional agency, that is given the consequentialist task of promoting value.

7

In this concluding treatment of "Ethical Life" I will sketch Hegel's conception of normal ethical agency and the role that institutions play in the realization of value. Ethical Life is a system of value with institutional and individual sides. The individual side of this system is in one sense "ruled" by the institutional side. This is a feature of Ethical Life that runs counter to the *agential self-sufficiency* requirement and that thus runs counter to a deontological reading of Hegel's ethics. This relation is captured in Hegel's claim about "the *ethical powers* which govern the lives of individuals" (*PR* §145). These powers are values (or value spheres) that were represented in the ancient world "as gods who have being in and for themselves" (*PR* §145A). In operationalizing the values, institutions are responsible for promoting value, and thus they have a largely consequentialist character. This is not to say that all the actions of institutions are evaluated through a calculation of expected consequences, let alone utility, but there is a marked focus on the overall achievement of the Good. Even in the justice system, where we might expect Hegel to be the most unyielding in an insistence on the strict right being carried out, he shows a surprising willingness to make the system of punishments flexible depending on the consequences for social order.[25]

Ethical *individuals* are in the position of honoring their gods, which means honoring/instantiating the relevant institutional values. Ethical Life assumes full compliance from individuals, so normally there is no need for individuals to promote value instead of honoring it. In these contexts, to honor or instantiate the value *is* to promote it, for other individuals recognize my actions and I recognize theirs as instantiating the institution's values. For an agent in a normal ethical action, there is no responsibility to go above and beyond doing what is right according to that normal context. The *sufficiency of honoring value* claim holds for individuals. This deontological character- ization might seem to run counter to Hegel's claim that Ethical Life gives us an account of "necessary relations" rather than moral duties. But in that same passage he also writes that he is leaving behind an account of duties that "adduce[s] the further consequences which this duty may have with refer- ence to other ethical relations and to welfare and opinion" (*PR* §148). This restriction of the case of action to the normal context rules out a strong promoting element to guide *individual* actions in Ethical Life. Individual agency is also deontological because there is a (limited) sense of *agential self-sufficiency* that is preserved at this level. The family and civil society, in particular, are structured by the modern conception of freedom so as to give a central place to individual self-directedness/independence. The institutions that "rule" the individuals also enable them to direct their own lives and thus to have a sphere of freedom *from* direct institutional control.

Since the institutions of Ethical Life are contexts of suitable compliance, it might seem that we should also conceive of the actions of institutions themselves as honoring rather than promoting value. Part of the problem here is that an institution as a whole is not defined by a single value or action. Insofar as it has the task of *maintaining* the whole structure of value within the institution, it could be seen *to that extent* as honoring the values. But along with maintaining the structure, the institutions are also responsive to changes in self-understandings that disrupt the structure. At the institutional level agency must therefore be seen as promoting the underlying values of the institutions when it comes to new developments. To take the somewhat non- standard case of family and marriage (where unlike in civil society or the state the institution itself has no official representative), if the underlying values are those of love, intimate household community, independent well-functioning children, etc., these values would be promoted rather than simply honored in the case where existing law is changed to allow for new family configurations. Though the impetus for such change is sometimes seen as coming from deontological questions of justice, the Hegelian view would be that such changes are right insofar as the purposes or values characteristic of the institution are promoted thereby. That is, we evaluate those changes as justified based on the overall consequences (in terms of the relevant values) that result from the changes. At the moment of their inception these changes may appear to some as dishonoring the values because the promotion does perturb existing practice (think of those who object to gay marriage).

The payoff of the two-level dynamics in Ethical Life can be seen in the way in which this picture satisfies the intuitions behind consequentialism and deontology that I outlined in section 1. On the consequentialist side, the intuitions are that ethical action serves the greater overall value and that there is a system of value that determines what actions are best. In the two-level approach, the greatest overall value is realized in the actions on first-order values that are close to home (especially those of the family and professional life) in part because individuals are motivated to energetically pursue goals, to realize value, when that value is their *own* family, honor, and economic well-being. Ethical action is thus guided by a system of value, but one which puts a premium on individual satisfaction, or on the particularity so essential to modern institutions. By what Hegel calls the cunning of reason, and by the self-conscious direction of the institutional authorities, individual actions that seem to be oriented by the particular good of individual agents and families also conduce to the greatest overall good.

On the deontological side there is the intuition that objective value is too theoretical a consideration to guide an agent's willing, and the intuition that good overall consequences cannot make an inherently wrong action right. On the first intuition about objective value, it is important to understand that value, mutual recognition, and first-person belief all go together in a single package for Hegel. A society's values are shaped and reshaped through processes of recognition, direct and indirect, and through the practice of modern conscience as the right to act on one's conviction. Determinate first-order values are hardly the philosopher's invention, though perhaps it is true that individuals have a much more inchoate sense of their realization of value than we represent when we theorize ethical action. The second-order valuing that deontologists prize can also be considered part of the objectively good without a mystifying metaphysical conception of the nature of such value.

On the second deontological intuition, we have seen that Hegel too thinks that right is right, apart from individual calculation of the consequences. But it is on this question of the finality of the deontological right that the trickiest issues arise for whether all these intuitions can be packed into a single theory. Hegel does not think that the law can command individuals how to think morally[26] and he admits that conscience may be the best guide when the external ethical world is morally bankrupt, so it would seem that consequentialist claims at the institutional level cannot override the individual's conviction about what is inherently right. On the other hand, Hegel puts the authority to override limited right in the hands of the state. Finally, Hegel is an amoralist in a certain sense when it comes to world history. It is a complex question, and one that cannot be treated here, whether Hegel takes this view of world history on consequentialist grounds, looking to the greater good that can be opened up by new world-historical figures who do not honor existing norms but rather promote emerging value.

The two-level structure that I have presented in this paper will no doubt remind some readers of the structure of rule consequentialism, and so a few words of comparison are in order here. In rule consequentialism the rules are assessed in terms of consequences, while individual action is assessed in terms of rules. In Ethical Life as I have presented it, the institutions are assessed in terms of consequences and individual action is assessed largely in terms of how well it fits the institutional norms. Despite this structural similarity, the comparison is in fact quite misleading. We can see this if we consider that rule consequentialism often goes with the thought that consequentialism is "self-effacing." This is the idea that although consequentialism may be true as a matter of philosophy, of theory, it would lead to worse outcomes if consciously pursued by agents themselves. Rule consequentialism builds this fact into the theory, having agents act on rules (full stop) while justifying the rules through the consequences. Turning to Hegel's individuals and institutions, we see that there is no such problem in the relations of individuals and institutions to value. There is no real tension here between following rules and maximizing consequences, for the individual acts or purposes that are nested within the overall purposes of the institutions. The same values justify both actions, so that there is not the same kind of disconnect between rules and consequences as there is on the rule-conse-quentialist picture. The trick to Hegel's two-level structure is that the individual can honor the values through particular objects of concern and (relatively) fixed duties, while institutions can promote the values in a way that is responsive to consequentialist considerations. Because everything is done in terms of purposes, even though the agent's actions are (usually) at one remove from the aims of the institution, the two levels of justification are naturally interlocking.[27] Though it is not the norm, agents can even take as their primary reason for action the value-promotion structure of the institution itself. One can stay married, for instance, because one thinks of the institution of marriage as promoting certain values, and one wants to support the institution. We hope that this is not the main reason that one acts on in one's marriage, but there is no pressure to *exclude* it from deliberation. There is no pressure parallel to that on the agent of rule consequentialism who must exclude the consequentialist element from his deliberations.

Can we say, finally, that Hegel is a consequentialist *or* a deontologist? No, in the end we have to say that he is both. I have argued, however, that the consequentialist dimension does have a certain priority within the *Philosophy of Right*. The first step in that argument was to show how the rational will realizes first-order value in material practical inferences. The basic legal conditions for that realization of value are deontological, and are based in abstract universal recognition. But we have seen that starting with the discussion of value at the end of Abstract Right, the aspects of value promoting and value honoring both have prominent roles. The transitions between the stages of right are consequentialist in their use of limited negation in the service of greater, more comprehensive value. With the transition to the Good itself Hegel puts his teleological cards on the table, and the transition to Ethical Life is an attempt to incorporate our deontological intuitions about second-order value within an institutional structure oriented by consequences. It should be clear from what we have seen that freedom for Hegel is a very protean value, coming in first- and second-order versions and always eluding our grasp when we try to catch it directly. Freedom is constantly in development, and though we know that it is working through us toward realization, we should not be so sure that we know what that development will mean before it actually happens.

Notes

1. Without an independent definition of the Good prior to the right, we would be "unable to avoid labeling as consequentialist the deontological theorist who says that the right thing for an agent to do is bring about the best state of affairs

that he can, where the best state of affairs always consists in the agent's doing his duty, which in turn consists in his performing tokens of act types that are intrinsically right and refraining from performing tokens of act types that are intrinsically wrong" (Shaw 2006: 7).

2. Fairly categorizing Kant's own theory is no simple task. I am deeply sympathetic to the project among some Kantian ethicists of the past 30 years that have put Kant's account of value at the forefront. I have been especially influenced by Herman 1993.

3. Philip Pettit makes this point especially clearly (Baron et al. 1997: 136, 140).

4. The characterizations in this paragraph draw on Pettit's discussion in Baron et al. 1997. I engage more closely with Pettit's position in section 4.

5. I have addressed this in Moyar 2010.

6. See Smart's comments in Smart and Williams 1973: 10.

7. Value, and in particular the value of freedom, is often invoked in the literature on Hegel's ethics, but to my knowledge there is little to no agreement about how to work out the details of his theory of value.

8. Citations from Hegel's *Philosophy of Right* (*PR*) using § refer to the section numbers. I have used Hegel 1991 as the basis for the English translations.

9. Brandom explicitly links his inferentialism to Hegel's own doctrine of the inference, so in one sense there is no need to argue for the relevance of Brandom's theory to Hegel's project (the case of Sellars is more complicated).

10. It is not my aim here to develop this distinction in detail, but rather to give a general picture of how to think of value on Hegel's picture. There are admittedly problems with the addition and multiplication models, but they do give us a good first gloss on two one-sided moments of the concept.

11. Hegel states quite clearly in the 1819–1820 lectures on the philosophy of right that this three-part structure is the structure of the inference. "1. Allgemeinheit, 2. Besonderheit, 3. Einzelnheit. Diese Totalität des Begriffs, Subjektivität, alles Vernunftige ist der Schluss" (Hegel 1983: 61).

12. This is the same point that Hegel makes in reference to marriage in *PR* §168.

13. See Siep 1979; Williams 1992, 1997; and Pippin 2000.

14. This phrase has come into currency in connection with Hegel through Brandom 1994.

15. I go into this distinction in much more detail in Moyar 2011: ch. 5.

16. The Wallace and Miller translation of the *Philosophy of Spirit* (Hegel 1971) inexplicably leaves out "of the *substance*," an omission that has contributed to the oversight of the crucial connection of recognition and substance for Hegel.

17. I am not saying that the category of substance in general should be read in terms of value, but that when substance is used in an ethical context Hegel is referring to objective value. There are many complicated issues here, and I will only say that substance and value as I read them here are *functional* concepts, and that they do not introduce any metaphysically "queer" entities into the world.

18. This is best illustrated by Hegel's depiction of the Roman world in the *Phenomenology*; see Moyar 2007a for a discussion.
19. See Honneth 1996: ch. 2 for an excellent discussion of this theme in Hegel's pre-*Phenomenology* writings.
20. In this opposition of valueless and substantial we have one important piece of evidence that value and substance are closely related in the ethical sphere.
21. I should note, lest it draw undue attention, that there is no word in the original German corresponding to "promote."
22. The *Science of Logic* also contains a crucial discussion; see Moyar 2007b.
23. All citations using ¶ refer to the paragraph numbers in Miller's translation of Hegel's *Phenomenology of Spirit* (Hegel 1977).
24. I analyze this passage in much more detail in Moyar 2011: ch. 1.
25. I have in mind the discussion at *PR* §218.
26. I am referring to the claim that Hegel makes in *PR* §213.
27. The institutions can adjust according to the changes in practice at the individual level without that forcing a collapse between the two levels (as in the argument against rule consequentialism).

References

Baron, Marcia W., Pettit, Philip, and Slote, Michael (1997) *Three Methods of Ethics.* Oxford: Blackwell.

Brandom, Robert (1994) *Making it Explicit.* Cambridge, MA: Harvard University Press.

Hegel, G. W. F. (1971) *Hegel's Philosophy of Mind: Being Part Three of the "Encyclopaedia of the Philosophical Sciences"* [1830], trans. A. V. Miller. Oxford: Clarendon Press.

Hegel, G. W. F. (1977) *Phenomenology of Spirit,* trans. A. V. Miller. Oxford: Oxford University Press. (Abbreviated *PS.*)

Hegel, G. W. F. (1983) *Philosophie des Rechts: Die Vorlesung von 1819/20 in einer Nachschrift,* ed. Dieter Henrich. Frankfurt: Suhrkamp.

Hegel, G. W. F. (1991) *Elements of the Philosophy of Right,* ed. Allen W. Wood, trans. H. B Nisbet. Cambridge: Cambridge University Press. (Abbreviated *PR.*)

Herman, Barbara (1993) *The Practice of Moral Judgment.* Cambridge, MA: Harvard University Press.

Honneth, Axel (1996) *The Struggle for Recognition,* trans. Joel Anderson. Cambridge, MA: MIT Press.

Moyar, Dean (2007a) "Hegel's Pluralism: History, Self-Conscious Action, and the Reasonable." *History of Philosophy Quarterly* 24(2): 189–206.

Moyar, Dean (2007b) "Urteil, Schluss und Handlung: Hegels logische Übergänge im Argument zur Sittlichkeit." *Hegel-Studien* 42:51–79.

Moyar, Dean (2010) "Hegel and Agent-Relative Reasons. " In Arto Laitinen and Constantine Sandis, eds., *Hegel on Action*. Basingstoke: Palgrave Macmillan, pp. 260–280.

Moyar, Dean (2011) *Hegel's Conscience*. Oxford: Oxford University Press.

Pippin, Robert (2000) "What is the Question for which Hegel's 'Theory of Recognition' is the Answer?" *European Journal of Philosophy* 8(2): 155–172.

Shaw, William (2006) "The Consequentialist Perspective." In James Dreier, ed., *Contemporary Debates in Moral Theory*. Oxford: Blackwell, pp. 5–20.

Siep, Ludwig (1979) *Anerkennung als Prinzip der praktischen Philosophie: Untersuchungen zu Hegels Jenaer Philosophie des Geistes*. Freiburg: Alber.

Smart, J. J. C., and Williams, Bernard (1973) *Utilitarianism: For and Against*. Cambridge: Cambridge University Press.

Williams, Robert (1992) *Recognition: Fichte and Hegel on the Other*. Albany, NY: SUNY Press.

Williams, Robert (1997) *The Ethics of Recognition*. Berkeley: University of California Press.

2

The Empty Formalism Objection Revisited
§135R and Recent Kantian Responses

Fabian Freyenhagen

Like two giant boxers exchanging punches, but neither landing the knock-out blow, Kantians and Hegelians seem to be in a stand-off on what (in contemporary parlance) is known as the "Empty Formalism Objection." Kant's ethics is charged with being merely formal and thereby failing to provide the kind of specific guidance that any defensible ethical system should have the resources to provide. Hegel is often credited with having formulated this objection in its most incisive way, and a wealth of Kantian responses have been deployed to answer it. In this paper, I take up the objection as it appears in §135R of *Elements of the Philosophy of Right* in order to scrutinize the contemporary debate between the two camps. I propose that there are, in fact, three different, albeit connected objections and examine (what I take to be) the best Kantian replies to them. I will neither adjudicate which of these replies is the most accurate interpretation of Kant's texts, nor trace the particular historical context in which Hegel takes up Kant's ethics, nor the way the empty formalism objection fits into Hegel's wider system. This is partly because of constraints of space, and partly because many of the contemporary Kantian replies – for better or for worse – treat the empty formalism objection as a self-standing philosophical problem, irrespective of its historical context or systematic place in Hegel's theory. My limited aim here is to show that, even if one grants – for argument's sake – the legitimacy of such a non-contextual approach, significant difficulties remain.

Hegel's Philosophy of Right: Essays on Ethics, Politics, and Law, First Edition.
Edited by Thom Brooks.
© 2012 Blackwell Publishing Ltd. Published 2012 by Blackwell Publishing Ltd.

1   Empty Formalism in the *Philosophy of Right*

What we now call the empty formalism objection finds, perhaps, its most
pithy statement in Hegel's *Philosophy of Right*, about midway through the
discussion of "Moralität" (third section, "The Good and Conscience"). I
will concentrate here on this statement, drawing on the rest of the book and
Hegel's other works only when necessary.

Still, some minimal textual contextualization of the empty formalism
objection within the *Philosophy of Right* is in order. Hegel's argument is at a
point where it has been suggested that the good provides an objective
standard by which the will should be guided (see §133). Specifically, the will
faces the good as an obligation or duty (*Pflicht*) which we are meant to obey
for its own sake, since the good here is contrasted to all specific determinations of the will that have proved unsuitable guides for genuinely free willing
in the preceding discussion and, hence, what remains is only the general
abstract essence of goodness that we ought to respect as such. The question
then becomes what this means concretely for our conduct (see §134). The
problem which arises is that for any conduct we require specific guidance in
form of detailed content and ends to orientate our wills, but such specific
guidance is not contained in, and presumably can also not be derived from,
the mere idea of duty for duty's sake (see §135). It is not that we have no idea
what this content or these ends could be – presumably drawing on the earlier
discussion of abstract right and welfare, Hegel suggests that we should do
what is right and work for the happiness of ourselves and others (see §134).
Rather, the point is that even such abstract and general guidance as this
cannot be derived and is not contained in the idea of duty for duty's sake.
Hence, this idea lacks any content and consists merely in an empty identity,
forcing people to turn to their conscience for any specific guidance, which,
however, has pitfalls of its own (which Hegel then goes on to discuss; see
§§136–140; see also §141).

It is in this context that Hegel, in the remark to §135, turns to his critique of
Kant's moral philosophy. He begins the remark with praising Kant: specifically, he credits him with having introduced the idea of autonomy, that is, the
idea that morality requires the ability not just to reflect on and choose among
one's impulses, inclinations, and desires (what Kant calls "negative freedom"), but also the ability to be motivated by pure practical reason alone – in
short, to act on the requirements of reason for the sake of these requirements
alone and thereby to achieve unconditional self-determination in one's

willing. This praise is followed by what we now call the empty formalism objection. Kant is faulted for turning his important insight into a one-sided position, absolutizing the moral standpoint. Doing so lands one with empty formalism for the following reasons:

> From this point of view, no immanent doctrine of duties [*Pflichtenlehre*] is possible. One might indeed bring in material *from outside* and thereby arrive at *particular* duties, but it is impossible to make the transition to the determination of particular duties from the above determination of duty as *absence of contradiction*, as *formal correspondence with itself*, which is no different from the specification of *abstract indeterminacy*; and even if such a particular content for action is taken into consideration, there is no criterion within the principle for deciding whether or not this content is a duty. On the contrary, it is possible to justify any wrong or immoral mode of action by this means. – Kant's further form – the capacity of an action to be envisaged as *universal* maxim – does yield a more *concrete* representation [*Vorstellung*] of the situation in question, but it does not in itself [*für sich*] contain any principle apart from formal identity and that absence of contradiction already referred to. – The fact that *no property* is present is in itself no more contradictory than is the non-existence of this or that individual people, family, etc., or the complete *absence of human life*. But if it is already established and presupposed that property and human life should exist and be respected, then it is a contradiction to commit theft or murder; . . . But if a duty is to be willed merely as a duty and not because of its content, it is a *formal identity* which necessarily excludes every content and determination. (*PR* §135R; emphasis original; translation altered)

This passage contains a whole barrage of criticisms.[1] While I will return to some of the more specific points later, it is useful here to distill the main elements of this passage, and I propose that it boils down to three general claims:

1. *No immanent doctrine of duties:* it is not possible to arrive at a doctrine of duties on the basis of the mere idea of duty for duty's sake or the formal identity of rational willing proposed in the categorical imperative.
2. *No criterion for testing potential duties:* even if candidate duties are provided from the outside, testing for whether there is consistency in rational willing (or for whether they can be willed as a universal law) does not provide a criterion for determining whether or not the candidate duties are genuine duties.

3. *False positives:* immoral acts could successfully pass the test for consistency in rational willing and the maxims involved could be universalized.[2]

These three criticisms are interconnected. For example, criticism 3 is a way of amplifying criticism 2: testing for consistency of rational willing is not just useless (as criticism 2 has it), but even dangerous.[3] Also, as the discussion of these three criticisms will show, they form a kind of dialectic, with one leading to the other by way of Kantian replies.

The criticisms are meant to be immanent ones – Hegel is trying to show how the Kantian position is problematic on its own terms and implodes, when fully thought through (albeit it can also be rescued to some extent by being sublated in Hegel's own position). Hence, Kantians will have to recognize themselves in the characterization offered. While I will suggest later that Hegel might well be accused of presenting an incomplete picture, the basic characterization that has gone into the three criticisms above seems correct. Specifically, Kantians would have a hard time denying that the moral law, as Kant thinks of it, consists in a merely formal requirement of reason. It is crucial to Kant's argument that, if there can be a moral law at all, it has to exclude all empirical ends and cannot be a "material principle," since neither such ends, nor material principles have the required universality and necessity for lawfulness (*G* 4: 399–402, 419–421; *KpV* esp. 5: 21–28). Hence, if there can be a moral law at all, then it must be formal in the sense of neither relying on empirical ends nor being a material principle. As such, it can only consist in the very idea of lawfulness itself – that is, in demanding that rational willing is consistent with itself and that one's subjective principle of action (one's maxim) can be willed to be a universal law. In short, Hegel latches onto the key move in Kant's argument for the categorical imperative, specifically the formula of universal law.[4] Moreover, Kantians would also accept that all human action requires specific ends and guidance. Kant repeatedly admits that all actions are directed at ends (*G* 4: 427; *MS* 6: 384–385; see also *KpV* 5: 34) and our (lower-level) maxims involve specific content and specific ends, or at least specific action types done for specific types of ends (such as making false promises as a way to promote one's interests, or committing suicide when one expects more suffering than happiness from living on). Hence, the problem of empty formalism cannot be simply sidestepped by denying the background assumptions leading to it.

Instead, Kantians have to take this problem head-on. In what follows, I will discuss (what I take to be) the best defenses against each of the three claims made by Hegel.

2   Kantian Reply Strategies

2.1   An immanent doctrine of duties

It is a controversial issue how, if at all, duties are derived within Kant's moral philosophy and what role, if any, the categorical imperative plays in this. I cannot do justice to all the different interpretations here. Instead, I shall concentrate on the three most promising avenues: (1) a sidestepping maneuver based on ascribing moral realism to Kant; (2) a reply that concedes that an immanent doctrine of duties is not possible, but denies that it was Kant's intention to provide one; and (3) a final, more elaborate defense, according to which there is a sense in which Kant's ethics does contain an immanent doctrine of duties, after all.

2.1.1   One recent suggestion has it that Kant is a moral realist who takes our moral duties as given, so that he neither needs to, nor attempts to, offer a doctrine or derivation of duties (see, e.g., Stern 2009: section III.1, with further references). On this view, the categorical imperative is meant only to be a useful tool to counteract our tendency to rationalize away the fact that a specific moral duty applies to us,[5] and its defense in section III of the *Groundwork* is only about assuring us about the obligatory nature of moral duties for finite rational beings such as us.

Insofar as Hegel is commonly read as a moral realist himself,[6] this interpretation of Kant's ethics would mean that there is actually no disagreement between Hegel and Kant when it comes to the impossibility of offering a doctrine of duties on the basis of the mere idea of duty for duty's sake. Moral realist or not, Hegel would just have misunderstood Kant, although the empty formalism objection might still be applicable to what we nowadays describe as Kantian constructivism (which is a form of moral anti-realism) and any attempts to derive specific duties from this perspective. Moreover, perhaps Hegel's first criticism could be recast to throw into doubt the usefulness of the categorical imperative for counteracting our attempts to rationalize away our obligations – this, however, would effectively collapse it into the second criticism (to which I return below in 2.2). In this way, the overall thrust of Hegel's first criticism would have been sidestepped or at least diverted.

2.1.2 Those who want to keep more distance from either Hegel or moral realism have to offer alternative reply strategies. A familiar first move is to insist that the *Groundwork* should not be understood to do anything more than what it says on the tin: to clarify and ground the highest principle of morality (*G* 4: 392). In the preface to this work, Kant states that he is not concerned with the application of the moral law (and thereby, one presumes, not concerned with arguing for or with deriving specific duties). Such application would be the work of "practical anthropology," not of "metaphysics of morals" and even less of the preliminary study of its foundations (*G* 4: 388; see also 412; *MS* 6: 217). In this sense, the examples of duties discussed in the *Groundwork* are just illustrations in the process of clarifying the highest principle of morality, not actually derivations of specific duties (such as the duty to not make false promises as a way to promote one's interests, or the duty to not commit suicide when one expects more suffering than happiness from living on). Kant takes it to be uncontroversial that the duties used in the examples are accepted as "actual duties" (*G* 4: 424) – no derivation is necessary to show this. He also accepts as given the customary division into self- and other-regarding duties of either a perfect or imperfect kind (*G* 4: 421; see also 423–424), reserving his right to revise it later (*G* 4: 421 n.). The closest Kant comes to offering arguments for specific (ethical) duties is in the second part of the *Metaphysics of Morals*, the "Doctrine of Virtue" (*Tugendlehre*) (about which more below).

However, this first move merely shifts the problem, since the real question is not so much whether or not Kant attempts to provide or derive an immanent doctrine of duties in this or that book, but whether his moral philosophy has the resources to do so. One response to this question is to concede that if what is at issue is the possibility of deriving a doctrine of duty from the mere idea of duty for duty's sake, then Kant does not attempt it and anyway cannot provide it (nor could anyone else). Still, this concession does not damage Kant's ethics, since he does not attempt to offer an immanent doctrine of duties. In fact, Kant himself would reject such an immanent doctrine as misconceived – unless we bring in knowledge about human beings, their needs and vulnerabilities, a doctrine of duties for human beings cannot be provided, and that is why such a doctrine and the specific duties we face fall within practical anthropology, not metaphysics of morals.

Actually, even the discussion of specific duties in *Metaphysics of Morals* is merely due to the fact that "a metaphysics of morals cannot dispense with principles of application and we shall often have to take as our object the particular *nature* of human beings, which is cognized only by experience, in order to *show* in it what can be inferred from universal moral principles" (*MS* 6: 217; emphasis original). In other words, the specific duties discussed in the Doctrine of Virtue are not derived merely from the idea of duty for duty's sake, but owe their existence to practical anthropology.[7]

If one adopts this response strategy, then the decisive disagreement with Hegel is whether or not his second criticism is correct – that is, whether or not the mere idea of duty for duty's sake, and thereby the categorical imperative, contains a criterion for testing maxims. The first criticism is correct as far as it goes, but it just does not go far at all, since Kant was well aware that this mere idea did not contain a doctrine of duties.

2.1.3   A third reply strategy is similar to the second, but less concessive. It consists in emphasizing that some content and even some (albeit general) duties are contained in the mere idea of duty for duty's sake, and that, although anthropological knowledge and perhaps even sociology are required to derive more specific duties from this content, this idea frames this derivation and, in this sense, Kant's ethics contains an immanent doctrine of duties. Part of this defense relies on the thought that the very concept of duty only makes sense as applied to finite rational creatures and that hence knowledge about human beings (as finite rational creatures) is admissible, at least as long as it is merely descriptive and no normative ideas other than the form of the moral law (or, what comes to the same thing, the mere idea of duty for duty's sake) is appealed to (see, e.g., Herman 1993: 122).[8] In this sense, even the anthropological (and sociological) knowledge invoked is not really outside material – only other normative ideas, or substantive duties would be. Also, for the most general elements of the doctrine of duties even such knowledge would not be required: we can derive some content from the mere idea of duty for duty's sake, specifically the objective end of humanity.

To substantiate this response, it is useful to begin by noting how Kant actually proceeds in the Doctrine of Virtue to arrive at the specific duties he puts forward. What is striking is that the formula of universal law, which Hegel seems to have in mind when making his empty formalism objection, does not figure prominently. Instead, the formula of humanity features repeatedly in the reasoning,[9] as does the idea of two obligatory ends, the perfection of oneself and the happiness of others (on which more below). Insofar as humanity as end in itself is an objective end contained in the idea of the categorical imperative itself and insofar as the two obligatory ends follow from this idea (at least in conjunction with some anthropological knowledge), Hegel's first claim could be rebutted and there is a doctrine of duties immanent in the mere idea of duty for duty's sake, after all.

On this third reply strategy to Hegel's first criticism, defending Kant would, hence, involve showing that humanity as an objective end is contained in the idea of a categorical imperative and that the two obligatory ends also follow from this idea. These are complex issues, so my discussion of them here is going to be a high-altitude sketch only.

Objective and obligatory ends   The key move in the transition to the formula of humanity in the *Groundwork* is the connection between the idea of the moral law and the will of a fully rational being (G 4: 426). Kant extends his analysis of what is involved in rational willing beyond what he already says about it in Parts I and II up to this point, suggesting that all willing is directed at ends (G 4: 427). However, since we are looking at rational willing as such, the ends in question cannot be empirical ends, from which, as we have already seen, the moral law is supposedly independent. Rather, we need to consider whether there are any ends which "hold equally for all rational beings" (G 4: 427). Such ends would be what Kant calls "objective ends." They are *analytically differentiated* from subjective ends, that is, the particular ends on which finite subjects actually act, although in practice it can happen that a particular subject makes an objective end his or her subjective end. Kant's formal principle of morality, the categorical imperative, has only to abstract from subjective (and thereby contingent) ends, but not from objective (and thereby necessary) ends.

In the *Groundwork*, Kant argues that there is at least one objective end, namely, humanity (by which Kant understands the rational nature of human beings, that is, their capacity of rational and autonomous choice).[10] The argument for this, in a nutshell, is the following (see, especially, G 4: 427–428, 435, 437–438, 440). Absolute worth (that is, unconditional goodness) is an objective end, an end that holds for all rational beings. Whatever makes it possible is such an end too. The only thing of absolute worth in the world is a good will (this premise is taken from Part I of the *Groundwork*; see 4: 393–394). The capacity for autonomous choice is required for a good will, since a good will is a will which aims at morality for moral reasons, and such reasons cannot be based on inclinations, since the latter are – by (their) nature – orientated toward self-love, which can differ from and even conflict with morality (*G* Part I and 4: 444; *KpV* 5: 22–27, 33ff). In fact, the capacity for autonomy is required for a good will not as an independent precondition, but constitutively (*G* 4: 444) – willing autonomously consists in willing what is absolutely good and vice versa. Consequently, the capacity for autonomy is an objective end, and, as the idea of humanity consists in this capacity, humanity is an objective end.[11] As such, we have to treat humanity in all our action always as an end in itself, not merely as a means – and that is exactly what the formula of humanity requires.

The problem facing Hegel is that Kant seems here to be doing exactly what Hegel denies is possible: to derive some content from the mere idea of good willing (which, in the case of human beings, comes to the same as the mere idea of duty for duty's sake – as Hegel concedes, at least for argument's sake in *PR* §§133–135). Admittedly, what is derived here is not yet some specific duty but "only" an objective end. Still, this objective end plays an important part in generating specific ethical duties in the Doctrine of Virtue – for example, the arguments for the duty not to murder or maim oneself, the duty to oneself not to lie, and the duty against false humility rest centrally and explicitly on the claim that undertaking such acts would be to treat humanity in one's own person as a mere means (*MS* 6: 423, 429–430, 434–436). Similarly, duties to others, such as the duty of respect, are based on the same consideration as applied to others: we have this duty since otherwise we would treat others as mere means and disregard the dignity with which their humanity endows them (*MS* 6: 462, 466).

Turning to the two obligatory ends of one's own perfection and the happiness of others, Kant's argument here too is probably best constructed as relying heavily on the formula of humanity, at least in the case of the first obligatory end. To say that one's own perfection is an obligatory end is to say that we have a duty to develop and protect our capacities. Specifically, this means that we have a duty to preserve our body, to develop our moral capacity to act, to cultivate our natural powers and faculties as well as moral predispositions. The argument in support of the thesis that this is an obligatory end could just be seen as an extension of the argument that humanity is an end in itself. Thus, if our capacity for autonomy is an objective end because it is required for there to be absolute worth, then whatever makes this autonomy possible is also an objective end. Protecting and developing our capacities is required to sustain and actualize auton-omy, and, hence, our own perfection is obligatory as an end. Admittedly, this judgment relies on some knowledge of human beings – that they are born in such a way that their capacities need to be developed, that they have vulnerabilities and needs which make it necessary to protect their capacities, and so on. Still, the knowledge required here is of a very general nature and, at least in part, just an extension of the very idea of a finite, embodied rational agent.

Why is the perfection of others not also an obligatory end? Well, Kant thinks that we cannot directly promote the perfection of others – for perfection requires that agents set their own ends in the light of their understanding of duty, and such end-setting no one can do for someone else (*MS* 6: 386). Still, we can and should help others to be *in the position* to perfect themselves – and this thought leads us to the second obligatory end, the happiness of others, since sensuous creatures that we are, we would have difficulties to work toward our own perfection, if we were unhappy, and to avoid the latter we require the help of others.

If the happiness of others is an obligatory end for us, then this means that we have the duty to promote the ends of others, at least as long as these ends are morally permissible. The argument in Kant's text builds more on the idea of the formula of universal law and thereby presents an even more direct counterexample to Hegel.[12] If I takes the maxim of self-love and test it by way of the categorical imperative, then I realize that universalizing the maxim requires me to include the happiness of others among my ends (*MS* 6: 393; see also *KpV* 5: 34). I can rationally will to promote my own happiness only if I also accept the happiness of others as a reason for action.[13] One might think that it follows from this that we have a general duty to promote everybody's happiness, including our own. However, for Kant it cannot be a duty to do something that we are anyway going to do, independently of having a duty to do it. Consequently, promoting one's own happiness cannot be a duty, since it is an end every human being has "by virtue of the impulses of his nature" (*MS* 6: 385f; see also 387, 451). Thus, we naturally tend to promote our own happiness anyway, but this is permissible only if we are willing to promote other people's happiness, too.[14] Hence, the happiness of others is an obligatory end for us and so is the duty to promote their ends (subject to the constraint that the ends they pursue to attain happiness are morally permissible ends). Again, merely certain general facts about human nature (such as that they naturally seek their own happiness) play a role in this argument.

Kant uses these two obligatory ends to derive some of our more specific ethical duties in the Doctrine of Virtue, particularly the duty to search one's conscience, the duties to develop and increase one's natural and moral perfection, the duties of beneficence, and the duty to oneself regarding non-rational beings (see especially *MS* 6: 441, 443, 445–447, 451–453). To take the latter as an example, Kant argues that we have a duty not to wantonly destroy natural beauty and not to be cruel to animals because doing either of these acts weakens or undercuts our work toward moral perfection. Specifically, it blunts dispositions important for morality, such as, presumably, our sensitivity to suffering of sensuous creatures, which human beings also are, after all.[15]

Insofar as both obligatory ends are clearly linked to the categorical imperative, this imperative frames the derivation of duties, while it is not by itself sufficient for the purpose of deriving specific duties. Instead, we need to draw on the specific nature of human beings and their circumstances – that they have needs, that they interact in various ways, that their capacities need to develop, etc. Nonetheless, no purported or candidate duties are brought to the derivation from the outside, nor any other normative ideas beyond what is contained in the concepts of duty for duty's sake, good will, and rational beings with wills. In this sense, one could argue that Kant's ethics contains an immanent doctrine of duties. While based on a formal principle of morality, it is not devoid of moral content, but includes a way to derive specific duties by reference to this principle and the general facts about human beings relevant to its application – or, at least, this is what Kantians would argue (see, in particular, Herman 1993, 2007).

What is striking about this is that Hegel must have been aware of Kant's claim about the two obligatory ends. In fact, his very denial (in *PR* §§134–135) that the duty to promote the happiness of oneself and of others follows from the idea of duty might be understood as a direct attack on Kant's claim that there is an obligatory end to promote the permissible ends of others.

Still, Hegel probably thought that he had undermined the argument at an earlier stage and, hence, did not need to engage with this downstream material. For example, his worry might have been that the arguments for the obligatory ends rely on the argument for the formula of humanity, and he would have taken issue with a number of the premises in that argument, such as the claim that the only thing of absolute worth is a good will or the thesis that moral reasons cannot be based on inclinations.[16]

Instead of following up the wider debate between Kantians and Hegelians that such a challenge to the key Kantian premises would entail, I want to take up a more direct Hegelian rejoinder. Even if Hegelians were to accept for argument's sake that some ends can be derived from fairly minimal premises within Kant's ethics, they would argue that the ends in questions are too general and vague to get to the kind of specific duties and guidance that would be required for actual ethical practice (see MacIntyre 1998: 96–97). What it is to respect another person will vary enormously from one age to the next and from one society to the next – it will be different in twelfth-century Japanese society from twenty-first-century Sweden, and it will be different from contemporary Cairo to the contemporary Bronx, New York. Similarly, the duty to help those in need will vary enormously with context, notably with institutional context.[17] Is there a state-run and coercively enforced redistributive mechanism in place to help those in need? If so, does the duty to help others extend merely to compliance with this mechanism or does it go beyond it? Are there perhaps two duties here (one to comply with just institutions and one of charity)? And what if there is no such mechanism or one that is problematic in one of various ways? Will not the duty to help those in need change quite fundamentally in this different context? And if so, in which way are we still talking of one and the same duty that is merely applied differently in different contexts?

In reply, Kantians might begin by conceding some element of contextuality, although they would probably maintain that this is really only an application issue.[18] It might well be true that what it is to treat someone with respect and as end in itself will vary from one age to the next and from one society to the next, but the general duty of respect is invariant, and the rest is just about specifying its detailed implications or the practical rules of implementing it. Still, Kantians would not accept more than this, and would present the following counter to the Hegelians. If one makes moral norms and duties too context-specific, one opens the floodgates to relativism and, perhaps more importantly for a Hegelian, one cannot demonstrate that the specific practices and institutions are rational. To avoid this, we have to be able to show how the specific moral duties fit with the demands of reason – and the categorical imperative is meant to show just this. It brings out the choice-worthy aspects of maxims (and practices), and without it, we fall into either dogmatism or relativism – neither of which are suitable for Hegel's aim of *rational* reconciliation. As Ameriks puts it:

> But the crucial point here is that his superior concreteness can be a real advantage only if the content is *correct*. At this point, rather than lapsing into social relativism, as he is too often still charged with having done, Hegel tends to fall back on bounds set by pure morality: our commitment to *Sittlichkeit* is to be restrained by a Kantian respect for man as an end in himself. In this way

Hegel can properly criticize ancient slave culture as well as the similarly objectionable *Sittlichkeit* of some modern societies, but only at the price of relying on what seem to be the very abstract principles he meant to transcend. (Ameriks 2000: 314)

In sum, Kantians are happy enough to concede that we need what Herman has called "middle theory" – which includes not just general anthropological knowledge but also knowledge about the particular social context – in order to arrive at specific duties.[19] Still, if we gave up on framing this derivation of duties by the categorical imperative (and the objective and obligatory ends), then we would give up on any rational grounding altogether.

At this point, Hegelians will counter that the categorical imperative does precious little work in the actual derivation of duties. Instead, when Kant in his time and Kantians nowadays say that they derive duties, they, in fact, just fall back on the ethical life that surrounds them (or the remnants thereof) (see MacIntyre 1998: 191, 197, 207–208). Rather than holding social practices to an independent critical standard, they, perhaps unwittingly, rely on contextually given norms and turn into defenders or, at most, reformers of the status quo (as they see it). Presumably, this reassertion of the basic objection is partly due to the fact that Hegelians think that the categorical imperative does not actually provide a workable criterion with which to test maxims or candidate duties. And in this way the debate about the first criticism by Hegel merges into the debate of his second criticism, to which I will turn now.

2.2   A criterion for testing the candidate duties

Kant suggests at one point that an important function of the categorical imperative is to counteract our tendency to rationalize our past behavior and future actions in such a way as to let us get away with breaches of what we – at least in the abstract – already know is morally wrong (*G* 4: 405). The categorical imperative can do this counteracting work, since we can use it to test our maxims and, presumably, also any purported duty for whether or not they are genuinely morally permissible or required. It would thus be a serious blow, if Hegel was right that the categorical imperative is unsuitable for this purpose because it does not actually contain a criterion that rules genuine maxims (and candidate duties) in and problematic ones out. Moreover, it would be a blow to Kantians, whichever of the three reply strategies sketched above they adopt.

Hegel's criticism is specifically directed against the formula of universal law, that is, the categorical imperative to "act only on that maxim through which you can at the same time will that it should become a universal law" (G 4: 421). In effect, Hegel says that this formula does not go beyond the mere idea of duty as the lack of contradiction. There is truth in this assertion insofar as Kant would presumably admit that the formula of universal law is about whether or not one can will *without contradiction* that one's maxim become universal law. Specifically, for Kant, there are two kinds of cases of contradiction at stake: (1) one cannot will the maxim to be a universal law because its universalization cannot be conceptualized (that is, there is what is nowadays called a "contradiction in conception"); or (2) the maxim is conceivable as universal law, but its universalization can still not be willed by rational beings (that is, there is "a contradiction in willing").[20] A strict duty is one where universalizing a maxim contrary to it would generate a contradiction in conception, while a wide duty is one where universalizing a maxim contrary to it would avoid this problem, but instead generate a contradiction in willing. Kant's famous example of false promise-making (purportedly) illustrates contradictions in conception – I cannot even conceive of a world where false promise-making were a universal maxim because in such a world there would be no promising and, hence, there could not be false promise-making (see G 4: 422). The classic Kantian example of a contradiction in willing is the maxim of refraining from helping others in need (see G 4: 423): a world based on the universalization of this maxim would be radically deficient because finite rational beings, such as us human beings, are dependent on others, and, consequently, it would be irrational to will the maxim in question to be a universal law.[21]

Hegel does not discuss contradiction in willing, perhaps because he thinks that if the contradiction in conception test fails, the whole enterprise is doomed – after all, strict duties would then not be accounted for. What he does discuss (and repeatedly so) is a variant of the false promising example from the *Critique of Practical Reason*, the Deposit Example (*KpV* 5: 27; see *PS* ¶437; *PR* §135R). In this example, Kant imagines that someone placed a deposit with another person, but subsequently died and left no record of it. For the person with the deposit, this would be an occasion to act on the maxim "to increase my wealth by every safe means," but this person might test whether or not this is a permissible maxim by asking whether or not the maxim could be willed as a universal law. Kant says it could not be so willed, since in a world where it was a universal law that people did not return unrecorded deposits when it is safe to keep them, "there would be no deposits at all" (*KpV* 5: 27) or at least no unrecorded ones. One might object here to specific aspects of the example or to Kant's reasoning, but Hegel presses a deeper point: without the premise that property is a morally permissible institution and theft morally problematic, the mere fact that someone does not return a deposit to his or her owners (or to the heirs) cannot be shown to be morally problematic, for there is nothing with which this act or the underlying maxim could come into contradiction. To recall the passage from the *Philosophy of Right*, neither denying the right to existence of a particular group, nor rejecting such a right for humanity as whole, nor saying that there should be no institution of property leads to a contradiction, unless we already assumed what would have to be shown: that we have a duty to preserve or at least not endanger human life and a duty to respect people's property. Without these presuppositions, neither a contradiction in conception nor a contradiction in willing could be generated.

Kantian replies to this could emphasize the following two points. First, if they adopt the third reply strategy sketched in the previous section, they could argue that Kant pulls off the trick of generating content from the mere idea of duty for duty's sake, or at least from this idea in conjunction with some anthropological knowledge. Thus, not returning a deposit as a means for self-enrichment is morally problematic since it disregards an objective end by treating another rational being as mere means, not as an end in itself. Insofar as rational willing is committed to this objective end, there is something after all with which the maxim to disregard human life or someone's property is in contradiction, namely, this objective end. Hegel is right insofar as generating a contradiction requires something with which the maxim can come into conflict, but he is wrong in overlooking that the categorical imperative, despite being a merely formal principle, contains something with which maxims and candidate duties can come into conflict. To put it in Herman's terms, the categorical imperative contains immanently a criterion of choice worthiness (the objective end of humanity, the obligatory ends of one's own perfection and of the happiness of others) and, while this criterion might have to be supplemented by knowledge about human beings and their circumstances, it plays a major role in identifying which maxims are permissible and which ones are not (see Herman 1993, esp. chs. 7 and 10).

Second, Kantians could argue that the Hegelian worry is misconceived, even independently of any of the reply strategies already sketched – that is, they could claim that the objection can be answered, even if we do not invoke the earlier points about objective and obligatory ends. Specifically,

Hegel seems to assume that we would first need to show that promising or property are justifiable institutions in order to show that acting contrary to them is morally problematic. Walsh puts this Hegelian worry – in the context of the false promising example – as follows:

> We may agree that in these circumstances [i.e., when the maxim to make false promises to further one's desires would be universalized] the whole institution of giving and accepting promises would collapse without possibility of revival. But it does not follow that a world without promises would be morally inferior to the existing world; all that Kant demonstrates is that you cannot both accept the institution of promise-keeping and repudiate something which necessarily goes with it, namely that a person who makes a promise intends to carry it out. Hegel is quite right that it is a presupposition of Kant's argument that it is right to keep the promises: the very conclusion his appeal to the universalisation test is supposed to justify. (Walsh 1969: 23)[22]

What is misconceived here, the Kantians could argue, is that we are supposed to deal with a contradiction in conception, not a contradiction in willing (where the rational acceptability of institutions might play a role). The contradiction in the case of the maxim of false promise-making is that the maxim both relies on the existence of an institution (here promise-making) and, if adopted as universal law, makes its existence impossible. This suffices to strike the maxim down, independently of the merits or demerits of the institution in question. A justification of the institution is neither assumed, nor necessary, since the agent in invoking the institution already accepts it in a sufficient sense: he or she cannot both want to use it and undermine the possibility of its existence.[23]

Admittedly, such a contradiction does not show that the institution in question (say promise-making or private property) is morally permissible. Still, this is neither necessary to defeat the maxim, nor is the testing of that maxim meant to be an evaluation of the institution. The latter would involve either a different maxim (such as one about introducing or complying with the institution in question) or a different argument altogether – such as Kant's argument for private property in the Doctrine of Right, which is more like a transcendental argument with regard to external freedom than about universalizing a maxim that involves making use of an institution. In this sense, it might well be right to say that testing the specific maxim is not suitable to test whether or not the institution involved is morally permissible. Yet, testing specific maxims of individuals would be the wrong place to look for an evaluation of institutions, and Kant can offer other mechanisms for evaluating institutions and whether or not they should exist.

A more promising Hegelian line is to argue that it is misleading to evaluate an institution and the maxim making use of it wholly independently of each other – such a strict division of labor is likely to generate blind spots or overlook important moral elements. Basically, what the contradiction in conception test might be good at is showing that free riding is impermissible. Still, even if it were good at showing this, it could be seen to give the wrong result, since not all free riding or non-compliance with institution is obviously impermissible. Imagine a society in which one can own and sell other human beings as slaves. Common sense morality (within modern liberal societies) would criticize this society as morally problematic, and Kantian moral theory would want to vindicate this. Now, imagine that someone in this society bought slaves in order to set them free. If the maxim acted on by this person would be universalized, then it might well fail the contradiction in conception test, since in a world in which everybody acted on this maxim, there would (soon) be no slaves to buy and sell anymore. Still, does this mean that the person freeing the slaves violated a strict duty? This seems absurd. At most, we might want to say that the even better course of action is not to partake in the buying and selling of human beings at all, but to try to undermine this practice by other means. But even then, would we want to say that the chosen conduct is morally impermissible rather than merely suboptimal? The contradiction in conception seems to produce here a false negative, that is, it excludes something as a violation of a strict duty that is not obviously such a violation.[24]

Kantians would tend to say here that there was something wrong *not* with the test provided by the categorical imperative but, rather, with the *formulation* of the maxim – for example, the maxim should not be described as buying slaves in order to free them, but as acting against unjust institutions by legally permissible means. Still, in order for this reply not to be merely ad hoc, Kantians would have to provide clear limits and guidance on maxim formulation, and do so without smuggling in substantive ethical content. In this way, the discussion has to move on to what Kantians can reply to Hegel's third criticism.

2.3 False positives (and negatives)

What has been said so far in response to Hegel might also *seem* sufficient to answer his claim that Kant's testing procedure yields false positives (that is, his claim that it can be used to justify immoral acts).[25] If, after all, there is some content to the formal idea of duty (most notably, the objective end of humanity and the obligatory ends of one's own perfection and other people's happiness) and if contradictions in conception might actually have some bite as a criterion, then it is unlikely that it is possible to justify any wrong or immoral mode of action by means of the categorical imperative. Killing, deceiving, and robbing people will run counter to the objective end of humanity, and possibly involve the agent contemplating these acts in a maxim that both invokes the existence of institutions (such as promising, property, etc.) and, if universalized, makes their existence impossible.

However, there might be more to this third claim by Hegel than is let on by the brief remark in the *Philosophy of Right*. When we turn to the *Phenomenology of Spirit*, we can see Hegel making a similar point: "Just because the criterion [of rational consistency] is a tautology, and indifferent to the content, one content is just as acceptable to it as its opposite" (PS ¶430). More specifically, it turns out that the objection here is, at least in part, related to what is sometimes called the Act-Description Problem. As Hegel argues in the context of the discussion of the Deposit Example (¶437; see *KpV* 5: 27 and above), nothing prevents me from stopping to describe the object as deposit or the rightful property of someone else and viewing it, instead, as "my rightful property" or "an unowned object" – or so Hegel claims:

> If I should keep for myself what is entrusted to me, then according to the principle I follow in testing laws, which is a tautology, I am not in the least guilty of contradiction; for then I no longer look upon it as the property of someone else: to hold on to something which I do not regard as belonging to someone else is perfectly consistent. Alteration of the *point of view* is not contradiction; for what we are concerned with is not the point of view, but the object and content, which ought not to be contradictory. Just as I can – as I do when I give something away – alter the view that it is my property into the view that it belongs to someone else, without becoming guilty of contradiction, so I can equally pursue the reverse course. (*PS* ¶437; emphasis original)

The crucial point in this argument is that changing my description of the object in question is not contradictory and, hence, not excluded by the testing procedure. In this sense, it seems again as if the criterion provided by rational consistency (or willing my maxim as universal law without contradiction) is not sufficient as criterion and might not exclude immoral acts and maxims.

One way to capture Hegel's point somewhat differently is to say that Kant faces a dilemma when it comes to the input into the test that the categorical imperative supposedly provides: if the moral law just consists in the requirement that we should not act other than on a maxim that could be a universal law, then any maxim can be made to conform to the moral law, if suitably described (the Act-Description Problem);[26] if, on the other hand, there are constraints on what kind of maxims (or act descriptions) are the right ones to be tested, then Kant's ethics is not formal, but contains substantive constraints after all.

It may help to consider an example. A man we might call "Eric Cantona" is leaving the football pitch in anger and while walking toward the changing room a fan from the opposite team insults him.[27] Cantona could consider whether it is permissible to act on the maxim "Whenever I am insulted by someone, I will kick them." Now, one would expect this maxim to fail the categorical imperative, and to do so under the more demanding requirement of the contradiction in conception test – after all, to avoid such behavior would be a strict duty, not a wide one. It is actually less obvious than it should be how the argument would run, but we could always have recourse again to the formula of humanity. Also, even if the universalization of this maxim would not lead to a contradiction in conception, it would, at the very least, generate a contradiction in willing – for who could rationally will a world in which everybody just kicked someone else whenever they are insulted? Let us grant then that the specified maxim would be excluded as impermissible. Still, Cantona does not test the suggested maxim, but instead considers a maxim with much more specific detail: "Whenever I, a French player with the number 7 of the football club Manchester United, am insulted by the Crystal Palace fan Matthew Simmons on 25 January 1995 in the Crystal Palace football stadium, I will kick the amassed matter at space x." Here, it seems very difficult, if not impossible, to claim that there is a contradiction in conception or in willing – for I can consistently conceive and perhaps even rationally will a world where everyone who is the French Player with the number 7 of the football Club Manchester United, is permitted to kick the amassed matter at space x when they are insulted by the Crystal Palace fan Matthew Simmons on the 25th January 1995 in the Crystal Palace football stadium. As there is only going to be – at most – a one-off application of this maxim, even if it were universally adopted by everyone, it seems that it does not undermine any important institutions, or in other ways run counter to many of the usual things Kantians say would make passing the universalizability test impossible. Moreover, the description is, at once, specific and vague, and in such a way that none of the important moral elements that one would normally flag up come into view.

There are a number of things Kantians say in response to the Act-Description Problem, not all of which are necessarily compatible with each other. I will start here with the most important and generally accepted line of response. Testing maxims for conformity with the categorical imperative is first and foremost a test to assess maxims for action from the deliberative, first-personal perspective (rather than a third-personal assessment of rightness of action). The first-personal perspective brings certain constraints on maxim formulation with it. The maxims need to be at least minimally rational, where this means that they must conform to the hypothetical imperatives in question (rules of skill (technical) and counsels of prudence (pragmatic)) – otherwise they fail as principles of willing and action, quite independently of their moral permissibility. The maxims to be tested also have to be those that the agent sincerely believes he or she actually acts on. Finally, we are interested only in action types, not specific acts – that is, we are interested in, for example, deception for personal gain, not the specific time of day this takes place. These three constraints are not substantive in a way that takes anything away from the formalism of Kant's ethics, since they are part of the very idea of maxims as subjective principles of action and the particular first-personal use to which we put the categorical imperative – if we want to know whether the behavior we intend to undertake and the specific reasons for why we undertake it are permissible, we had better make sure that we test the relevant maxim, that is, one which sincerely describes what we are up to, which involves the required means, and which is sufficiently general to allow for whichever specific variation is required to then put it into practice. These constraints are not independent moral constraints, but constitutive norms of the very process of testing our maxims for moral permissibility.[28]

Let us return to the Eric Cantona Example and look specifically at the second constraint mentioned, sincerity. If the maxim is formulated in such a specific way as my example above was – "Whenever I, a French Player with the number 7 of the football Club Manchester United, am insulted by the Crystal Palace fan Matthew Simmons on the 25th January 1995 in the Crystal Palace football stadium, I will kick the amassed matter at space x" – then it must be part of the intention that it stands and falls with this specificity. Thus, Cantona was not permitted to kick the Crystal Palace fan on his adopted maxim, if he had just found out that he was in fact not French. Yet, it would seem that Cantona would have proceeded to kick the fan, even if he had discovered this fact. Hence, it seems that the maxim he ascribed to himself is not the maxim he did, in fact, (set to) act upon, as he would have admitted, if pressed. The actual sincere maxim would have not depended so much on specific details as the imagined one did, and Cantona could have known this. Yet, this means that the imagined one was insincere and as such unsuitable anyway for testing it as a maxim for action he was actually going to adopt. In this way, a lot of maxims, which look like they would pass the test of the categorical imperative because they are too specific or idiosyncratic would be disallowed even before this test is applied.[29] Consequently, a significant first step toward overcoming the Act-Description Problem is to recognize that the maxims to be tested have to meet the requirement that they are sincerely held and instrumentally rational (as well as stated in terms of action types).

The Act-Description Problem concerns not just the objection that impermissible maxims could pass the categorical imperative as long as they are specified in a particular way. Rather, this problem (or, at any rate, a related problem) is also about the fact that some action descriptions, on which it seems perfectly permissible to act, do not pass the universalizability test. We have already encountered one example earlier (see section 2.1.2), but let us take another, even more innocent-looking example here. The maxim "Whenever I eat cake with friends, I ought never to take the first piece" is non-universalizable (it even leads to a contradiction in conception), but it still seems morally permissible. So, the categorical imperative seems to give counterintuitive results also by way of false negatives.

The Kantian reply we have considered already will help here too. Thus, if I think about it, what I actually want to know is whether I can rationally will to be respectful or generous, not (primarily) whether or not this will mean to never take the first piece of cake. If we tested this more general maxim ("I will be respectful to my friends" or "I will act as a good friend acts"), then the answer generated by way of the categorical imperative would fit our intuitive answer, namely, that it is morally permissible to be respectful toward our friends and to act as good friends do (at least, other things being equal, that is, as long as we do not neglect some other, more urgent duties in doing so). Moreover, if an agent actually thought that what mattered was never to take the first piece of cake (rather than friendship or respectful treatment of others), then the categorical imperative would rightly show this person that this concern is morally problematic – or, to put it slightly differently, such a concern (never taking the first piece of cake) would be shown to miss the point of both (1) what is important about friendship or treating others respectfully and (2) what it is to act in a permissible and good way (see Timmermann 2007: appendix C).

Moreover, this reply strategy also suggests that one could disagree with Hegel's claim that an alteration of a point of view or redescription of something (say, from Smith's rightful property to my rightful property) is not a contradiction. After all, at least if I intentionally alter my point of view or redescribe something, then I also act on a maxim – say the maxim "Whenever it is to my advantage, I will redescribe things, actions or maxims so as to make my behavior and willing appear to be compatible with the categorical imperative." One could argue that this maxim would itself not pass the categorical imperative, and to act on it would display insincerity not in the practically self-defeating sense of not really testing the maxim I genuinely want to act on, but in the direct moral sense of aiming at deception.

Still, there is something unsatisfying about the Kantian reply strategy, for the problem is not just that the maxim tested was not sincerely held or might have involved an impermissible deception strategy, but that – even if it had been sincerely held in all its specificity and was not adopted to deceive – the action it proposed is morally problematic: assuming that the deposit really ought to be returned, then this part of it has been lost track of in the response considered so far to the Act-Description Problem. The categorical imperative would be suitable only to pick up on the second-order maxim of deception, but absent such a maxim and insincerity, the presence of either too much specificity or too much vagueness (or both) in the description means that the testing process would not pick up on the morally salient features and would not yield the result of excluding what is morally impermissible and allowing what is permissible. Similarly, if we think back to the slave-freeing example, it seems as if the maxim "I will buy slaves in order to free them" could be sincerely held (and is instrumentally rational and formulated in terms of action types), but would still come out as impermissible on that formulation. In other words, the categorical imperative does not exclude impermissible and pass permissible actions, unless they are sincerely and correctly described in the first place.

Herman suggests a reply to worries such as these when she accepts that human beings need not just to know the categorical imperative, but also be to educated in rules of moral salience to realize that they are in a moral situation and to identify the features that require moral deliberation (1993: ch. 4).[30] This represents a break with what Kant says in his more optimistic moments about the categorical imperative, namely, it is a break with his claim that everyone could know (or, at least, be assured of) what is morally required of them just in virtue of the compass the categorical imperative provides (*G* 4: 404; see also *KpV* 5: 27, 35–37).[31] Still, there are other passages where Kant acknowledges that certain sensibilities and the capacity of moral judgment are required as background conditions of moral agency (*MS* 6: 399–402), and in some places he even admits that we require experience in sharpening these sensibilities and the capacity to judge in order to recognize what we have to do in specific situations and be motivated to act accordingly (see, most notably, *G* 4: 389).

However, if we need rules of moral salience, or moral sensibilities to correctly describe the situation and to make correct use of the categorical imperative, then one might again question whether the categorical imperative still does any useful work. If I have described the situation correctly so as to bring the morally salient features in view and I am generally disposed to act morally, then why does this not suffice by itself to settle what I have to do? Why do I still need to consult the categorical imperative? In fact, many of the paradigm examples of morally right behavior – such as the actions of those who helped Jews to escape persecution and death during the Nazi reign – did not involve any appeal to the categorical imperative or much reflection at all, but simply the perception of the need of others and the danger they were in (see Halter 1998). On the other hand, knowledge of and appeal to the categorical imperative did not stop people from carrying out some of the most paradigmatic evil acts – Eichmann famously claimed to have always tried to live according to the requirements of the categorical imperative and quoted it in his defense (see Arendt 1994: 135–136).

In reply, it could be argued that one reason why testing my maxim by way of the categorical imperative might still be required or, at least, be useful is that even if I have the morally salient features clearly in view, I might not yet know how to adjudicate between them and the categorical imperative test could help with this task, at least once the situation is described correctly. Probably, Kantians would not claim that we would, in all cases, actually have to go through the procedure, but merely that we could and that doing so would yield the right results. Moreover, as already mentioned, given our tendency to rationalize away what we know is morally required, actually going through with testing our maxims by way of the categorical imperative is an important counterweight to this tendency.

Perhaps more worrying are the following two objections. First, if Kant's optimism is indeed unfounded and has to be given up in the way Herman suggests, the issue of culpability becomes much trickier, since luck now plays a much bigger role in whether or not the individual is fully capable of describing the situation and using the categorical imperative correctly. There are related repercussions, such as the fact that the alleged advantage of the categorical imperative over the counsels of prudence – that the requirements of the former, but not of the latter, are always "quite easily seen and without hesitation by the most common understanding" as well as "within everyone's power at all times" to satisfy – disappears, and with it also goes the reasonableness of the moral demands to "command compliance from everyone, and indeed the most exact compliance" (*KpV* 5: 36).[32]

Second, one other important lesson from this discussion is that the earlier Kantian argument that the categorical imperative (or the objective end of humanity) could and should be used to test for the permissibility of social practices is now shown to rest on presuppositions that call the viability of its employment for this purpose into question. How could the categorical imperative provide a critical standard of this sort, if it actually turned out that using it correctly relied on having been brought up to recognize morally salient features? Presumably, if social practices are morally problematic, the moral upbringing and education in that society may well be problematic too. If so, the purported advantage of abstract morality over concrete ethical life – that the former, but not the latter, offers us the resources to evaluate our social practices on the basis of a standard independent from them – evaporates, at least for those within these practices. And if the social world contains some non-corrupted normative resources and upbringing after all, then no appeal to context-transcendent standards will be required.

In sum, something of Kant's enlightenment optimism – the optimism that we can all use our own reason unassisted, whatever our upbringing or social context – is required to keep the Kantian and Hegelian positions apart, but one could reasonably disagree about the viability of this view and even Kantians seem to have given up on this optimism. To stay with the boxing analogy with which I started, it looks like the result is a split decision points victory for the Hegelians.

Acknowledgments

For comments and criticisms on earlier drafts, my thanks go to audiences in Newcastle and Stirling. Special thanks are due to Thom Brooks, Rowan Cruft, Wayne Martin, Bob Stern, and the fellow members of the Cambridge

Forschungskolloquium (Manuel Dries, Martin Eichler, Raymond Geuss, Michael Hampe, Richard Raatzsch, Jörg Schaub, and Christian Skirke).

Notes

1. In fact, Hegel goes on to point to the *Phenomenology of Spirit* for a discussion of further antinomies that the Kantian position gives rise to (*PR* §135R, referring to *PS* ¶¶596–631).
2. One might ask here by which means we are to ascertain that the maxims are immoral, given that they purportedly pass the categorical imperative. One way to argue here is that Hegel (rightly) takes Kant to be trying to vindicate common sense morality, so that it would be a problem, if a maxim that is immoral by the lights of common sense would pass the categorical imperative (or if one seen as permissible would fail to pass it).
3. One could read Hegel's passage to entail the stronger claim that the categorical imperative contains *no criterion whatsoever*, not merely that it contains no criterion for testing potential duties. While the text is not conclusive, one downside of this stronger reading is that the third criticism would then make little sense – if there is no criterion whatsoever, there is no test and, hence, nothing would pass the categorical imperative, not even immoral acts.
4. The formula of universal law states: "act only in accordance with that maxim through which you can at the same time will that it become a universal law" (*G* 4: 421; see also 402, 437; *KpV* 5: 30).
5. Kant mentions at one point that the categorical imperative has such a counter-acting function (see *G* 4: 405). I take this up below (in section 2.2).
6. See, e.g., Knowles 2002: 215, with reference to *PR* §140R; see also Wood 1990 and Stern 2007.
7. In fact, some commentators think of the book *Metaphysics of Morals* as something more like Kant's practical anthropology and not really as a treaty in metaphysics of morals, which would deal mainly or even exclusively with a priori concepts and justification (see, e.g., Timmermann 2007: appendix F).
8. One possible objection to this strategy, which I will not be able to discuss here, is to doubt that the distinction drawn between descriptive and normative content is defensible, especially when anthropological and sociological knowledge are counted among the former.
9. The formula of humanity states: "Act in such a way that you always treat humanity, whether in your own person or in the person of any other, never simply as a means, but always at the same time as an end" (*G* 4: 429).
10. See, e.g., *G* 4: 439, where Kant directly equates "humanity" (*Menschheit*) with "rational nature" (*vernünftige Natur*). Thus, Kant means by "humanity"

something else than merely the human biological species. For him, humanity consists in the capacity to reason and to be moved to action by pure practical reason alone. It is a normative ideal, not merely a descriptive category.

11. For example, Kant writes that "autonomy is therefore the ground of the dignity of human nature and of every rational nature" (*G* 4: 436).

12. Still, the argument could also be run by way of the formula of humanity – presumably, to treat others as ends in themselves includes respecting and promoting their (permissible) ends.

13. A similar argument might be at the back of Hegel's mind when he claims that the welfare of all is a value for us (see *PR* §125; see also Knowles 2002: 187–189, although he does not mention this parallel to Kant). On the sense of rational willing at play here, see n. 26 below.

14. Although we do not have a direct duty to promote our own happiness, Kant admits that we have an indirect duty to promote it. If we are unhappy or lack means (say, when we are extremely poor), this may make it difficult or impossible to act morally. Hence, we have an indirect duty to avoid pain, adversity, and want, since we have a moral duty to preserve our moral agency and integrity (*MS* 6: 388; see also *G* 4: 399). This is only indirectly a duty to our own happiness, since directly it is a duty to preserve our "moral integrity" (*MS* 6: 388).

15. It is not my intention here to suggest that this argument is successful or plausible, but merely to highlight that the obligatory end of one's own perfection plays a recognizable role in Kant's and Kantian reasoning.

16. In fact, Hegel does elsewhere take issue with these premises. For example, he is often read to attack the central Kantian idea that morally worthy action requires that we do not act from inclination (see, e.g., Knowles 2002: 178–184, with reference to *PR* §§123–124; see also Rawls 2000: 333, 335). See Herman 2007: ch. 1 for a reply that emphasizes that Kantian autonomy might require only that my desires and inclinations be shaped by moral considerations, not that I act without or against them.

17. I take the issue of (institutional) context dependence to be at least part of the point of Hegel's discussion of "Love thy neighbour as thyself" in the *Phenomenology of Spirit* (see ¶425). See also MacIntyre's discussion of how circumstances alter what character traits are counted as virtues or vices (1998: 206) and change moral concepts (1998: ch. 1, esp. pp. 1–2).

18. See, e.g., Herman 2007, esp. ch. 2; see also her 1993: ch. 4.

19. On middle theory, see Herman 1993: 233–240. It is "the translation of a formal conception of value into terms suitable to the particular contexts of human action and deliberation" (240).

20. See, e.g., O'Neill 1989; for the textual basis underpinning this distinction, see *G* 4: 424. One common way to think about the categorical imperative is to ask whether or not we could conceive and rationally will a world in which one's

maxim is a natural law governing this world and determining human nature (see, e.g., Rawls 2000: 168–169). This approach takes its lead from a variant of the universal law formula, namely, the law of nature formula which states that we should "act as if the maxim of your action were to become by your will a universal law of nature" (*G* 4: 421). I will adopt this practice in the discussion which follows.

21. A comment on "rational willing" might be in order here. What Kant must mean by our inability to will the universalization of a maxim is not something that one simply cannot actually will, since there are things that one can actually will that are problematic (think of Hare's example of the imaginary Nazi who actually wills to be killed if he were a Jew, or of someone who is in such dire straits that he or she would agree to anything in order to be fed and housed). Rather, the contradiction in willing test is about what a *fully rational being* would be able to consent to. For this reason and in this sense, I speak of "rational willing" here. This should also bring out that rational here is more than taking the required means to further one's long-term self-interest – one can be rational in this (weaker) sense and not accept a moral duty to help others in need that goes beyond strict mutual advantage. A fully rational being, unlike us finite ones, would not be motivated by self-interest, but only by what pure practical reason required. To mark the difference to the weaker sense of rationality, some Kantians speak of "reasonable" to denote the stronger one (see Rawls 2000: 164–165).

22. Other commentators make a similar point; see, e.g., Houlgate 1991: 95–97; Westphal 1995: 490; and Knowles 2002: 206.

23. The exact nature of the contradiction is debated among Kantians, with the two leading interpretations being that a contradiction in conception is about (1) logical contradiction or (2) practical contradiction (acting in such a way as to undermine the very possibility of achieving the end one sets out to achieve by so acting). Fortunately, we need not enter into this debate here, since the response sketched in the main text is open on both interpretations. For further discussion, see Korsgaard 1996: ch. 3; Herman 1993: 136–143.

24. There is another objection here, although it is not clear, whether it is Hegel's or Hegelian (see also Henrich 1994, esp 102–103). It is, arguably, implausible to think that the most important reason for why physical abuse or torture is wrong is that we cannot universalize a maxim that aimed at them or at making use of them. In fact, it is also implausible to think that the only or even most important reason why physical abuse and torture are wrong is that they undermine our moral agency. If this is true, then one could argue that contradictions in conception or willing are not an adequate test for the (im)permissibility of maxims, since they do not reveal the right reasons why acting on the maxim is wrong. Especially on a Kantian picture, it is also those reasons which we want to know about and then act on. To Hegel's credit, he seems to acknowledge that

inflicting bodily harm is bad in itself (not just in virtue of resting on non-universalizable maxims or undermining our moral agency; see *PR* §48R). Admittedly, if those who ascribe moral realism to Kant are correct, then he could accept this too (although running the categorical imperative test would still not provide us with knowledge of the right reasons why inflicting bodily harm is wrong).

25. I will return to the issue of false negatives (mentioned in the previous section).
26. See also MacIntyre 1998: 197–198; Knowles 2002: 205–206.
27. As they say at the end of movie trailers, "any resemblance to persons living or dead is purely coincidental."
28. Admittedly, we might not test our maxims at all, but this would be a moral failing in at least some instances and one which has little to do directly with the Act-Description Problem. Also, we might test the false maxims (e.g., we might be deceived about our own motives). Kant cannot exclude this. For him, the best we can do is to describe the actions and motives as sincerely and as accurately as possible. The point in this context is that this requirement of sincerity already weeds out maxims of the sort that could yield false negatives or positives, and, hence, is an important resource in responding to the Act-Description Problem – or so the Kantians argue.
29. To repeat, the maxims in question would be ruled out even before testing them with the help of the categorical imperative, not because they conflict with substantive moral norms imported from the outside, but because they are incompatible with the constitutive requirements of acting and wanting to test the maxim one intends to act on (as well as the first-personal perspective involved in this).
30. See especially the following concession: "An agent who came to the CI procedure with no knowledge of the moral characteristics of actions would be very unlikely to describe his action in a morally appropriate way. Kant's moral agents are not morally naive. In the examples Kant gives of the employment of the CI procedure (G[, 4:] 422–423), the agents know the features of their proposed actions that raise moral questions *before* they use the CI to determine their permissibility. It is because they already realize that the actions they want to do are morally questionable that they test their permissibility. It is hard to see how any system of moral judgment that assessed maxims of action could work with morally naive or ignorant agents" (p. 75).
31. Herman is aware that her proposal "does not preserve the idea of a simple technique for maxim assessment," but suggests that this "loss (if it is a loss) will be more than made up if the CI procedure [that is, testing maxims by way of the categorical imperative] can be made to work" (1993: 131).
32. To claim that the purported advantage disappears is not to say that there are no other contrasts between the categorical imperative and counsels of prudence that might remain.

Abbreviations

Works by Hegel

PR   *Elements of the Philosophy of Rights,* trans. H. B. Nisbet, ed. Allen W. Wood. Cambridge: Cambridge University Press, 1991. Original work *Grundlinien der Philosophy des Rechts* [1821], repr. in *Werke,* vol. 7. Frankfurt: Suhrkamp, 1986.

PS   *Phenomenology of Spirit,* trans. A. V. Miller. Oxford: Oxford University Press, 1977. Original work *Phänomenologie des Geistes* [1807], repr. in *Werke,* vol. 3. Frankfurt: Suhrkamp, 1986.

Works by Kant

G   *Groundwork of the Metaphysics of Morals.* In *Practical Philosophy,* trans. and ed. M. J. Gregor. Cambridge: Cambridge University Press, 1996, pp. 41–108. Original work *Grundlegung der Metaphysik der Sitten* [1785], 4: 395–463.

KpV   *Critique of Practical Reason.* In *Practical Philosophy,* trans. and ed. M. J. Gregor. Cambridge: Cambridge University Press, 1996, pp. 137–271. Original work *Kritik der praktischen Vernuft* [1788], 5: 1–163.

MS   *The Metaphysics of Morals.* In *Practical Philosophy,* trans. and ed. M. J. Gregor. Cambridge: Cambridge University Press, pp. 362–603. Original work *Metaphysik der Sitten* [1797], 6: 203–493.

References

Ameriks, K. (2000) "The Hegelian Critique of Kantian Morality" [1987]. Repr. in *Kant and the Fate of Autonomy.* Cambridge: Cambridge University Press, pp. 309–337.

Arendt, H. (1994) *Eichmann in Jerusalem: A Report on the Banality of Evil* [1964], rev. and enlarged edn. New York: Penguin.

Halter, M. (1998) *Stories of Deliverance: Speaking with Men and Women who Rescued Jews from the Holocaust,* trans. M. Bernard. Chicago: Open Court.

Henrich, D. (1994) *The Unity of Reason: Essays on Kant's Philosophy.* Cambridge, MA: Harvard University Press.

Herman, B. (1993) *The Practice of Moral Judgement*. Cambridge, MA: Harvard University Press.

Herman, B. (2007) *Moral Literacy*. Cambridge, MA: Harvard University Press.

Houlgate, S. (1991) *Freedom, Truth and History: An Introduction to Hegel's Philosophy*. London: Routledge.

Knowles, D. (2002) *Hegel and the Philosophy of Right*. London: Routledge.

Korsgaard, C. M. (1996) *Creating the Kingdom of Ends*. Cambridge: Cambridge University Press.

MacIntyre, A. (1998) *A Short History of Ethics: A History of Moral Philosophy from the Homeric Age to the Twentieth Century* [1967], 2nd edn. London: Routledge.

O'Neill, O. (1989) *Constructions of Reason*. Cambridge: Cambridge University Press.

Rawls, J. (2000) *Lectures on the History of Moral Philosophy*, ed. B. Herman. Cambridge, MA: Harvard University Press.

Stern, R. (2007) "Freedom, Self-Legislation and Morality in Kant and Hegel: Constructivist vs. Realist Accounts." In E. Hammer, ed., *German Idealism: Contemporary Perspectives*. London: Routledge.

Stern, R. (2009) "The Autonomy of Morality and the Morality of Autonomy." *Journal of Moral Philosophy* 6(3): 395–415.

Timmermann, J. (2007) *Kant's Groundwork of the Metaphysics of Morals: A Commentary*. Cambridge: Cambridge University Press.

Walsh, W. H. (1998) *Hegelian Ethics* [1969]. Bristol: Thoemmes.

Westphal, K. R. (1995) "How 'Full' is Kant's Categorical Imperative. " *Jahrbuch für Recht und Ethik/Annual Review of Law and Ethics* 3: 465–509.

Wood, Allen W. (1990) *Hegel's Ethical Thought*, Cambridge: Cambridge University Press, pp. 127–173.

3

On Hegel's Critique of Kant's Ethics
Beyond the Empty Formalism Objection

Robert Stern

In the current literature on Hegel and Kant, an uneasy truce seems to have broken out in the trench warfare between Hegelians and Kantians over Kant's ethics. On the one hand, at least some commentators on Kant have started to take seriously the critical fire directed by Hegel at Kant's treatment of the Formula of Universal Law as the "supreme principle of morality," and so to that extent have accepted the force of Hegel's so-called "empty formalism" objection.[1] On the other hand, the Kantians' response has been to beat a tactical retreat on this issue, and to press forward on a new front, by arguing that the Formula of Universal Law (henceforth FUL) was never *meant* to stand alone as the supreme principle of morality, and that once it is put together with Kant's other formulae (particularly the Formula of Humanity (FH)), this can resolve the formalism problem, so that Hegel's point regarding the FUL can safely be conceded, while Kant's position *as a whole* can be saved. One attraction of this more concessive approach,[2] it may seem, is that both sides can then go away happy: Hegelians can be content that, rather than simply being dismissed, Hegel's objections to Kant have been taken seriously and to some extent accepted as valid, while Kantians can be pleased that the damage caused by Hegel can nonetheless be shown to be limited and only narrowly focused, and that overall Kant's ethics with its several related formulae remains intact.

In this paper I want to consider whether the questions at issue between Kant and Hegel can really be satisfactorily resolved in this manner. I will suggest that in fact Hegel's concerns go deeper than this concessive response to the empty formalism objection allows, and that these deeper concerns

Hegel's Philosophy of Right: Essays on Ethics, Politics, and Law, First Edition.
Edited by Thom Brooks.
© 2012 Blackwell Publishing Ltd. Published 2012 by Blackwell Publishing Ltd.

have still not been dealt with by the Kantians who adopt this less resolute approach – where, put briefly, those concerns resemble those of the particularistic intuitionist, and so will extend to *any* attempt to uncover a "supreme principle of morality," whether this is the FUL *or* the FH. However, I will also suggest that hopes for peace between the two camps should not be abandoned entirely: for, I will argue, on a certain understanding of what Kant was up to in seeking to identify the "supreme principle of morality," his position may be made more compatible with the sort of particularistic intuitionism which I claim is favored by Hegel, so that a truce of sorts may be viable after all – albeit one that requires further concessions on the Kantian side, but where these concessions are ones (I will argue) that Kant himself may well have been happy to make.

   I will begin by briefly recapping the history of the hostilities as they have been conducted in the recent literature thus far, and say more about the strategy adopted by the more concessive Kantians (section 1). I will then show why Hegel would not be satisfied by their position (section 2), and explore whether a further rethinking of Kant's approach might give rise to a more lasting peace (sections 3 and 4).

1   Hegel's Empty Formalism Objection and the Concessive Kantian Response

In the *Groundwork of the Metaphysics of Morals*, Kant sets out to identify and establish "the *supreme principle of morality*" (*GMM* 47/*Ak* 4: 392), which he initially claims to be the following: "*act only in accordance with that maxim through which you can at the same time will that it become a universal law*" (*GMM* 73/*Ak* 4: 421; all emphases original).[3] It is this that has come to be called Kant's Formula of Universal Law.[4]

   In picking out the FUL as the supreme principle of morality, Kant stresses that, unlike other candidates for this role that have been put forward by previous philosophers,[5] the FUL is a *formal* principle, not a material one. This, Kant claims, must be the case if the principle is really going to reflect the categorical nature of dutiful moral action, of the sort that common sense morality takes for granted as an essential part of moral life, for such action must not involve any expectation that performing it will help the agent to realize some non-moral end. It therefore follows, Kant argues, that what determines the will must be the formal properties of the maxim on which the agent acts, namely whether or not some sort of *contradiction* would be involved in acting in this way, where Kant locates the contradiction in the idea that if others adopted this maxim as their own too, acting on it would somehow become impossible, so that as a maxim for action it would undermine itself in this way.

Now, put at its simplest, Hegel's empty formalism objection is that precisely because Kant is operating here in purely formal terms, by trying to determine what is right and wrong by testing to see whether a maxim does or does not lead to a contradiction when universalized in this way, the FUL cannot in fact plausibly be used to give any *content* to morality, and so cannot really constitute the supreme principle of morality at all.[6] In order to demonstrate the FUL's uselessness in this respect, Hegel and Hegelians have introduced a series of puzzle cases, where the FUL seems to deliver either no result at all or one that is clearly mistaken, which Hegel and Hegelians take to show that the FUL is too flimsy to bear any normative weight, and so is in practice empty and always in need of further "content" or supplementation. Thus, as Hegel puts it in the *Phenomenology*, "The criterion of law which Reason possesses within itself fits every case equally well, and is thus in fact no criterion at all."[7] In order to bring out the problem, Hegel gives various examples, where the FUL seems either to yield conflicting results and so is indeterminate, or to yield so-called "false negatives,"[8] in seeming to rule out actions that we would ordinarily accept as perfectly morally legitimate.

To illustrate the indeterminacy claim, Hegel refers to Kant's own "deposit" case, where Kant considers someone who has had someone else's money entrusted to him, and who avariciously desires to keep it or is also in great need.[9] Hegel argues that the FUL cannot be used to determine one's duty in this case, for it cannot determine whether or not property or a social system without property is a morally good thing, as the contradictoriness of both options can be argued either way.[10] And to illustrate the false negatives claim, Hegel mentions the examples of fighting for your country, and of helping the poor, neither of which (he claims) can be universalized:[11] for if everyone defended their own country, no one would attack other people's countries, so that there would be no defending to be done, while if everyone helped the poor, no one would be in poverty, so that acts of benevolence would be prevented if universalized, seeming to suggest (absurdly) that maxims like "help the poor" are immoral insofar as they would fail the FUL test.

It is perhaps not surprising, however, that the response of some readers of Kant to these Hegelian objections has been rather dismissive.[12] For, in relation to the deposit case, Hegel may seem to have simply misunderstood how the FUL is meant to function, which is in relation to the *maxim* on which a person proposes to act, and whether or not so acting, if universalized, would lead to an undermining of the kind of trust required to keep the institution of property going on which they themselves rely: it therefore seems irrelevant that the FUL is indeterminate when it comes to deciding whether or not the institution of property *itself* is contradictory in some way – indeed, the Kantian may well agree with Hegel that it is hard to know what this could even mean. Now, to this, perhaps, the Hegelian might respond that surely if I am trying to decide whether to keep some property, I need first to know whether property is a good or bad thing. However, again the Kantian might reasonably deny this, arguing that it is sufficient to know that keeping the property is wrong if I can see that in keeping it, I would be free-riding or exploiting the good will of others – so that again, the contradictoriness or otherwise of property *itself* is irrelevant here.

And, when it comes to Hegel's supposed "false negatives," Kantians have responded by arguing that Hegel has misunderstood the maxims that would realistically be involved, and failed to show that these would genuinely fail the FUL test. For, it is pointed out, in order to count as a maxim, something like "help the poor" must have some specified end in view, and when this is spelt out in the morally admirable case (e.g., "help the poor in order to abolish poverty"), then there is no difficulty in the fact that, by everyone helping the poor, the end of so doing would be achieved – quite the contrary, in fact.

However, notwithstanding the plausibility of these Kantian responses, and the further ingenuity that has been used to deal with related complexities, there remains a feeling to which the more concessive Kantians are also sensitive, that Hegel was still on to something in raising his concerns, however much he may be convicted of somewhat misrepresenting and oversimplifying the way in which Kant presents the FUL as working. For, it can be argued on Hegel's behalf, that in an important sense he can use these Kantian responses to his own advantage. Thus, in relation to the property case, it may indeed be right to say that the FUL is not designed by Kant to adjudicate on the question of whether it is right or wrong for people to possess private property:[13] but isn't this *itself* a limitation? Surely anything purporting to be a "supreme principle of morality" *should* be able to adjudicate on such an issue, which has clear moral as well as political implications? Isn't it precisely a fault of the FUL that it is too narrow in this respect, and silent on this sort of question, which can plausibly be regarded as just one instance of many such cases concerning institutions? (For example: Is democracy more morally legitimate than any other political system? Is monogamy a better system of marriage from the moral point of view than polygamy? Is there any moral significance to marriage at all?) And second, in relation to the "help the poor" case, the Kantian response may also be said to highlight a deeper difficulty for their position, which is the notoriously problematic issue of determining how exactly maxims are to be framed and determined, where an agent might find she can come up with a different outcome for the FUL test by adjusting the maxim by which she proposes to act in ways that do not really alter the moral situation – for example, by making her maxim more specific in various ways, it might then become universalizable, but where what is still fundamentally a morally wrong action is being licensed, so that the problem of false results for the test re-emerges.

In addition to these ways in which Hegel's empty formalism objection may continue to be pressed, it can also be argued that there is a yet deeper worry underlying it, which is that the FUL is inadequate as the supreme principle of morality taken on its own, because something more substantive is required if we are to understand *why* there is any moral significance in acting on maxims that are universalizable – why this *matters* from a moral point of view. The problem might be put as a dilemma for the Kantian: on the one hand, he could answer this question by relating the FUL to considerations such as equality, fairness, or free-riding,[14] but then it is not clear why "treat others fairly" is not the supreme moral principle and the FUL merely a test for whether or not in acting a certain way one would be doing so; or he could treat the FUL as somehow prior in itself, but then make its moral relevance mysterious.

Now, while some commentators on Kant have continued the tradition of remaining unimpressed by these sorts of Hegelian considerations, others have accepted their force, and have given up the attempt to defend the FUL as a candidate for the supreme principle of morality in its own right. However, rather than then abandoning Kant's project in the *Groundwork* and elsewhere altogether, they have instead insisted that Hegel was being myopic in concentrating on *just* the FUL in the first place, and that the more significant ethical principles for Kant are given in the other moral formulae, particularly perhaps the so-called Formula of Humanity: "*so act that you use humanity, whether in your own person or in the person of any other, always at the same time as an end, never merely as a means*" (*GMM* 80/*Ak* 4: 429). The suggestion is that once the FH is made central in this way, Kant has a candidate for the supreme moral principle that can be said to overcome the difficulties faced by the FUL, in being more determinate; in recommending actions that better fit our intuitive moral judgments; and in making a clear connection to the sorts of values (such as our rational nature as agents) that make the moral basis for the principle readily apparent.[15]

And, on their side, commentators on Hegel have been generally prepared to accept this kind of Kantian approach, where in exchange for Kantian concessions regarding Hegel's critique of the FUL, they have been willing to allow that this critique is indeed rather narrow and that, using his other formulae, Kant may be able to escape the charge of empty formalism made against the FUL on its own.[16] In this way, therefore, a kind of stable consensus between both sides has emerged, with some ground being conceded on both sides.[17]

I now want to argue, however, that this consensus is premature,[18] and that Hegel's concerns do not *just* apply to the FUL and its peculiarities, but to *any* attempt to propose a "supreme principle of morality," *even* the less "formal" FH. Once the full extent of these concerns are considered, therefore, I will argue that if we are still searching for some consensus between Kant and Hegel, it must involve more than just this move from the FUL to the FH, or any other of Kant's proposed formulae.

2   Hegel's Intuitionism: Against a "Supreme Principle of Morality"

On the view of Hegel I want to put forward in this section, Hegel's objection to Kant may be compared with a form of intuitionism, where this is to be understood not primarily as an epistemological doctrine ("we know moral truths or propositions by intuition"), but as a doctrine that rejects the idea that morality has any single highest principle, and thus the view that there might be any "supreme principle of morality" at all, whether that is the FUL, the FH, or any other principle of a Kantian or non-Kantian kind (such as the utilitarian principle of maximizing happiness or well-being).[19] As generally conceived, intuitionism of this sort stands between those theories that think there is *one* highest moral principle that underpins all others, and those theories that say there are no moral principles *at all*, not even the many prima facie principles that the intuitionist allows, where this latter position is a form of strong particularism.[20]

A broad sympathy with the ideas behind an intuitionism of this sort is reflected in many aspects of Hegel's work. At the highest and most abstract structural level, Hegel is deeply preoccupied with the categories of universality, particularity, and individuality, where he argues throughout that any position that becomes too general and abstract will become empty, while any that focuses too much on the specificity of the individual case will lose sight of what is common between individuals, where the inadequacies of each of these sides will then cause us to oscillate to the extreme of the other. What is needed, therefore, across all philosophical positions (so, for example, in metaphysics, epistemology, philosophy of nature, philosophy of religion, philosophy of art, as well as ethics and political philosophy) is a standpoint that enables us to move between these extremes, and thus a theory that combines elements of generality with a sensitivity to the particularities of the situation. It is therefore scarcely surprising, then, that while Hegel opposes those who reject all talk of duties and rules as too abstract and general in favor of an inarticulable moral "feeling," he equally opposes attempts to reduce the complexity of the details of the moral situation to a simple principle to be applied to all cases, where one has thereby abstracted too much away from any differences between them. In his ethical writings, Hegel therefore makes no attempt to offer any "supreme principle of morality," as if particular duties were to be derived from or grounded in such a principle: it is these particular duties that must be treated as fundamental, as the higher principle is too abstract to serve plausibly as their foundation or basis – only if we "already had determinate principles concerning how to act" (Hegel, PR, §135A, p. 163/HW VII: 253–254), could we know how to operate with such a principle, rendering its claims to supremacy highly dubious.

Hegel's most extended discussion of the issues raised here can be found in the *Phenomenology*, in his analysis of a rationalistic approach to ethics that forms part of the "Reason" chapter as a whole, in the subsections on "Reason as lawgiver" and "Reason as testing laws."[21] In the first of these subsections, Hegel attacks a rationalism that lays down certain particular principles as *absolute* rather than as provisional, and thus tries to treat them as exceptionless and simple to apply, rather than as guidelines that require sensitivity to where they can go wrong. He thus considers the examples "Everyone ought to speak the truth" and "Love thy neighbor as thyself." In the former case, Hegel argues, this principle is plausible only if we are conscious of our own fallibility in knowing the truth, so that rather than being a principle we can use straightforwardly to determine our behavior, it in fact requires us to take our epistemic condition into account in a way that can be far from easy. Likewise, when it comes to the principle "Love thy neighbor as thyself," Hegel argues that we must exercise judgment in deciding what is genuinely in the best interest of the individual we are dealing with, where simply giving him what he wants or what would make him happy is not what is required: "I have to distinguish what is bad for him, what is the appropriate good to counter this evil, and what in general is good for him: i.e. I must love him *intelligently*. Unintelligent love will perhaps do him more harm than hatred" (*PS* 255/*HW* III: 314). But, Hegel claims, this may mean that in some situations it might be best if I did nothing to aid the individual, so that "this acting for the good of others which is said to be *necessary*, is of such kind that it may, or may not, exist; is such that, if by chance the occasion offers, the action is perhaps a 'work' and is good, but also perhaps not" (*PS* 256/*HW* III: 315).

Now, for the sort of rationalism that Hegel is considering at this stage of the *Phenomenology*, this is a frustrating outcome, as it cannot see how such provisional rules that require such complex judgments to apply can really count as genuine moral laws: "This law [of loving thy neighbor as thyself], therefore, as little has a universal content as the one we first considered [i.e., of telling the truth], and does not express, as an absolute ethical law should, something that is valid in and for itself" (*PS* 256/*HW* III: 315). Frustrated by this outcome, reason then adopts another strategy of trying to find a more absolute position in ethics, by moving from particular moral principles, to some general moral principle that perhaps stands above them, on which all lower-level principles are to be grounded and against which they are to be tested: "[Consciousness] takes up their *content* simply as it is, without concerning itself, as we did, with the particularity and contingency inherent in its reality; it is concerned with the commandment simply as a commandment, and its attitude towards it is just as uncomplicated as is its being a criterion for testing it" (*PS* 257/*HW* III: 317). However, Hegel argues, by attempting to base these particular principles on a single principle that is supposedly more fundamental than they are, we in fact invert the true order of priority, for the latter is no more than an abstraction from the former. Consciousness acknowledges this by the end of the subsection, in returning to a position that accepts (for example) that we "hit moral bedrock"[22] by recognizing that stealing someone's property is wrong because it belongs to them and so should not be appropriated, where seeking for some more general moral and genuinely "absolute" principle to underlie it can lead only to a distortion in our moral attitudes.[23]

Of course, given the complex dialectical structure of the *Phenomenology*, Hegel should not be simply taken as stating his final position here, or straightforwardly expressing his *own* view at all, as he is just laying out the next phase in the development of consciousness as it moves through the stages on its "highway of despair"; and consciousness will certainly need to move beyond the pre-modern view of the ethical that it returns to at this point, which treats morality as involving "the unwritten and infallible law of the gods" (*PS* 261/*HW* III: 322). Nonetheless, I would claim, this basic critique of abstract rationalism is preserved within Hegel's final position, and is reflected in the structure of the *Philosophy of Right*, where as I have noted, there is no attempt to offer anything equivalent to a "supreme principle of morality."

Moreover, Hegel's commitment to an intuitionist position of this sort is indirectly confirmed when it is seen that he is sensitive to a worry that one might therefore have about the *Philosophy of Right*, which is often said to arise for intuitionism more generally: namely, that it must end up treating the normative realm as nothing but a "heap of unconnected duties."[24] Now, for some philosophers this may not be a matter of concern; but Hegel, of course, is a systematic philosopher par excellence, and his conception of philosophy as a science is tied directly to the idea that it can find a rational structure in what otherwise may appear to be a random set of phenomena.[25] Indeed, in the early *Natural Law Essay* of 1802–1803, this is precisely the issue that he thinks drives us from an empiricist approach that is happy to treat laws and principles as a "heap" in this manner, to an a prioristic approach like Kant's, which then tries to reduce the "many" to a "one."[26] However, Hegel makes plain here that he thinks this approach is itself distorted and cannot succeed; instead, he suggests (in a way that then points to his procedure in the *Philosophy of Right* itself) that we must achieve a systematic and structured account of our various duties and moral principles in a *different* way, that can do without any such supreme principle to guide it.[27] Thus, like other intuitionists, Hegel suggests that there are way of finding necessary interrelations between the various duties in an organic manner that makes them amenable to rational and philosophical treatment, but *without* being committed to the search for a single "master" principle in order to do so – where this is precisely the project that is carried out (I would argue) in the *Philosophy of Right*, through Hegel's consideration of freedom and the will. Hegel thereby produces an account of the normative realm that is certainly more than a "heap of unconnected duties," but which also avoids the need to present any single principle of morality as somehow "absolute" or "supreme" as the method by which this is achieved.

Thus, interpreted in this way, while in these and related discussions, it is certainly the FUL as the "supreme moral principle" that Hegel criticizes, there is no reason to think that his criticisms apply *only* to that in particular:

in fact, his critique seems general enough to apply to *all* attempts to come up
with such a principle, whether that is the FUL, or the FN, or some other
Kantian or non-Kantian candidate.[28] And if this is right, then the move by
those concessive Kantians from the FUL to the FH cannot really be taken to
address Hegel's fundamental concerns; to do this properly, a more radical
view of Kant's position will need to be adopted.[29] It is that which I will now
attempt to offer and defend.

3   Kant on the Supreme Principle of Morality: Socratic or Pythagorean?

In order to do so, I will now appeal to a helpful distinction drawn by J. B.
Schneewind, between conceptions of moral theory that are *Socratic* and
those that are *Pythagorean*.[30]

What Schneewind means by the Socratic picture is the idea that, while
people have always had moral opinions and beliefs, what is still required is
for philosophers to find an undeniable foundation to those beliefs which
will make them indubitable, where without this ordinary moral thinking
will always remain insufficiently secure and warranted. By contrast, the
Pythagorean[31] picture holds that the truths of morality have already been
discovered and known as a result of divine revelation, so that ordinary moral
thinking has no need of philosophy to play any such systematizing and
grounding role. Rather, the task for philosophy is a different one, which is to
help frail human beings keep to the moral path:

> Belief that the Noachite revelation was the origin of moral knowledge itself
> would make it natural to ask why we have moral philosophy anyway . . . The
> answer to [this] question lies in human sinfulness. Our nature was damaged
> by the Fall. It not only dimmed our faculties, lessening our ability to
> understand God's commands and accept them. It also unleashed the pas-
> sions. Evildoers, driven by their lusts, seek to avoid the pangs of conscience, so
> they blind themselves to its clear dictates. They also strive to veil and confuse
> the moral thoughts of those whom they wish to entangle in their wicked
> schemes. Bad reasoning is one of their basic tools. Now reason is one of God's
> gifts to humanity. Among other things it enables us to hold on to at least some
> of the moral knowledge we need, once revelation has ceased. If reason makes
> moral philosophy possible, pride leads men to try to outdo one another in
> inventing schemes and systems of morality, and morality itself gets lost in
> their struggles. Since the causes of the misuse of reason and of bad philosophy

are now ingrained in our nature, there will be no final triumph of good philosophy until after the last judgment. But the battle must be kept up. Moral philosophy is to be understood as one more arena for the struggle between sin and virtue. (Schneewind 1998: 537)

As Schneewind notes, even when God played less of a role within the Pythagorean story in the more modern period, it was still accepted by some that "the basic truths of morality are readily accessible to human reason" (1998: 541), so that the task of philosophy was still conceived as correcting for our tendency to stray from the moral path, rather than to give our ordinary moral thinking a grounding it needs and would otherwise lack.

Now, within the Socratic approach, there is a clear pressure toward the view that in order for philosophy to play its role properly, it needs to come up with a "supreme principle of morality," as this is precisely the way in which our messy and insufficiently reflective ordinary ways of thinking about moral issues can be made properly systematic and given a stable grounding. This pressure was clearly felt strongly by J. S. Mill, who puts forward his case for the principle of utility in precisely these terms:

> there ought either to be some one fundamental principle or law, at the root of all morality, or if there be several, there should be a determinate order of precedence among them; and the one principle, or the rule for deciding between the various principles when they conflict, ought to be self-evident.
>
> To inquire how far the bad effects of this deficiency [of failing to have identified this principle] have been mitigated in practice, or to what extent the moral beliefs of mankind have been vitiated or made uncertain by the absence of any distinct recognition of an ultimate standard, would imply a complete survey and criticism of past and present ethical doctrine. It would, however, be easy to show that whatever steadiness or consistency these moral beliefs have attained, has been mainly due to the tacit influence of a standard not recognized. Although the non-existence of an acknowledged first principle has made ethics not so much a guide as a consecration of men's actual sentiments, still, as men's sentiments, both of favour and of aversion, are greatly influenced by what they supposed to be the effects of things on their happiness, the principle of utility, or as Bentham latterly called it, the greatest happiness principle, has had a large share in forming the moral doctrines even of those who most scornfully reject its authority. Nor is there any school of thought which refuses to admit that the influence of actions on happiness is a most material and even predominant consideration in many of the details of morals, however unwilling to acknowledge it as the fundamental principle of morality, and the source of moral obligation. (Mill 1972: 3)

Mill then immediately goes on to mention Kant, assuming without question that Kant too was looking for the "one fundamental principle or law" that is needed here, but criticizing the FUL for its failure to fulfill this role adequately, which is why something more like the principle of utility is needed (see Mill 1972: 3–4).[32] By placing Kant alongside himself within the Socratic tradition, Mill therefore has no difficulty in making Kant's outlook seem as at odds with any form of intuitionism as his own self-consciously sets out to be, making any possible reconciliation with Hegel seem irredeemably bleak.[33]

However, as Schneewind notes, there are perhaps good grounds for criticizing Mill's assumption here, and for in fact thinking of Kant not as operating with Mill's Socratic picture, but rather as working with something more like the Pythagorean one.[34] For, when Kant comes to explain why his attempt to come up with the "supreme principle of morality" is needed, he does not express any sense that without it ordinary morality is in jeopardy, in failing otherwise to have a proper systematic structure or rationale; on the contrary, he seems to think that ordinary moral thought is in perfectly good order just as it is. Where the supreme principle is needed, rather, is in the Pythagorean fight between good and evil within the human breast, as a way of helping us avoid the kind of bad faith and self-deception that can so easily allow us to become corrupted in our actions, where at one level we know perfectly well what we should do, based on the various principles imparted to us through our ordinary moral education which come prior to any philosophizing.

Kant's position here can be seen most clearly, perhaps, in the *Groundwork*, particularly in sections I and II, which is where Kant sets about identifying the FUL (and related formulae) as the "supreme principle of morality." In those sections, Kant presents himself as proceeding *analytically*, starting from our commonly shared moral conceptions. In these sections, therefore, Kant seems more than happy to accept that we have a good grasp of morality without any need for philosophy, where he does not expect us to find the Formula of Universal Law to be revisionary of that grasp in any way – indeed, if it were, he would allow that it would be an objection to his claim that it constitutes the supreme principle that he is looking for here. Kant therefore does not see himself as adding to our ordinary moral understanding, or to be offering some sort of philosophical perspective from which he can address those who lack it. Thus, Kant willingly accepts that in arriving at the Formula of Universal law, he is not teaching "the moral cognition of common reason" anything new, but simply making it "attentive to its own principles": "there is, accordingly, no need of science and philosophy to know what one has to do in order to be honest and good, and even wise and virtuous" (Kant, *GMM* 58/*Ak* 4: 404).[35] Kant therefore seems to take for granted that our moral practices are in good order and in no need of defense or justification, and that philosophy can proceed by simply reflecting on them, to bring out the fundamental moral principle on which they rely.

Nonetheless, it might be said, nothing in this shows that Kant was not proceeding in the Socratic manner.[36] For, one might consistently think that the only way to find the supreme principle of morality is to start from our ordinary moral beliefs and opinions, while still holding that unless and until some principle can be uncovered in this manner, those beliefs and opinions remain inadequate and limited, much as Mill claims, in arguing that "whatever steadiness or consistency these moral beliefs have attained, has been mainly due to the tacit influence of a standard not recognized," which it is then the philosopher's role to make explicit. Thus, one might hold that as far as it goes, the philosopher should certainly take ordinary moral thinking seriously and not seek to come up with anything too revisionary of that thinking; nonetheless, that thinking requires the services of philosophy and the principle it arrives at, if it is not to struggle with conflicts between lower-level principles; difficult moral cases where our ordinary moral convictions give out; and an unanswerable skeptical challenge to articulate what the basis is for our convictions on moral matters.

Now, of course, intuitionists have been doubtful that any proposed supreme moral principle will really bring the advertised benefits promised on these issues. But what is notable about Kant in this context is that, rather than making these sorts of claims for the value of identifying a supreme principle of morality, his focus lies elsewhere. For, the value Kant empha-sizes most in arriving at the supreme principle of morality is that we can then be led to be better moral agents, as rendering such a principle explicit will make it harder for us to deceive ourselves on moral matters, and so will help to keep us more securely on the moral path. Kant's approach in this respect therefore seems to be closer to the Pythagorean tradition than the Socratic one.

So, in the Preface, Kant claims that lying behind a "metaphysics of morals" is no mere "motive to speculation" (*GMM* 45/*Ak* 4: 389; see also p. 60 (4: 405)), but a more pressing practical need, "because morals themselves remain subject to all sorts of corruption as long as we are without that clue and supreme norm by which to appraise them correctly"

(*GMM* 45/*Ak* 4: 389). Kant clearly hopes, therefore, that by identifying the supreme principle of morality, he will be able to prevent the "corruption" of our moral lives by making our conformity to morality less "contingent and precarious" (*GMM* 45/*Ak* 4: 390), as we can then combat our inclinations more effectively by giving pure practical reason a clearer voice: for, without this, "the human being is affected by so many inclinations that, though capable of the idea of a practical pure reason, he is not so easily able to make it effective *in concreto* in the conduct of his life" (*GMM* 45/*Ak* 4: 389). Similarly, in the first section of the *Groundwork*, having identified the principle of universalizability in a preliminary way as the "supreme principle of morality" (*GMM* 56–57/*Ak* 4: 402), but having admitted that this principle is already implicit in our moral thinking (*GMM* 58/*Ak* 4: 403), Kant argues that nonetheless this philosophical exercise is valuable in making it harder for our inclinations to distort our view of what is right and wrong by twisting it to fit our interests (for example, as when I convince myself that it is somehow right for me to keep the money I have been mistakenly refunded by the bank because I need it more than they do, so that this will lead to more good overall and so is justified thereby, where the application of the Formula of Universal Law and related formulae would make it clear to me that what I am presenting to myself as the justification for the action does not carry any moral weight, and in fact merely masks a desire to further my interests that is lurking beneath the moralistic facade):

> Would it not therefore be more advisable in moral matters to leave the judgment of common reason as it is ... [and] not to lead common human understanding, even in practical matters, away from its fortunate simplicity and to put it, by means of philosophy, on a new path of investigation and instruction?
>
> There is something splendid about innocence; but what is bad about it, in turn, is that it cannot protect itself very well and is easily seduced. Because of this, even wisdom – which otherwise consists more in conduct than in knowledge – still needs science, not in order to learn from it but in order to provide access and durability for its precepts. The human being feels within himself a powerful counterweight to all the commands of duty, which reason represents to him as so deserving of the highest respect – the counterweight of his needs and inclinations, the entire satisfaction of which he sums up under the name of happiness. Now reason issues its precepts unremittingly, without thereby promising anything to the inclinations, and so, as it were, with disregard and contempt for those claims, which are so impetuous and besides so apparently equitable (and refuse to be neutralized by any command).

> But from this there arises a *natural dialectic*; that is, a propensity to rationalize against those strict laws of duty and to cast doubt upon their validity, or at least upon their purity and strictness, and, where possible, to make them better suited to our wishes and inclinations, that is, to corrupt them at their basis and to destroy all their dignity – something that even common practical reason cannot, in the end, call good. (*GMM* 59–60/*Ak* 4: 404–405)[37]

Thus, as Henrich puts it, Kant sees a problem for us in the fact that "man subtly refines the moral law until it fits his inclination and his convenience, whether to free himself from it or to use the good for the justification of his own importance" (Henrich 1994: 66).[38] Kant hopes that his identification of the supreme principle of morality as involving universalizability can play a significant role in helping us overcome this natural dialectic of practical reason,[39] where one significant criticism he has of other candidates for this supreme principle is that they will make this dialectic harder to resolve, by introducing hedonistic elements into morality itself, in such a way as to make moral self-deception easier for us to achieve.[40]

Thus, Kant's position seems Pythagorean, in that he clearly recognizes how our self-interested motivations can be powerful enough to lead us to view our actions in a spurious moral light, and believes his project in the *Groundwork* will make this harder. He is therefore addressing us as frail and easily corrupted moral agents, rather than dealing with the sort of Socratic questions raised by Mill. The value Kant claims for the FUL or his other formulae as candidates for the "supreme principle of morality" is the role they can play in helping us to unmask our bad faith on this issue, thereby making it harder to dodge the right course of action which our ordinary moral thinking has already made clear; and the advantage he claims for the FUL and his other formulae over other candidates is that, because they are not related to the happiness of the agent or based on merely empirical considerations, his formulae will serve this role better than those other candidates, which can make it too easy for us to stray or remain undecided. (For example, if keeping the money from the bank would make me *much* happier than the unhappiness caused by not returning it, perhaps I *ought* to keep it? Or, at least, perhaps the moral considerations could be argued either way?)

Seen in this light, therefore, the real significance of the formulae Kant offers is in a sense heuristic, where deploying them will make it very difficult for a moral agent to use spurious moral considerations as a smoke-screen for what are really his own interests, for all these formulae force us to consider the situation in a more objective manner in different but complementary respects, by abstracting from those interests and so take into account the perspective of all the others affected.[41] Considered in a Pythagorean light, therefore, we can give significance to Kant's search for a supreme principle of morality, while allowing us to think of that search in a way that is free of any ambition to reduce the plurality of prima facie duties that make up ordinary moral thinking to any single, underlying, formula in a Socratic manner, and so in a way that would bring it into conflict with a more intuitionistic approach.

4   Kant and Hegel: A Reconciliation?

Taken in this way, therefore, Kant's preoccupation with identifying a supreme principle of morality in the *Groundwork* need not set him at odds with Hegel's apparent resistance to anything resembling the Socratic project, and thus with Hegel's underlying intuitionism. Thus, whereas the move from the FUL to the FH was perhaps not sufficient in itself to settle their differences, this more Pythagorean treatment of Kant's position might be. However, just as some Kantians have resisted the former as too concessive, and have instead sought to defend the FUL, so one might expect some Kantians to resist the latter move from a Socratic to a Pythagorean picture of Kant as being too conciliatory as well. Nonetheless, I hope to have done enough here to at least suggest that such a reading of Kant can be made plausible; and to suggest, moreover, that when Kant's ethics are viewed in this manner, the Hegelian can find more common ground with them than has generally been supposed. Of course, the Hegelian can (and probably will) still quarrel with Kant's Pythagorean account of how it is that we get led astray in moral matters, and what role moral philosophy and moral theory can realistically play in keeping us on track; but these disagreements, even if they persist, are not those usually associated with the Kant–Hegel debate in this area. In this way, therefore, I hope to have shed new light on an old controversy, while perhaps also bringing it to a conclusion that will be satisfying to both sides.

Acknowledgments

I am grateful to Tony Burns and Fabian Freyenhagen for helpful comments on a previous version of this paper.

Notes

1. See, e.g., Wood 1999, esp. pp. 97–110; Lo 1981; Galvin 2009.
2. Needless to say, not *all* commentators on Kant have adopted this concessive approach to Hegel's criticism: some remain resolute, and have stuck to the more traditional response of defending the Formula of Universal Law itself against the formalism objection. For examples of this more resolute approach, see, e.g., O'Neill 1989a; Schnoor 1989; and Korsgaard 1996. Of course, resoluteness with respect to the FUL does not preclude these commentators from also taking the other formulae very seriously too, and relating all the formulae together in various ways.
3. See also *GMM* 57/*Ak* 4: 402.
4. The FUL is sometimes then immediately grouped together with the next formula Kant offers, which is known as the Formula of the Law of Nature (FLN): "*act as if the maxim of your action were to become by your will a universal law of nature*" (*GMM* 73/*Ak* 4: 421). The two formulae together are then sometimes called the Universal Law formulas. This in itself then immediately introduces a complexity into the debate with Hegel, as on the one hand Hegel himself mainly just concentrates on FUL rather than FLN or any combination of the two, which may seem to put Kant at an immediate disadvantage in an unfair way; on the other hand, it is not clear whether Kant's move from FUL to FLN is already a concession to worries about the formalism of FUL itself and thus a stepping back from the latter, while in practice most Kantians who adopt the concessive approach to Hegel's objections are prepared to admit that they apply to *both* FUL *and* FLN, where it is only really when Kant gets to the FH that they are dealt with properly. So, in order to avoid complicating my discussion too much at this stage, I will focus mainly on the problems with FUL, and assume for the sake of this discussion that moving just to the FLN would not really be enough to help on its own, though I do not attempt to argue this here.
5. Kant discusses those alternatives at two main places in his published writings: at *GMM* 90–92/*Ak* 4: 441–444, and *CPrR* 172–175/*Ak* 5: 39–41. They are also discussed at some length in Kant's lectures on ethics (translated in *LE*), e.g. Collins Lectures, *LE* 65–68/*Ak* 27: 274–278; Mrongovius Lectures, *LE* 239–246/*Ak* 29: 620–629; Vigilantius Lectures, *LE* 280–282/*Ak* 27: 517–519. For a thorough discussion of Kant's position on the issue, see Kerstein 2002: 139–159.
6. Hegel's critique of Kant's FUL occurs in four main places: *NL*/*HW* II: 434–532; *PS* 256–262/*HW* III: 316–323; *PR* §§133–136, pp. 161–164/*HW* VII: 250–254; and Hegel *LHP* III: 458–461/*HW* XX: 366–369. It also occurs more briefly in *EL* §§53–54, 100–102/*HW* VIII: 138–139.

7. *PS* 259/*HW* III: 319. See also *PR* §135, p. 162/*HW* VII: 252–253: "there is no criterion within that principle [of absence of contradiction] for deciding whether or not [some action] is a duty. On the contrary, it is possible to justify any wrong or immoral mode of action by this means."

8. Hegel himself does not give any examples of "false positives" on their own, i.e. cases where the FUL would license what are intuitively wrong acts (although, in the context of the indeterminacy objection, the fact that the FUL might be used to justify the abolition of property would perhaps count as such a false positive for Hegel, given his views on property). However, others have offered such examples, e.g. Brentano 1969: 50, where Brentano argues that the maxim of not accepting bribes is ununiversalizable and so should be rejected by Kant. For a response to Brentano, see Patzig 1959.

9. See Kant, *CPrR* 161/*Ak* 5: 27 and *OCS* 287–288/*Ak* 8: 286–287.

10. *NL* 125–126/*HW* II: 462–463; *PS* 257–259/*HW* III: 317–318; *PR* §135, pp. 162–163/*HW* VII: 252–253; *LHP* III: 460–461/*HW* XX: 368–369.

11. *NL* 127–128/*HW* II: 465–466; *LHP* III: 460/*HW* XX: 368.

12. Marcus Singer's reaction is perhaps typical, where he calls Hegel's objection "almost incredibly simple-minded" (1963: 251).

13. As David Couzens Hoy has pointed out, however, in his *Rechtslehre*, Kant does seem to claim that the absence of property is contradictory: see Hoy 1989: 218, where he refers to Kant, *MM* 404–406/*Ak* 6: 246–247.

14. These considerations are the ones usually put forward by proponents of the FUL as the basis for its moral significance: see e.g. O'Neill 1989b: 156: "In restricting our maxims to those that meet the test of the Categorical Imperative we refuse to base our lives on maxims that necessarily make of our case an exception. The reason why a universalizability criterion is morally significant is that it makes of our own case no special exception"; and Korsgaard 1996: 92: "What the test shows to be forbidden are just those actions whose efficacy in achieving their purposes depends upon their being exceptional." One further difficulty here is whether exceptional actions of this kind are always wrong (see Wood 1999: 108); another more exegetical worry is that while Kant himself mentions this as a central issue (see *GMM* 75–76/*Ak* 4: 424), it is hard to see how this can be made into the moral issue underlying some of his examples (e.g. suicide).

15. See Riley 1983: 38–50, where Riley speaks of the other formulae as adding "a bit of nonheteronomous teleological flesh to the bare bones of universality" (p. 49); Wood 1990: "it is a mistake for Hegel and other critics to fasten so exclusively on the FUL in their attempts to prove that Kantian ethics is empty of content . . . Hegel and other critics will have not shown Kantian ethics to be empty of content until they have demonstrated the emptiness of [the] other formulas along with that of FUL" (p. 156); Lo 1981: "Those philosophers who keep charging Kantian ethics with '*empty* formalism' only pay attention to [the FUL] and brush aside

[the other formulae] as though they were unworthy of consideration. This is completely un-Kantian because [the FH] is straightforwardly formulated in the *Groundwork* and is carefully applied in *The Doctrine of Virtue*. It seems clear to me that [the FH] is a practicable criterion for determining moral rightness or wrongness, and is by no means barren" (pp. 197–198).

16. See Smith 1989: 73–74, where Smith allows that it is probably correct "that Hegel's view of Kant derives from an undue attention to the first formulation of the Categorical Imperative, which emphasizes the universality of its form, and not enough from the second, which commands respect for persons or treating others as 'ends in themselves.' Had he done so, he might well have found in Kant a set of objective ends that he criticizes him for not having. Kant's moral theory may well be formal, but it need not be empty." See also O'Hagan 1987: 142: "The radical Kantian can escape the Hegelian ["emptiness"] charge only if he moves on to the [FH] formulation of the categorical imperative"; and Geiger 2007: 11, where Geiger accepts that on the traditional view of Hegel's critique of Kant, that critique is unfair in that "it focuses exclusively on the universal law formula of the categorical imperative and ignores its other formulations," and so he argues that battle must be properly joined elsewhere.

17. Another approach is to accuse Hegel (and other similar critics) of overlooking not the other formulations of the supreme principle of morality, but the "impure" aspects of Kant's ethics, and its incorporation of more empirical elements: see e.g. Louden 2000, esp. pp. 167–170. This approach, too, has the effect of the reducing the "gap" between the Kantian and Hegelian positions, though in ways that cannot be fully explored here. For further discussion see Westphal 2003.

18. Another way to challenge this consensus might be to argue that the Hegelian should not allow the Kantian to move beyond the FUL in this way, as to do so is inconsistent with the basis of Kant's position, such as his view of autonomy. Though I don't think Hegel ever says as much, I think this is perhaps why Hegel nowhere really discusses the other formulae in any detail, and only really focuses on the FUL: see e.g. *LHP* III: 260/*HW* XX: 367–368: "this freedom is at first only the negative of everything else; no bonds, nothing external, lays me under an obligation. It is to this extent indeterminate; it is the identity of the will with itself, its at-homeness with itself. But what is the content of the law? Here we at once come back to the lack of content." For a contemporary discussion of the difficulties involved in moving from the FUL to FH, given a certain understanding of what Kant means by autonomy, see Johnson 2007.

19. See Urmson 1975, who characterizes Prichard's brand of intuitionism as "attacking ... the view that there was some supreme moral principle from which all others could be derived" (p. 112); see Prichard 2002: 14; and also McNaughton 2002.

20. The relations between intuitionism (of the sort favored by W. D. Ross) and strong particularism (of the sort favored by Jonathan Dancy) are complex, as intuitionism certainly contains some particularistic elements, while nonetheless seeing more scope for moral principles in our ethical thinking than the strong particularist will allow. For a helpful discussion of the relation between intuitionism and particularism, see Hooker 2000.

21. Hegel's position here is prefigured in some of his earlier writings, e.g. *SC* 246/ *HW* I: 361–362: "A living bond of the virtues, a living unity, is quite different from the unity of the concept; it does not set up a determinate virtue for determinate circumstances, but appears, even in the most variegated mixture of relations, untorn and unitary. Its external shape may be modified in infinite ways; it will never have the same shape twice. Its expression will never be able to afford a rule, since it never has the force of a universal opposed to a particular."

22. I take this phrase from Philip Stratton-Lake's very helpful characterization of the intuitionist's position:

> If asked why we think lying is wrong, we might point to the fact that in lying we betray the trust the other person has placed in us to tell the truth, or that we harm the other person in some way. If someone then went on to ask us what is wrong with harming, or betraying the trust of others, most would find it difficult to find something further to say. To many it will seem as though we have already hit moral bedrock with considerations of fidelity and non-maleficience.
>
> It might be argued that betraying the trust of others is wrong because in doing this we are acting on a principle that could not be willed as a universal law, or because a society in which trust is respected will be a happier society than one in which it is betrayed. But such Kantian and consequentialist support will strike us as both irrelevant and unnecessary. Pre-theoretically we do not think that considerations of fidelity are morally salient for the reasons Kantians and consequentialists claim, but treat them as salient on their own account. (Stratton-Lake 2002a: 25–26)

See Kant, *GMM* 57/*Ak* 4: 403, where I think Stratton-Lake would want to argue that once we know that an act would involve breaking a promise, this in itself carries all the normative information we need, and that the appeal to universalizability considerations is therefore superfluous and unconvincing.

23. See Hegel, *PS* 262/*HW* III: 322: "Ethical disposition consists just in sticking steadfastly to what is right, and abstaining from all attempts to move or shake it, or derive it. Suppose something has been entrusted to me; it *is* the property of someone else and I acknowledge this *because* it *is so*, and I keep myself

unfalteringly in this relationship ... It is not, therefore, because I find something is not self-contradictory that it is right; on the contrary, it is right because it is what is right. That something *is* the property of another, that is fundamental; I have not to argue about it, or hunt around for or entertain thoughts, connections, aspects, of various kinds; I have to think neither of making laws nor of testing them."

24. See McNaughton 2002, esp. pp. 77–85. See also Stratton-Lake 2002b: xxxvi–xxxviii.

25. See *PR* 20–21/*HW* VII: 25: "For what matters is to recognize in the semblance of the temporal and transient the substance which is immanent and the eternal which is present. For since the rational, which is synonymous with the Idea, becomes actual by entering into external existence [*Existenz*], it emerges in an infinite wealth of forms, appearances, and shapes and surrounds its core with a brightly coloured covering in which consciousness at first resides, but which only the concept can penetrate in order to find the inner pulse, and detect its continued beat even within the external shapes."

26. See *NL* 108/*HW* II: 442: "But since this empirical science finds itself [immersed] in a multiplicity of such principles, laws, ends, duties, and rights, none of which is absolute, it must also have before it the image of, and need for, [both] the absolute unity of all these unconnected determinacies and an original simple necessity; and we shall consider how it will satisfy this demand, which is derived from reason, or how the absolute Idea of reason will be presented in its [different] moments [while] under the domination of the one and the many which this empirical knowledge cannot overcome."

27. See *NL* 175/*HW* II: 524: "It is this individuality of the whole, and the specific character of a nation [*Volk*], which also enable us to recognize the whole system into which the absolute totality is organized. We can thereby recognize how all the parts of the constitution and legislation and all determinations of ethical relations are completely determined by the whole, and form a structure in which no link or ornament was a priori present in its own right [*für sich*], but all came about through the whole to which they are subject."

28. David Couzens Hoy has recently noted this aspect of Hegel's position: "[Hegel's] criticisms are intended to show the limitations of the Kantian approach to moral experience that turns it into a deduction of principles. Hegel's strategy is not to offer an alternative set of principles, and, more importantly, it is not to offer an alternative 'grounding' of these principles in one meta-principle like the categorical imperative or the utility principle. In our more contemporary parlance, I am suggesting that Hegel is not offering an alternative 'foundational' account to Kant's (like the utility principle)" (Hoy 2009: 167–168). I think similar considerations apply to Bradley's position, which also takes an intuitionist line in criticizing the Kantian view, stressing the priority of particular duties over any single general formula: see Bradley 1927:

156–159 and 193–199. A different view has been taken by Tony Burns, who sees Hegel as holding a "natural law theory [which] incorporates a definite hierarchy of moral principles," where "at the top of this hierarchy there is a primary principle of morality or justice," which "is a version of what is probably best described as the principle of equity and reciprocity" (Burns 1996: 60). While I would agree, as mentioned above, that Hegel's position is certainly *structured*, I would dispute that it is hierarchical in this manner, and that any such "primary principle" can be found in the textual references that Burns gives.

29. A more moderate response might be to say that Kant himself is a pluralist rather than a monist here, in offering several principles rather than one (not *just* the FUL, but also the FN and the Formula of Autonomy, and other sub-formulae). Whilst it is of course true, however, that Kant does offer a variety of principles in this way, he is quite explicit about them all amounting to "so many formulae of the very same law" (*GMM* 85/Ak 4: 436), and so always presents himself as seeking and finding *a* supreme principle of morality (no matter how difficult it has then been for commentators to unite the various formulae in the way that Kant seems to require).

30. Schneewind introduces this distinction in the final chapter of his 1998: 533–554. See also Schneewind 2010b. As he notes, a related distinction can be found in Griffin 1996: 131–132.

31. Schneewind calls this second picture "Pythagorean" because the early modern account of why ordinary moral thinking has already attained the truth about moral matters is that it is has been revealed to us by God; but this opens up the question of why Pythagoras, who was Greek, should have been credited by Aristotle and others as the first to think about virtue – where one ingenious solution to this problem was to claim that Pythagoras was Jewish or was at least incorporating Jewish ideas.

32. In an influential essay in which she offers a critique of moral theory, Annette Baier accepts this Millian picture of Kant's ambitions, as do many such critics: see Baier 1989, esp. p. 36.

33. See also Schneewind 2010a: 44, where he contrasts the position of the utilitarian and the intuitionist as follows: "for the utilitarian the paradigm moral problems are those in which we do not know what we ought to do, and in which the solution comes as soon as we do know; while for the intuitionist the central sort of problem is that in which the agent knows what he ought to do but finds it difficult to bring himself to do it. His problem is one of will or feeling."

34. See Schneewind 1998: 543–548; 2010b: 119–120. For a related discussion of Kant in terms of Schneewind's distinction, see Krasnoff 2004.

35. For similar remarks, see *GMM* 66/Ak 4: 412, where Kant comments that "common moral appraisal" is "very worthy of respect"; and *CPrR* 153 n./Ak 5: 8: "who would even want to introduce a new principle of all morality and, as it

were, first invent it? Just as if, before him, the world had been ignorant of what duty is or in thoroughgoing error about it."

36. See Kant's own reference to Socrates at *GMM* 58/*Ak* 4: 404.

37. See also *CPrR* 143n./*Ak* 5: 8: "But whoever knows what a *formula* means to a mathematician, which determines quite precisely what is to be done to solve a problem and *does not let him go astray* [my emphasis], will not take a formula that does this with respect to all duty in general as something that is insignificant and can be dispensed with" (translation modified). And see *LE* 136–137/*Ak* 27: 359.

38. For further discussion of Kant's position here, see also Guyer 2000, and Shell 2009: 129–131, where she writes that "The goal of science is not to teach common moral understanding something new, but to enhance the force and staying power of the knowledge it already possesses" (p. 131). Rawls adopts a similar perspective in Rawls 2000: 148–149, as does Geiger 2010. More generally, see Nussbaum 2000, where Nussbaum sets out to defend moral theory, but does so in Pythagorean terms: "*Theory*, then, *can help our good judgements by giving us additional opposition to the bad influence of corrupt desires, judgements, and passions*" (p. 252; emphasis original).

39. Kant did not think that this would be enough on its own, however: the more metaphysical speculations of section III of the *Groundwork* are also required to complete the job, in order to answer questions that may arise concerning the status of the moral law, questions that may prevent frail human beings from keeping to the moral path.

40. See *GMM* 65/*Ak* 4: 411: "on the other hand a mixed doctrine of morals, put together from incentives of feeling and inclination and also of rational concepts, must make the mind waver between motives that cannot be brought under any principle, that can lead only contingently to what is good and can very often also lead to what is evil"; and also *MM* 370–371/*Ak* 6: 215–216: "If the doctrine of morals were merely the doctrine of happiness ... [a]ll apparently *a priori* reasoning about this [would come] down to nothing but experience raised by induction to generality, a generality ... still so tenuous that everyone must be allowed countless exceptions in order to adapt his choice of a way of life to his particular inclinations and his susceptibilities to satisfaction and still, in the end, to become prudent only from his own or others' misfortunes."

41. See *GMM* 75–76/*Ak* 4: 424: "If we now attend to ourselves in any transgression of a duty, we find that we do not really will that our maxim should become a universal law, since that is impossible for us, but that the opposite of our maxim should instead remain a universal law, only we take the liberty of making an *exception* to it for ourselves (or just for this once) to the advantage of our inclination. Consequently, if we weighed all cases from one and the same point of view, namely that of reason, we would find a contradiction in our own will, namely that a certain principle be objectively necessary as a universal law and yet subjectively not hold universally but allow exceptions."

Abbreviations

Works by Hegel

EL   *The Encyclopaedia Logic: Part I of the Encyclopaedia of Philosophical
     Sciences with the Zusätze*, trans. T. F. Geraets, W. A. Suchting, and
     H. S. Harris. Indianapolis: Hackett, 1991.

HW   *Werke in zwanzig Bänden, Theorie-Werkausgabe*, ed. Eva Mol-
     denhauer and Karl Markus Michel. Frankfurt: Suhrkamp,
     1969–1971. (References are to volume number and page number.)

LHP *Lectures on the History of Philosophy*, trans. E. S. Haldane and
     Frances H. Simson, 3 vols. Originally published London: Kegan
     Paul, 1892–1896; repr. Lincoln: University of Nebraska Press,
     1995.

NL   *On the Scientific Ways of Treating Natural Law, on its Place in
     Practical Philosophy, and its Relation to the Positive Sciences of Right*,
     in *Political Writings*, ed. L. Dickey and H. B. Nisbet, trans. H. B.
     Nisbet. Cambridge: Cambridge University Press, 1999, pp.
     102–180.

PR   *The Philosophy of Right*, trans. H. B. Nisbet. Cambridge: Cambridge
     University Press, 1991.

PS   *Phenomenology of Spirit*, trans. A. V. Miller. Oxford: Oxford
     University Press, 1977.

SC   "The Spirit of Christianity and its Fate." In *Early Theological
     Writings*, trans. T. M. Knox. Philadelphia: University of Pennsyl-
     vania Press, 1971, pp. 182–301.

Works by Kant

Ak   *Kants Gesammelte Schriften*, ed. Royal Prussian (later German,
     more recently Berlin-Brandenberg) Academy of Sciences. Berlin:
     Georg Reimer; subsequently Walter de Gruyter, 1900–. (References
     are to volume and page numbers.)

CPrR *Critique of Practical Reason*, in *Practical Philosophy*, ed. and trans.
     Mary J. Gregor. Cambridge: Cambridge University Press, 1996, pp.
     133–272.

GMM *Groundwork of the Metaphysics of Morals*, in *Practical Philosophy*,
     ed. and trans. Mary J. Gregor. Cambridge: Cambridge University
     Press, 1996, pp. 37–108.

LE   *Lectures on Ethics*, ed. Peter Heath and J. B. Schneewind, trans.
      Peter Heath. Cambridge: Cambridge University Press, 1997.
MM   *The Metaphysics of Morals*, in *Practical Philosophy*, ed. and trans.
      Mary J. Gregor. Cambridge: Cambridge University Press, 1996,
      pp. 353–604.
OCS   *On the Common Saying: That may be Correct in Theory, but It is of
      No Use in Practice*, 8: 286–287. In *Practical Philosophy*, ed. and
      trans. Mary J. Gregor. Cambridge: Cambridge University Press,
      1996, pp. 287–288.

References

Baier, Annette (1989) "Doing without Moral Theory?" Repr. in Stanley G. Clarke and
    Evan Simpson, eds., *Anti-Theory in Ethics and Moral Conservativism*. Albany, NY:
    SUNY Press, pp. 29–48.
Bradley, F. H. (1927) *Ethical Studies*, 2nd edn. Oxford: Oxford University Press.
Brentano, Franz (1969) *The Origin of our Knowledge of Right and Wrong*, ed. Oskar
    Kraus and Roderick M. Chisholm, trans. Roderick M. Chisholm and Elizabeth H.
    Schneewind. London: Routledge & Kegan Paul.
Burns, Tony (1996) *Natural Law and Political Ideology in the Philosophy of Hegel*.
    Aldershot: Avebury.
Galvin, Richard (2009) "The Universal Law Formulas." In Thomas E. Hill, Jr., ed.,
    The Blackwell Guide to Kant's Ethics. Oxford: Wiley-Blackwell, pp. 52–82.
Geiger, Ido (2007) *The Founding Act of Modern Ethical Life: Hegel's Critique of Kant's
    Moral and Political Philosophy*. Stanford: Stanford University Press.
Geiger, Ido (2010) "What is the Use of the Universal Law Formula of the Categorical
    Imperative?" *British Journal for the History of Philosophy* 18: 271–295.
Griffin, James (1996) *Value Judgment*. Oxford: Oxford University Press.
Guyer, Paul (2000) "The Strategy of Kant's *Groundwork*." In *Kant on Freedom, Law,
    and Happiness*. Cambridge: Cambridge University Press, pp. 207–231.
Henrich, Dieter (1994) "The Concept of Moral Insight into Kant's Doctrine of the
    Fact of Reason." In Richard Velkley, ed., *The Unity of Reason: Essays on Kant's
    Philosophy*. Cambridge, MA: Harvard University Press, pp. 55–87.
Hooker, Brad (2000) "Moral Particularism: Wrong and Bad." In Brad Hooker and
    Margaret Little, eds., *Moral Particularism*. Oxford: Oxford University Press, pp. 1–22.
Hoy, David Couzens (1989) "Hegel's Critique of Kantian Morality." *History of
    Philosophy Quarterly* 6: 207–232.
Hoy, David Couzens (2009) "The Ethics of Freedom: Hegel on Reason as Law-
    Giving and Law-Testing." In Kenneth R. Westphal, ed., *The Blackwell Guide to
    Hegel's "Phenomenology of Spirit."* Oxford: Wiley-Blackwell, pp. 153–171.

Johnson, Robert N. (2007) "Value and Autonomy in Kantian Ethics." In Russ Schafer-Landau, ed., *Oxford Studies in Metaethics*, vol. 2. Oxford: Oxford University Press, pp. 133–148.

Kerstein, Samuel J. (2002) *Kant's Search for the Supreme Principle of Morality.* Cambridge: Cambridge University Press.

Korsgaard, Christine M. (1996) "Kant's Formula of Universal Law." Repr. in *Creating the Kingdom of Ends.* Cambridge: Cambridge University Press, pp. 77–105.

Krasnoff, Larry (2004) "Pythagoras Enlightened: Kant on the Effect of Moral Philosophy." In: Natalie Brender and Larry Krasnoff, eds., *New Essays on the History of Autonomy: A Collection Honouring J. B. Schneewind.* Cambridge: Cambridge University Press, pp. 133–153.

Lo, Ping-cheung (1981) "A Critical Reevaluation of the Alleged 'Empty Formalism' of Kantian Ethics." *Ethics* 91: 181–201.

Louden, Robert B. (2000) *Kant's Impure Ethics: From Rational Beings to Human Beings.* Oxford: Oxford University Press.

McNaughton, David (2002) "An Unconnected Heap of Duties?" Repr. in Philip Stratton-Lake, ed., *Ethical Intuitionism: Re-evaluations.* Oxford: Oxford University Press, pp. 76–91.

Mill, J. S. (1972) *Utilitarianism.* In *"Utilitarianism," "On Liberty" and "Considerations on Representative Government,"* ed. H. B. Acton. London: J. M. Dent.

Nussbaum, Martha (2000) "Why Practice Needs Ethical Theory: Particularism, Principle, and Bad Behaviour." In Brad Hooker and Margaret Little, eds., *Moral Particularism.* Oxford: Oxford University Press, pp. 227–255.

O'Hagan, Timothy (1987) "On Hegel's Critique of Kant's Moral and Political Philosophy." In Stephen Priest, ed., *Hegel's Critique of Kant.* Oxford: Oxford University Press, pp. 135–159.

O'Neill, Onora (1989a) "Consistency in Action." Repr. in *Constructions of Reason.* Cambridge: Cambridge University Press, pp. 81–104.

O'Neill, Onora (1989b) "Kant after Virtue." Repr. in *Constructions of Reason.* Cambridge: Cambridge University Press, pp. 145–162.

Patzig, Günther (1959) "Der Gedanke eines Kategorischen Imperatives. " *Archiv für Philosophie* 6: 82–96.

Prichard, H. A. (2002) "Does Moral Philosophy Rest on a Mistake?" Repr. in *Moral Writings,* ed. Jim MacAdam. Oxford: Oxford University Press, pp. 7–20.

Rawls, John (2000) *Lectures on the History of Moral Philosophy.* Cambridge, MA: Harvard University Press.

Riley, Patrick (1983) *Kant's Political Philosophy.* Totowa, NJ: Rowman & Littlefield.

Schneewind, J. B. (1998) *The Invention of Autonomy: A History of Modern Moral Philosophy.* Cambridge: Cambridge University Press.

Schneewind, J. B. (2010a) "Moral Problems and Moral Philosophy in the Victorian Period." Repr. in *Essays on the History of Moral Philosophy.* Oxford: Oxford University Press, pp. 42–61.

Schneewind, J. B. (2010b) "No Discipline, No History: The Case of Moral Philosophy." Repr. in *Essays on the History of Moral Philosophy*. Oxford: Oxford University Press, pp. 107–126.

Schnoor, Christian (1989) *Kants kategorischer Imperativ als Kriterium der Richtigkeit des Handelns*. Tübingen: J. C. B. Mohr.

Shell, Susan Meld (2009) *Kant and the Limits of Autonomy*. Cambridge, MA: Harvard University Press.

Singer, Marcus George (1963) *Generalization in Ethics*. London: Eyre & Spottiswoode.

Smith, Steven B. (1989) *Hegel's Critique of Liberalism*. Chicago: University of Chicago Press.

Stratton-Lake, Philip (2002a) "Introduction." In Philip Stratton-Lake, ed., *Ethical Intuitionism: Re-evaluations*. Oxford: Oxford University Press, pp. 1–28.

Stratton-Lake, Philip (2002b) "Introduction." In David Ross, *The Right and the Good*, ed. Philip Stratton-Lake. Oxford: Oxford University Press, pp. ix-l.

Urmson, J. O. (1975) "A Defence of Intuitionism." *Proceedings of the Aristotelian Society* 75: 111–119.

Westphal, Kenneth R. (2003) "Objective Gültigkeit zwischen Gegebenem und Gemachtem: Hegels kantischer Konstruktivismus in der praktischen Philosophie." *Jahrbuch für Recht und Ethik* 11: 177–198.

Wood, Allen W. (1990) *Hegel's Ethical Thought*. Cambridge: Cambridge University Press.

Wood, Allen W. (1999) *Kant's Ethical Thought*. Cambridge: Cambridge University Press.

Part II
Politics

4

Hegel and the Unified Theory of Punishment

Thom Brooks

1 Introduction

G. W. F. Hegel's theory of punishment has been most often thought to fit within a particular penal camp. The most popular interpretation is that this theory is retributivist because criminals should be punished only where deserved in an effort to "annul" crime. Others believe this theory is a theory of moral education whereby criminals come to understand their crimes as wrongs in an effort to reform their behavior. These interpretations all fail to acknowledge the novelty of Hegel's theory of punishment. Hegel's originality consists in offering the first *unified* theory of punishment. A unified theory of punishment aspires to offer a single, coherent theory of punishment that brings together retributivist, deterrent, and rehabilitative elements without substantial conflict. We can find similar unified theories of punishment amongst Hegel's earliest defenders, the British Idealists (or "British Hegelians"), who helped to popularize Hegel's philosophical contributions in the late nineteenth century. Thus, Hegel's novel theory of punishment marks the beginning of a new tradition concerning how we might think about punishment.

The structure of this chapter will be as follows. I will begin with a presentation of the key idea behind Hegel's unified theory of punishment before considering its discussion in his *Philosophy of Right*. I will then focus on the reception of his theory of punishment by the British Idealists before

Hegel's Philosophy of Right: Essays on Ethics, Politics, and Law, First Edition.
Edited by Thom Brooks.
© 2012 Blackwell Publishing Ltd. Published 2012 by Blackwell Publishing Ltd.

concluding with a few remarks on the contemporary prospects of a unified theory of punishment.

2   The Key Idea

The key idea in Hegel's unified theory of punishment can be found in *The Science of Logic*. He offers a crucial example meant to illustrate his conception of a "ground":

> Punishment, for example, has various determinations: it is retributive, a deterrent example as well, a threat used by the law as a deterrent, and also it brings the criminal to his senses and reforms him. Each of these different determinations has been considered the *ground of punishment*, because each is an essential determination, and therefore the others, as distinct from it, are determined as merely contingent relatively to it. *But the one which is taken as ground is still not the whole punishment itself.* (Hegel 1969: 465; emphases added)[1]

This illustration is most revealing and it is telling that virtually all presentations of Hegel as a retributivist fail to discuss this passage.[2] Hegel distinguishes three different approaches to punishment that continue to serve as the primary views today: retribution, deterrence, and rehabilitation. Penal theorists too often choose one of these approaches and defend it against the others. Thus, the retributivist who defends the view that punishment must be deserved will criticize proponents of deterrence who might allow an innocent person to be punished if this would have a deterrence effect. And so on.

Hegel's original contribution is to argue that penal theorists have adopted the wrong strategy. They should not seek to promote a single approach as acceptable, unlike rival approaches. Instead, penal theorists should recognize that each approach (retribution, deterrence, rehabilitation) is a different and legitimate facet of justified punishment. Therefore, deterrent theorists are not wrong to argue that just punishment ought to make crime less, not more, likely. Rehabilitation theorists are also not wrong to claim that just punishment should help criminals reform themselves and reduce recidivism. Finally, the retributivist is correct to argue that punishment must be deserved for a crime and set in proportion to it. These are all valid elements of just punishment. We should not choose one against the others, but aspire to build a theory that can accommodate the core of each approach.

Nor is this statement a one-off from Hegel. In his earlier essay on natural law, he states:

> in the case of punishment, one specific aspect is singled out – the criminal's moral reform, or the damage done, or the effect of his punishment on others, or the criminal's own notion of the punishment before he committed the crime, or the necessity of making this notion a reality by carrying out the threat, etc. And then some such single aspect is made the purpose and essence of the whole. The natural consequence is that, since such a specific aspect has no necessary connection with the other specific aspects which can be found and distinguished, there arises an endless struggle to find the necessary bearing and predominance of one over the others. (Hegel 1975: 60)[3]

Hegel highlights the problem well. Penal theorists commit an error in taking one of the three different aspects of punishment as *the* only approach to determining just punishments. In other words, punishment is not retributivist, deterrent, *or* rehabilitative, but rather a combination of the three. It is then a mistake to consider only one aspect as encompassing "punishment" in its fullness. This mistake – namely, the view that punishment is either retributivist, a deterrent, or rehabilitative but not in any combination – has led to the present conflict. The conflict is between penal theorists and concerns their seemingly perpetual standoff regarding which single approach to punishment is the best. Instead, we should recognize the merit in each element of punishment and attempt to offer a unified theory that brings them together in a coherent way.

It is not difficult to see why penal theorists have gone astray. Different approaches to punishment appear to endorse conflicting principles. The retributivist and deterrence proponent are good examples. The retributivist argues that punishment should be deserved for and in proportion to a crime. The deterrence proponent argues that punishment should deter potential criminals. The project of punishing the deserving may not bring about general deterrence and, thus, an important element of retributivism may conflict with a core idea in deterrence. Likewise, the project of general deterrence may support our punishing undeserving persons and, thus, an important element of deterrence may conflict with a core idea in retributivism. If important elements of one approach may often conflict with core ideas of a second approach, then it may become difficult to discern how best to resolve this conflict. This explains why it is unsurprising that many penal theorists may find the idea of a unified theory of punishment a non-starter whatever its intuitive appeal.

There have been past attempts to offer "hybrid" theories of punishment that included retributivist and consequentialist elements, but these have never been "unified" in any substantive sense. A good example is offered by John Rawls. He speaks of the backwards- and forward-looking considerations relevant to just punishments in his essay "Two Concepts of Rules" (1999). These considerations play particular roles in the justification of a practice and particular actions falling under any such practice. For Rawls, we accept forward-looking considerations in justifying penal institutions (1999: 22). We ask, why punish rather than forgive? Rawls suggests that the consequences pertaining to forward-looking considerations help shape our answer. This explains why penal institutions are just (and also perhaps why pardons are not unjustified). There remains the concern that these considerations might permit the punishment of innocent people, but Rawls claims this is not a criticism of the larger institution of punishment, but rather a concern about particular actions – namely, the decision to punish any specific individual – falling under the institution of punishment. These concerns about how we determine whether to punish an individual, as opposed to the concerns about whether we have penal institutions, fall under the remit of backward-looking considerations that look very similar to retributivist concerns (1999: 22–23). We can endorse a hybrid theory of punishment that can accommodate retributivist and non-retributivist concerns, and without the worry that it might punish innocent persons.

There has been much debate on whether this strategy is successful. For example, we might object that penal institutions are justified entirely on grounds of desert. This is not a mere rule that applies solely to practices within the institution of punishment, but speaks to the larger purposes of punishment more generally. The objection continues: if non-retributivist considerations alone ground the practice of punishment, why do they fall silent on how we determine individual punishments? In other words, suppose all punishments were determined with reference only to retributivist backward-looking considerations. Rawls assumes that determining punishments in this way is compatible with the view that the longer-term consequences of determining punishments in this way will be positive. If this is the case, then perhaps he is guilty of running together competing ideals. This is because imposing what is deserved may not always entail positive consequences: in some cases, it may even threaten political stability.

A more common approach has been to argue that retributivism and other considerations fit together differently. Backward-looking considerations offer a standard by which we determine whether someone should be punished and forward-looking considerations help us decide the severity of punishment. Some have even attributed a similar view to Hegel and understand it to be "retributivist" or "modified retributivism" (see Tunick 1992: 162–164). This characterization seems incorrect. These views often claim that the necessary desert is an indication of the moral serious-ness of the crime. This amount of seriousness speaks to the relevant criminalization. We would expect moral seriousness to play an important role in determining the severity of punishment given its importance in justifying criminalization and being a necessary element of punishable desert. However, this desert is merely necessary, but not sufficient and non-retributivist features may play a more prominent role. Thus, the actual punishments imposed by such understandings of retributivism may well endorse non-retributivist functions, leaving them "retributivist" in name only. While I would not reject this view, it is a mistaken understanding of what a retributivist theory of punishment is and a mischaracterization of Hegel's project.

We have seen that Hegel appears explicit: we ought not to endorse any one approach to punishment. Instead, we should embrace the three main approaches to punishment as part of a larger, unified theory. Why have many not held this view of Hegel before? We turn to this question now before considering its contemporary prospects.

3   Punishment in the *Philosophy of Right*

Most Hegel scholars reject the view that he held a unified theory of punishment. The great majority claim he held a retributivist view and it is easy to see why (see Findlay 1958: 312–313; Cooper 1971; Stillman 1976; Primoratz 1989: 69–81; Wood 1990: 108–124; Inwood 1992: 232–235; Tunick 1992; Anderson 1999). One reason is the difficult writing style we find with Hegel, or as one commentator claims: "A punishment is an annulment, a cancellation or a return to a previous state of affairs . . . All this, of course, is obscure. It is by Hegel" (Honderich 1976: 45). A more central reason is the limited context within which Hegel's theory is discussed. For example, David Cooper argues: "In this essay I discuss Hegel's theory of punishment for its own sake. I am not concerned with its relation to the rest of the *Philosophy of Right*, and even less with its place in the dialectic as a whole" (1971: 151). Since Cooper, the great majority of commentators have largely followed his lead. Whereas Cooper claims he will discuss Hegel's treatment of punishment to the exclusion of his other possibly related arguments in the *Philosophy of Right*, Cooper does not even consider Hegel's full treatment of punishment within this work, limiting himself entirely to the discussion of punishment that appears in the section "Abstract Right." Such a view has been widely held as largely unproblematic. This is because this section is where we find the longest treatment of the subject and also because it is widely held that his discussions elsewhere about punishment add little to his account. For example, Peter Stillman argues:

> for neither morality nor society yet exist at the level of abstract rights, where Hegel primarily discusses punishment. Hegel does introduce further, non-abstract right aspects of punishment later – a law code, some concern with intention, pardon, crimes against the state, and a system for the adminis-tration of justice – but these produce only minor additions and no essential changes to the theory of punishment at abstract right – except, of course, to make the abstract into the concrete and existent. (1976: 170 n. 5)

Scholars agree that Hegel has much to say about punishment. They remain divided only on the question of relative weight: should we give much weight to comments on punishment beyond the section "Abstract Right"? Most agree that we should not; I believe that we should. I will make this case here.[4]

3.1   The system

Hegel viewed his *Philosophy of Right* as a part of his larger philosophical system. Readers are presumed to have some familiarity with his logic which provides a foundation for the system (see *PR* §§4R, 8R). For Hegel, logic develops itself through clarifying categories that correspond to reality (Hegel 1969: 37). The necessary relationship of one category to the next is essential to the self-development of logic, such that each conceptual "movement" is justified and not arbitrary (Hegel 1991: §99A). The devel-opment of these movements charts the progress we make in clarifying categories from an abstract to a more concrete and true conception of reality. Peculiar to this development is the claim that each conceptual advance contains all those preceding it. Therefore, the starting point of logic's development is not left behind through progress, but remains preserved throughout the complete development (Hegel 1969: 71).

This development culminates in what Hegel calls "the Idea," or "truth" (*PR* §§10, 21). Each conceptual advance is "true" in relation to the Idea as a whole (see *PR* §§2, 31R).[5] For Hegel, the Idea is more than a simple aggregate of its numerous developments, but an interrelated whole (Hegel 1969: 514–515, 827). Each individual development toward this whole is "abstract" or "incomplete" (Hegel 1969: 198, 414). The closer each development is to this whole, the more "actual" or "concrete" it is.

These general features of his philosophical system are important to bear in mind when interpreting the *Philosophy of Right*, as its subject matter is the concept of right and the manner through which it develops into an "Idea of right" (*PR* §§1, 29). In other words, the central focus is on each development of right leading from an abstract to a more concrete comprehension, with the final development able to account for each previous determination and not vice versa. Hegel's project is to discover the various determinations of right in their proper context (*PR* §§2R, 19). The initial, or abstract, determination of right is not removed from a higher comprehension; but, instead, it serves as a necessary presupposition for all further developments (*PR* §32A). For Hegel, right is not developed independently, but through the will of human beings (*PR* §4). The will is reason that seeks external expression through reflective involvement with the world, rather than only with itself (*PR* §§4, 13A).

For Hegel, our comprehension of right must begin from its most basic conception, abstract right. Its focus is the existence of personality, that is "the capacity for right" (*PR* §§33, 36). Hegel attempts to explain how our will first manifests itself externally in property ownership. What is central to his discussion is the activity of the will, not the physical acquisition of property (*PR* §§55R, 217R; see §§41A, 49R). In possessing property, my will enjoys an external sphere in which it can be recognized by other human beings (*PR* §§51, 57R). This recognition becomes manifest in a relation to other persons, will to will (*PR* §71). The relation takes the form of a contract whereby each individual will finds common ground with another will, forming a common will uniting them (*PR* §78A). The creation of a common will develops one's capacity for right beyond one's pure subjectivity. As a result, Hegel says, "The rational aspect of property is to be found not in the satisfaction of needs but in the superseding of mere subjectivity of personality" (*PR* §§41A, 71R, A).

For Hegel, it is an open question whether or not persons who freely create a common will honor their agreements. Thus, contracts remain "susceptible to wrong": the violation or non-performance of certain contractual agreements (*PR* §81A). In Hegel's view, the creation of a common will is a positive thing as individuals come to agreement. Indeed, he argues "it is the nature of humanity to press onward to agreement with others" (Hegel 1977: 43). Persons who are unable to come to agreement with others are akin to animals, unable to base their judgments on anything beyond their own feelings. When we decide not to honor contractual agreements, this is a negative movement as our willful activity prioritizes arbitrary choice over common agreement.[6] Hegel calls this "wrong" as right exists only contingently, asserted and denied at the discretion of private individuals (*PR* §§81, 82).[7]

3.2   "Punishment" in abstract right

This background helps us approach Hegel's first comments on punishment in the *Philosophy of Right*. As a response to wrong, Hegel argues that right must be made effective. He says:

> But the truth of [wrong] is that it is null and void, and that right re-establishes itself by negating this negation of itself. Through this process of mediation whereby right returns to itself from its negation, it determines itself as *actual* and *valid*, whereas it was at first only *in itself* and something *immediate*. (*PR* §82; emphases original)

We must address wrongs by overcoming purely arbitrary willful activity by refusing to recognize it as valid. In so doing, we cancel, or "negate," the influence of wrong on the development of right. Crucially, this discussion regards the reaffirmation of the common will as a superior arbiter of right rather than the purely subjective will.

With this discussion in mind, Hegel distinguishes three varieties of "wrong": unintentional wrong, deception, and crime.[8] Unintentional wrongs are simply mistaken agreements, the least harmful kind of wrong (*PR* §86A). Their relative harmlessness consists in the fact that no common will had ever been formed between the two parties. Deception, however, is a more serious wrong because no commonality is shared truly, as one party agrees to a contractual stipulation with another only through dishonesty (*PR* §§87–88).

The most serious wrong is crime, characterized by a criminal's rejection of another will's capacity for rights (*PR* §95). The criminal acts in such a way that he recognizes only himself as having a capacity for rights, interacting with others however he pleases. Hegel describes the proper response to crime as the "cancellation [*Aufheben*] of crime" (*PR* §101). Here he uses the German word *Aufheben* which is often translated into English as "sublation." According to his *Science of Logic, Aufheben* has "a twofold meaning . . . on the one hand it means to preserve, to maintain, and equally it also means to cause to cease, to put an end to" (Hegel 1969: 107). In the present context, the sublation of crime involves both (1) the cancellation of wrong and (2) the preservation of the common will. Thus, Hegel speaks of punishments as (1) "the negation of a negation" whose end is (2) "the restoration of right" (*PR* §§97A, 99).

Indeed, Hegel does refer to this "cancellation of crime" as "retribution" (*PR* §101). However, this is only the case, he adds:

> in so far as [retribution] . . . is an infringement of an infringement, and in so far as crime, by its existence [*Dasein*], has a determinate qualitative and quantitative magnitude, so that its negation, as existent, also has a determinate magnitude. (*PR* §101)

This relationship between crime and its punishment is not strictly equal, but equal "in terms of its *value*" (*PR* §100; emphasis original). It is important to note that this relationship is purely conceptual (*PR* §100R).[9] Hegel's discussion of punishment in abstract right is never meant to be understood as anything more than a theoretical treatment of the subject.[10] Indeed, his purpose has been only to demonstrate retribution as the *primary* ground justifying corrective treatments: "that which is *retributive* implies veritable imputation of guilt" (Hegel 1956: 128). When we impute guilt to deserving persons, we "honor" the criminal insofar as we treat her as rational by holding her responsible for what she does (*PR* §100R). For these reasons, Hegel rejects the justice of punishing the innocent on all grounds.

Yet, despite these retributivist claims, it is not clear how strongly Hegel adheres to them. On deterrence, he says famously: "To justify punishment in this way is like raising one's stick at a dog; it means treating a human being like a dog instead of respecting his honour and freedom" (*PR* §99A). However, I would like to suggest that Hegel's argument is only against deterrence as the *primary* justification, or "real ground," for punishing. In fact, Hegel is not opposed to various forms actual punishments may take in "their proper context" to be developed within a more substantive comprehension of right (*PR* §99R). Hegel's retributivism is no greater than the claims that punishment can be distributed only to guilty persons and that there is a relationship between the particular wrong and its punishment.

More importantly, it should be clear that if this was a complete account of Hegel's theory of punishment, it would be of little use to us. For example, punishments in abstract right arise in reaction to the existence of "wrong." By "wrong," Hegel refers to a willful disregard for mutual recognition. Punishments aspire to "restoring (abstract) right." However, the (abstract) rights punishments seek to preserve exist only contingently and at the discretion of private individuals. Indeed, this is also true for the act of punishing. For this reason, Hegel clearly states that acts of punishment at the level of abstract right are acts of revenge, as there is no designated penal power: "Where there is no state, there is revenge" (Hegel 1995: §46R).

Moreover, not only is there no proper judicial institutions available for the administration of justice, there are no *laws* either. If the majority of commentators on Hegel are correct to say that his theory of punishment is substantively contained in abstract right, then "crimes" and their corresponding "punishments" are matters entirely independent of the rule of law and judicial institutions. In addition, these commentators cannot make sense of a second commonly held thought about Hegel's theory of punishment: namely, that Hegel's complete view of punishment is laid out in his theory of civil society where his judicial system of courts transforms revenge into legal punishment. It is difficult to see how the courts can have a role in a theory of punishment that does not consider its relation to positive laws.

Finally, retributivism is a theory of punishment that gives pride of place to desert: the moral culpability of an offender. It is then highly curious that abstract right lacks any substantive analysis of desert. This analysis comes after abstract right in Hegel's later section entitled "Morality" (*Moralität*). Indeed, Hegel admits that in abstract right "it makes no difference what my principle or intention was" (*PR* §§106A, 113R). To be clear, it is very difficult to see the discussion on punishment in abstract right as a complete retributivist theory of punishment given that Hegel's consideration of purpose, intention, responsibility, and morality all appear elsewhere (see *PR* §§105–141). Not only does Hegel's theory of punishment presented in abstract right seem problematic as a theory of *legal* punishment, but it seems problematic as a distinctly *retributivist* theory as well.

3.3   Punishment beyond abstract right

The implications for how Hegel ultimately attributes punishments for violations of positive laws – rather than contractual stipulations – are rarely addressed specifically.[11] When we consider the use of punishment at the level of what Hegel calls "the objective actuality of right" as opposed to "abstract right," punishments are deserved only by persons who have transgressed a state's positive law.[12] Thus, *actual* punishments (or what we might call *concrete* punishments) are warranted by violations of law rather than abstract, contractual stipulations. One attractive feature of Hegel's theory for many commentators is its apparent flexibility on the final form that punishment may take. As stated above, punishments can be determined only approximately according to value, rather than to a strict equality (*PR* §101R). Hegel therefore rejects any imposition of the *lex talionis*.

However, Hegel does *not* hold that even a good state will always punish criminals to a degree that approximates to the seriousness of its corresponding crime. For example, he says: "It is not the crimes or punishments which change, but the relation between the two" (*PR* §96A). This changing relationship is the setting of the values of crimes and punishments (*PR* §101). It would be incorrect to believe Hegel held that the value is set only by the criminal per se in committing the crime, as is commonly claimed. In fact, the degree to which a crime poses a threat to the security of society may have a primary impact on the severity of the punishment (*PR* §218).[13] He says:

> The fact that an injury to *one* member of society is an injury to *all* the others does not alter the nature of crime in terms of its concept, but in terms of its outward existence ... its *danger to civil society* is a determination of its magnitude ... This quality or magnitude varies, however, according to the *condition* of civil society. (*PR* §218R)

Crucially, there are two different treatments of punishment that must be distinguished between an abstract, conceptual comprehension of crime and the magnitude of the actual punishment. On the one hand, in a certain respect, the "wrongness" of a particular criminal act is equal to other similar acts. However, on the other hand, *actual* punishments are distributed to violators of positive law, not abstract right. If this were not true, it would always be unjust to punish criminals differently for the same crime. On the contrary, Hegel argues that a society's penal code is "primarily a product of its time and of the current condition of civil society" (*PR* §218R). Civil society determines the severity of punishments because crimes attempt to negate "the validity of the laws": in some sense, punishments must seek to restore the validity of a society's laws, rather than abstract right per se.

Thus, legal punishment aspires to satisfy societal maintenance primarily. Punishment aims to both maintain and protect the continuation of the community against criminal actions that seek to undermine or forever damage the community as a community of *right*. This is not to say that Hegel's views on punishment are designed to punish all who challenge the state. There are clear limits on who can be punished – for example, only those who have broken a law – and clear limits on acceptable punishments. Remember that Hegel is not presenting a picture of any *existing* government, whether it be the United States, United Kingdom, or United Arab Emirates. Instead, this picture is of the Idea of the state: a just community that serves as our benchmark for a more perfect state.

Importantly, abstract right does reappear in this discussion. Recall that, for Hegel, speculative logic's self-development from an abstract to a more concrete and true conception of reality entails that each conceptual advance contains all those preceding it. Likewise, Hegel's account of punishment here in civil society "contains" the account of punishment in abstract right. He says:

> Just as right *in itself* becomes law in civil society, so too does my individual [*einzelne*] right, whose existence [*Dasein*] was previously *immediate* and *abstract*, acquire a new significance when its existence is recognized as part of the existent [*existierenden*] universal will and knowledge. (*PR* §217)[14]

In abstract right, wrongful acts must be punished or the crime "would otherwise be regarded as valid" (*PR* §99). Similarly, Hegel says: "it would be impossible for society to leave a crime unpunished – since the crime would then be posited as right" (*PR* §218R). Crucial to Hegel's theory of punishment is that punishments can be distributed only to deserving persons. Thus, actual punishments seek to address the existence of wrong as positive laws.

In addition, the general "equality" between the conceptual comprehension of crime and the magnitude of the actual punishment remains as a measure of a criminal's essential desert, but it may not always play a role in "the specific external shape" punishment takes (*PR* §101R). As a result, Hegel clearly recasts the retributivist core in his original treatment in abstract right where he endorses the view that (1) crime exists as the violation of abstract right, (2) only someone who performs a crime can be guilty, (3) only guilty persons are liable to punishment, and (4) all punishments must be proportional in value to their precipitating crimes. His later treatment qualifies these steps so that crime becomes a violation of positive law, rather than abstract right, strictly speaking. More importantly, he does not abandon the earlier view that the values of crime and its punishment are linked. The difference is that Hegel now adds an important twist: *civil society* – rather than only the criminal himself in acting – has a say in which punishment is most appropriate. Thus, Hegel's full theory of punishment is *not individualistic*, in a break from traditional retributivism.[15]

I believe there are further reasons that might cast doubt on Hegel's alleged retributivism. For example, Hegel says, "in civil society offenses can be punished more severely than they can be in the abstract, in and for themselves" (Hegel 1995: §114; see *PR* §218A). This fact may be particularly troubling given Hegel's views on war, as civil society may often find itself sentencing its criminals to punishments more severely than it might have in peace time, all else being equal (see *PR* §§218A, 324–329). For Hegel, there is no such thing as a punishment unjust in and for itself as such because they are all "proportionate to the conditions of their time; a criminal code cannot be valid for every age, and crimes are semblances of existence which can meet with greater or lesser degrees of repudiation" (*PR* §218A). None of these views coheres with retributivism which would claim instead that punishment cannot be just if it fails to cohere with a criminal's individual desert and, more importantly, the only justifiable punishment is one that is just in and for itself.

The specific determination of punishments is by professional judges presiding over jury trials (*PR* §§214R, 227A, 228R).[16] These decisions are to take account of the effect on society from a crime and "not solely the law" (Hegel 1995: §45). We might expect repeat offenders to receive punishments that do not take into account past offenses, as the criminal would have annulled these crimes through his punishment. In fact, Hegel argues that repeat offenders might deserve more severe punishments than someone committing the same offense for the first time, in the effort to prevent the performance of crimes from becoming a habit (Hegel 1995: §114). This may make some sense if we consider that one role of punishment is to reconcile the criminal with the community. By committing the same offense repeatedly, the criminal displays her resistance to reintegration with society and the need for a more severe than usual punishment to bring this about.

This chapter began with a passage well worth repeating in full:

> Punishment, for example, has various determinations: it is retributive, a deterrent example as well, a threat used by the law as a deterrent, and also it

brings the criminal to his senses and reforms him. Each of these different determinations has been considered the *ground of punishment*, because each is an essential determination, and therefore the others, as distinct from it, are determined as merely contingent relatively to it. *But the one which is taken as ground is still not the whole punishment itself.* (Hegel 1969: 465; emphasis added)

This passage coheres well with the presentation of punishment we find in the *Philosophy of Right*. One reason is that this passage makes clear that just punishment is not merely retributivist. We have already seen how Hegel's theory departs from more strict understandings of retributivism while maintaining a concept of desert redefined as criminal wrongdoing. A criminal is deserving of punishment not because of an immorality, but because of criminality. It is his performing a crime that is an issue.

A second reason is that this helps makes best sense of the special role that societal maintenance plays in his theory of punishment. The just punishment for crimes presupposes that our laws are themselves just. Together, these laws form a structure that makes political community possible over time. We punish crimes to the degree we as societal members believe they pose genuine threats to our just institutions. Therefore, we punish only those who have performed crimes (fulfilling a retributivist dimension) and the shape this punishment takes is that which will best serve societal maintenance and in proportion. Punishments that might *further* accommodate deterrence and/or rehabilitative effects have a special preference. This is because such effects would contribute to the goal of societal maintenance. If we have two available and legitimate punishments equal in value in all relevant respects aside from the fact that one of the punishments has a greater potential to rehabilitate the criminal, then a Hegelian theory of punishment will justify the punishment with the greater rehabilitative effect as such a punishment will further the aims of societal maintenance. We do not maintain our state for its own sake, but as a demand of justice punishing only those who have committed crimes within a proportional framework. Hegel's theory of punishment accommodates more functions than simply retributivism. These functions are justified within a certain structure where deterrent and rehabilitative functions are secondary to the necessity of desert and proportionality. Punishment is neither retributivist, preventative, nor rehabilitative, strictly speaking, but a *unification* of these three distinct functions within a rational framework. This reading fits best with his presentation of punishment in the *Philosophy of Right* and his other works.

4 The Reception amongst British Idealists

It is worth noting even briefly that this result should not be surprising. This is because Hegel's first interpreters in English held a very similar understanding of punishment. These persons were the British Idealists, sometimes referred to as "British Hegelians," and they wrote in the late nineteenth century until about the 1930s. While there are many differences between them, the British Idealists shared remarkable commonality with respect to their theories of punishment (see Brooks 2003; 2007b; 2009; 2010; 2011a; 2011b; forthcoming). Both major figures in this movement, such as Bernard Bosanquet, F. H. Bradley, and T. H. Green, as well as more minor figures, such as James Seth, all offer unified theories of punishment (see Green 1941: §§176–206; Bosanquet 1958: 167–217).

British Idealists defend Hegel's idea that societal maintenance justifies legal punishment, built upon just laws. While British Idealists accept societal maintenance, they did not argue that we should maintain laws of whatever society wherever we find them. Instead, they argued that the community and its laws do not exist independently, but that the laws exist for the benefit of the community's members. Individuals must find satisfaction in their community and its laws (Ritchie 1905: 321). Thus, Green argues that "the justice of the punishment depends on the justice of the general system of rights" and "the proper and direct object of state-punishment [is] ... the general protection of rights" (1941: §§189, 204).

British Idealists also agreed with Hegel on how punishments should be set in proportion to crimes. Seth argues:

> The view of the object of punishment gives the true measure of its amount. This is found not in the amount of moral depravity which the crime reveals, but in the importance of the right violated, relatively to the system of rights of which it forms a part ... The measure of the punishment is, in short, the measure of social necessity; and this measure is a changing one. (1907: 305)

Punishments are set in proportion to its object, crimes. Not all crimes are equal in value. The difference between the values of various crimes lies not in their immoral depravity, but the importance of the legal right threatened. Green agrees:

> a violation of a right, requires a punishment, of which the kind and amount must depend on the relative importance of the right and of the extent to which

its general exercise is threatened. This every theory of rights in detail must be followed by, or indeed implies, a corresponding theory of punishment in detail. (1941: §177)

Any theory of rights will require a theory of punishment. Punishment serves the end of protecting our rights. It is justified where rights are violated through criminal acts and set in proportion to the importance of this right viewed within the larger context of a system of rights.

Finally, British Idealists also accept a unified theory of punishment. Green says: "it is commonly asked whether punishment according to its proper nature is retributivist or preventative or reformatory. The true answer is that it is and should be all three" (1941: §178; see Seth 1892: 236; Ritchie 1902: 221; Mackenzie 1924: 430–432; Bosanquet 1958: 216). Not unlike Hegel, the British Idealists accept that all crime must be deserved if only in the sense that it can be justified only in relation to a crime. The purpose of punishment is to further just societal maintenance and, thus, the form that punishment may take can include deterrent and rehabilitative elements where this purpose is best served. Bosanquet says: "Deterrence and reformation are subordinate aspects implied within [punishment]" (1918: 207). These elements can play a useful role, but taken on a case-by-case basis.

My purpose here is primarily suggestive. I have argued that there is a core idea in Hegel's philosophy that has been overlooked. This idea is that he holds a unified theory of punishment. This theory brings together retribution, deterrence, and rehabilitation in one coherent view. I have argued that this theory is present in his several works and helps us to make sense of his comments on punishment in the *Philosophy of Right*. In this section, my purpose is not to offer a complete theory of punishment offered by British Idealists. Instead, I hope that the comments above, while merely suggestive and lacking further (and necessary) elaboration, make clear a central fact: the first leading exponents of Hegel's philosophy all seem to hold a theory of punishment that is distinctive in its similarities to the unified theory of punishment I have claimed is held by Hegel. Contemporary interpreters have not only been mistaken in their views about Hegel's theory of punishment, but they have been mistaken further to overlook earlier interpretations by those who first introduced Hegel to the English-speaking world as these early views more accurately characterize Hegel's theory of punishment.

5 The Prospects of a Unified Theory of Punishment

We should not be surprised that Hegel held a unified theory of punishment. One reason is that any reading beyond the comments in "Abstract Right" clearly state real tensions between his account and traditional retributivism. A second reason is that it is surely Hegelian to argue for a unified theory bringing together *three* distinct elements within a non-individualistic view. A third reason is that his early interpreters were virtually united in defending a unified theory of punishment. We must speculate why to some degree, but I would suggest that this is because they identified such a view in Hegel's work. Yet, something has gone wrong since the early twentieth century. This essay is an attempt to correct this error.

I conclude by noting that there is more than historical significance in this view. Sentencing guidelines often ask judges to weigh several penal principles in determining sentences. These include a view toward the criminal's desert, the public safety, the criminal's reform, and general deterrence. The strategy of some penal theorists is to criticize this Model Penal Code for holding inconsistent principles. This is the wrong strategy. Surely, there is much that would be attractive about a penal theory that defended just punishments as distributed only to those who are deserving, set in proportion to their crimes, and that favored options where there was an additional benefit of general deterrence and reduced risk of recidivism. The difficulty lies in formulating a theory that can coherently unify these seemingly different elements.

The Hegelian strategy offers a way forward. We should link just punishment with the corresponding law being just. Only criminals should be punished on account of their crimes. Proportionality can be set in relation to the importance of rights violated. This relation will be a changing one and we should not think any one punishment may be forever best for any crime, but recognize the importance of our current social conditions in making these determinations. The punishment itself should, wherever possible, incorporate elements that contribute to deterrence and rehabilitation. Much more work must be done to demonstrate this possibility and this is a major future challenge. However, Hegel shows us that such a possibility is conceivable and the British Idealists offer additional resources to further our creative imaginations.

Hegel defended a unified theory of punishment. So did the British Idealists. This has a historical importance in addressing past interpretations, but there is a larger importance in the promise such a view has to offer an exciting alternative to the theories of punishment which exist today. The future may be Hegelian after all.

Notes

1. See Hegel 1975: 60, 92, 120.
2. This is perhaps all the more troublesome given that Hegel's philosophy is systematic. In a philosophical system published in several books, any single book is but one part of the wider system. Interpretations that focus on one part to the exclusion of the rest of the system deny the systematic character that is undoubtedly a core feature of Hegel's philosophical writings, but also an essential element of his own self-understanding of his philosophical project. Discussions about punishment elsewhere in the system will have a relevance to what we find in the *Philosophy of Right*. It is a project for those that reject this perspective to justify why there should be continued neglect, rather than closer interest, in Hegel's comments on punishment beyond the *Philosophy of Right*.
3. Hegel will have more to say about punishment in the *Philosophy of Right*. I will turn to those comments in the next section. My concern here is first to establish the general picture and then to demonstrate that this picture best fits with Hegel's comments on punishment in the *Philosophy of Right* as well. Hegel's defence of a unified theory of punishment is a consistently held view across his work.
4. This section is a revised and expanded version of sections from Brooks 2007a: ch. 3.
5. Hegel 1991: §15R. See Hegel 1969: 755.
6. "Thus bad actions, for example, are merely subjective" (*PR* §27A).
7. *PR*, pp. 15, 18–19. Hegel repeatedly condemns grounding right solely with subjective inclinations (see *PR*, pp. 11–12, 15, 17–19; §§2R, 3R, 11, 15R, 17, 18, 25, 26A.)
8. These distinctions correspond to the logical categories of "simple negative judgement," "positive infinite judgement," and "negative infinite judgement."
9. "In the present discussion, we are solely concerned with the need to cancel crime – not as a source of *evil*, but as an infringement of right as right" (*PR* §99R).
10. "It is laughable to regard everything under the form of this abstraction as legal right; right is something entirely formal, (α) infinite in its variety, and without totality, and (β) without any content in itself" (Hegel 1979: 118).
11. For perhaps the best exception, see Nicholson 1982.
12. "The objective actuality of right" is manifest in "the Administration of Justice" (*PR* §210).

13. "An offense is intrinsically dangerous in proportion to the other offenses it makes possible ... since the security of civil society is thereby impaired, it can impose more severe penalties" (Hegel 1995: §114; see *PR* §§218R, A).
14. See *PR* §217R: "The original, i.e. immediate, modes of acquisition and titles (see §§54ff) are in fact abandoned in civil society, and occur only as individual accidents or limited moments."
15. My view contradicts that of Stillman, who claims that "the measure of [a criminal's] penalty is also derived from the criminal's act and will. For the penalty is derived from the specific content of the crime itself ... Since the punishment fits the crime, the criminal in committing the crime has chosen his punishment" (1976: 174).
16. See *PR* §116R and *ES* §531. See also Brooks 2004a, 2004b.

References

Anderson, Jami L. (1999) "Annulment Retributivism: A Hegelian Theory of Punishment." *Legal Theory* 5: 363–388.
Bosanquet, Bernard (1918) *Some Suggestions in Ethics*. London: Macmillan.
Bosanquet, Bernard (1958) *The Philosophical Theory of the State*. London: Macmillan.
Brooks, Thom (2003) "T. H. Green's Theory of Punishment." *History of Political Thought* 24: 685–701.
Brooks, Thom (2004a) "The Right to Trial by Jury." *Journal of Applied Philosophy* 21: 197–212.
Brooks, Thom (2004b) "A Defence of Jury Nullification." *Res Publica* 10: 401–423.
Brooks, Thom (2007a) *Hegel's Political Philosophy: A Systematic Reading of the Philosophy of Right*. Edinburgh: Edinburgh University Press.
Brooks, Thom (2007b) "Rethinking Punishment." *International Journal of Jurisprudence and Philosophy of Law* 1: 27–34.
Brooks, Thom (2009) "Muirhead, Hetherington, and Mackenzie." In William Sweet, ed., *The Moral, Social and Political Philosophy of the British Idealists*. Exeter: Imprint Academic, pp. 209–232.
Brooks, Thom (2010) "Punishment and British Idealism." In Jesper Rybergand J. Angelo Corlett, eds., *Punishment and Ethics: New Perspectives*. Basingstoke: Palgrave Macmillan, pp. 16–32.
Brooks, Thom (2011a) "Is Bradley a Retributivist?" *History of Political Thought* 32: 83–95.
Brooks, Thom (2011b) "What did the British Idealists do for Us?" In Thom Brooks, ed., *New Waves in Ethics*. Basingstoke: Palgrave Macmillan, pp. 28–47.
Brooks, Thom(forthcoming) *Punishment*. London: Routledge.

Cooper, David E. (1971) "Hegel's Theory of Punishment." In Z. A. Pelczynski, ed., *Hegel's Political Philosophy: Problems and Perspectives.* Cambridge: Cambridge University Press, pp. 151–167.

Findlay, J. N. (1958) *Hegel: A Re-examination.* London: George Allen & Unwin.

Green, T. H. (1941) *Lectures on the Principles of Political Obligation.* London: Longmans, Green.

Hegel, G. W. F. (1956) *The Philosophy of History.* New York: Dover.

Hegel, G. W. F. (1969) *Hegel's Science of Logic,* trans. A. V. Miller. New York: Humanities Press.

Hegel, G. W. F. (1975) *Natural Law: The Scientific Ways of Treating Law, its Place in Moral Philosophy, and its Relation to the Positive Sciences of Law,* trans. T. M. Knox. Philadelphia: University of Pennsylvania Press.

Hegel, G. W. F. (1977) *Phenomenology of Spirit,* trans. A. V. Miller. Oxford: Oxford University Press.

Hegel, G. W. F. (1979) *System of Ethical Life and First Philosophy of Spirit,* ed. H. S. Harris and T. M. Knox. Albany: SUNY Press.

Hegel, G. W. F. (1991a) *Elements of the Philosophy of Right,* ed. Allen W. Wood, trans. H. B. Nisbet. Cambridge: Cambridge University Press. (Abbreviated *PR.*)

Hegel, G. W. F. (1991) *The Encyclopaedia Logic: Part I of the Encyclopaedia of Philosophical Sciences with the Zusätze,* trans. T. F. Geraets, W. A. Suchting, and H. S. Harris. Indianapolis: Hackett.

Hegel, G. W. F. (1995) *Lectures on Natural Right and Political Science: The First Philosophy of Right,* trans. J. Michael Stewart and Peter C. Hodgson. Berkeley: University of California Press.

Honderich, Ted (1976) *Punishment: The Supposed Justifications.* Harmondsworth: Penguin.

Inwood, Michael (1992) *A Hegel Dictionary.* Oxford: Blackwell.

Mackenzie, J. S. (1924) *A Manuel of Ethics,* 5th edn. London: University Tutorial Press.

Nicholson, Peter P. (1982) "Hegel on Crime." *History of Political Thought* 3: 103–121.

Primoratz, Igor (1989) *Justifying Legal Punishment.* Atlantic Highlands, NJ: Humanities Press.

Rawls, John (1999) *Complete Papers,* ed. Samuel Freeman. Cambridge, MA: Harvard University Press.

Ritchie, D. G. (1902) *Studies in Political and Social Ethics.* London: Swann Sonnenschein.

Ritchie, D. G. (1905) *Philosophical Studies.* London: Macmillan.

Seth, James (1892) "The Theory of Punishment." *International Journal of Ethics* 2: 232–239.

Seth, James (1907) *A Study of Ethical Principles,* 9th ed. Edinburgh: William Blackwood & Sons.

Stillman, Peter G. (1976) "Hegel's Idea of Punishment." *Journal of the History of Philosophy* 14: 169–182.

Tunick, Mark (1992) *Hegel's Political Philosophy: Interpreting the Practice of Legal Punishment*. Princeton: Princeton University Press.

Wood, Allen W. (1990) *Hegel's Ethical Thought*. Cambridge: Cambridge University Press.

5

Hard Work
Hegel and the Meaning of the State in his Philosophy of Right

Kimberly Hutchings

We should therefore venerate the state as an earthly divinity and realize that, if it is difficult to comprehend nature, it is an infinitely more arduous task to understand the state.[1]

Thirty years ago, scholarly work on Hegel's *Elements of the Philosophy of Right* was obliged to deal with the charge that Hegel's view of the state made him an apologist for authoritarianism, fascism, and totalitarianism. In the intervening years, multiple interpretations of Hegel's political thought have put this charge to rest. It is now acknowledged that Hegel's account of the state in *PR* encompasses many liberal, republican, and social democratic as well as conservative elements, including the accommodation of individual rights, the rule of law, representative government, social welfare, and so on.[2] Of course, this does not mean that there is a consensus about the prescriptive implications of Hegel's political thought. Commentators identify Hegel as more and less liberal, republican, social democratic, or conservative. They disagree about what he means by freedom, about his view of the roles and the relation between the different elements of ethical life (family, civil society, state), about the significance of the monarch in the state's constitution, about the nature and extent of Hegel's commitment to social welfare or freedom of speech, and about the implications of his accounts of external sovereignty, international law, and international relations. But behind the debates in mainstream Hegel scholarship, there is a broad consensus that Hegel can now be counted as one of the good guys. However mistaken aspects of his political philosophy may be, he is essentially on the side of

Hegel's Philosophy of Right: Essays on Ethics, Politics, and Law, First Edition.
Edited by Thom Brooks.
© 2012 Blackwell Publishing Ltd. Published 2012 by Blackwell Publishing Ltd.

progress, which means, paradoxically, on the side of the earlier generation of his critics.

In the context of this emerging consensus on Hegel's reformist modernism, a new set of radical critiques of his work has emerged. This time, however, it is Hegel's modernism that is identified as the problem. Whereas the earlier generation of critics interpreted Hegel and his views on the state as a kind of atavistic throwback to an earlier era of Prussian triumphalism, the current generation sees them as exemplifying the fault-lines of the state in the present. In world history as the world's court of judgment, they find Hegel to be the spokesman of an imperialist and racist modernity. For thinkers such as Serequeberhan (1989), Bernasconi (1998), Hoffmeier (2001), Chanter (2010), Inayatullah and Blaney (forthcoming), Hegel's work is condemned for implicitly or explicitly justifying slavery, colonialism, and racism – charges as shocking as the earlier generation's accusations of fascism and totalitarianism.

In much of the mainstream literature on Hegel, those aspects of Hegel's arguments in *PR* that might seem to support this new line of critique are treated as peripheral embarrassments that can be dropped without compromising the major, positive content of Hegel's political thought.[3] Some of these defenses of Hegel are more persuasive than others, but it is not the aim of this chapter to adjudicate between them. Instead, I want to take these recent critiques of Hegel as a provocation to return to his treatment of the state in *PR* and what it may tell us about political communities self-consciously articulated in terms of a principle of self-determination and about the "hard work" involved in comprehending ourselves as citizens of such political communities. In this respect, following Durst's (2001) example, I will argue that it is illuminating to read *PR* in conjunction with Foucault's work on sovereign, disciplinary and biopolitical power.

The argument proceeds in three sections. In the first section I address the question of how to read the *PR*, bearing in mind what Hegel tells us in the Preface about the role of logic and history in his understanding of what political philosophy is and can do. In the second section, I turn to Hegel's treatment of the internal and external constitution of the state as the articulation of freedom. In the third section, I address the question of how Hegel's account of the historical education of self-consciousness, which culminates in identification with the state, remains instructive for the contemporary reader. This is not because Hegel's own views about how the state ought to be, are, or are not particularly persuasive as a normative model. Rather, it is because Hegel's account of the connections between the different dimensions of ethical life resonates with the ongoing experience of the complex fate of the state into the twentieth and twenty-first centuries. Some aspects of Hegel's state in *PR* may strike us as helpful, others as politically worrying, others as simply absurd, in formulating current theories of right and justice. But what remains compelling in his account is his insight into the kinds of social, educational, and political *work* needed to sustain a self-understanding of the state as the work of freedom.

1   Reading the *Philosophy of Right*

Philosophy is *exploration of the rational*, it is for that very reason the *comprehension of the present and the actual*, not the setting up of a *world beyond* which exists God knows where – or rather of which we can very well say that we know where it exists, namely in the errors of a one-sided and empty ratiocination (*PR* 20).

What kind of political philosophy is being done in *PR*? On the one hand, Hegel states very clearly in his Preface that he is engaging with what "is" rather than what "ought" to be (*PR* 21). On the other hand, the tone of much of his discussion is prescriptive, and he makes it clear that the kind of ethical life he delineates in Part 3 of the text (which deal with the institutions of family, civil society, and state) not only reflects the current stage of spirit's self-awareness, but is also a clear advance on other ways of organizing political community. For all readers, *PR* presents the puzzle of weighing up how much Hegel's system, especially his logic and philosophy of history, as opposed to either his specifically political theory or the demands of his particular political context, shape and direct his analyses of abstract right, morality, and ethical life. There are many plausible, non-metaphysical readings that rely on the possibility of abstracting Hegel's political theory, with its substantive claims about property, punishment, civil society, constitutional government, or international relations from the rest of his philosophical system.[4] Equally, there are strong arguments that *PR* makes sense only in the light of logical categories embedded in Hegel's non-foundational metaphysics.[5] Then again, more historically contextualist readings draw attention to Hegel's specific political commitments, the significance of the Prussian reaction to the ways in which the text was written, and the practical, educative functions the text was intended to serve.[6] Indeed, it has been argued recently that metaphysical readings effectively get things the wrong way round, and that Hegel's logic and philosophy of history are essentially the *product*, rather than the *ground* of his politics.[7]

Choices about how to read *PR*, as with all texts in political philosophy, reflect the assumptions, questions, and purposes of the reader. Many of the more "political theory" readings of Hegel emerge from the desire to find a corrective to utilitarian, contractarian, and deontological strands in contemporary political philosophy, and therefore need Hegel to be playing the same kind of prescriptive game as other modern political philosophers play. Systemic and contextualist readings, in contrast, are more interested in identifying Hegel's intentions at the time of writing, either in relation to the rest of his philosophical work or in terms of his particular political agenda. My own sympathies lie more with the latter two directions for reading Hegel's work, in large part because these modes of reading fit best with his own insistence on the integrity of his philosophy as a whole and his equally strong insistence that philosophy is always intimately bound up with its own time.

For me, the interest in Hegel's work resides in his claim that he has been able to uncover and comprehend the common rhythm immanent to the related domains of nature, spirit, and thought *because* of the time and place in which he was living and his own self-identification as a child of his time (*PR* 21). For Hegel, modernity was the first era in human history in which self-determination (freedom) was self-consciously articulated as the ground and end of social and political life, in law and institutions as well as in philosophical thought. He celebrated his era as a world-historical achievement, but he also focused his philosophical attention on the question of how social and political arrangements explicitly embodying freedom could be sustained. From his point of view, this is simultaneously a logical, historical, and practical question. It is a logical question insofar as Hegel's purpose is to unpack the meaning of ethical life as self-determination, through an immanent critique of the categories of its self-understanding in legal and institutional arrangements, and of the ways in which the latter had been grasped in the political and juridical thought of his day. It is a historical question insofar as this unpacking presupposes a set of historical developments that enabled the identification of spirit with freedom. This means that the philosopher is fundamentally engaged in grasping the universal implications of the particularities of his time. His raw material is the ways of organizing social, economic, and political life that he associates with these historical developments. And it is a practical question insofar as it is concerned with the social, legal, and institutional forms which can best embody and enable the idea of freedom which is claimed as their ground and end.

It is important to note that logic, history, and practice are not exclusive domains for Hegel; they may be analytically distinguishable, but speculative thought recognizes their immanent connection. This connection makes Hegel's work interesting for two reasons: first, because it opens up a distinctive understanding of the limitations on what political philosophy is and can do; second, because it provides a route into an immanent critique of Hegel's argument, in which the ongoing relevance of his difficult comprehension of the state can be argued for, even as aspects of his reading of his own time are put into question. When Hegel condemns contemporaries for "one-sided and empty ratiocination," he is not simply dismissing the value of utopian or prescriptive political thought. Rather, he is making the point that the *world beyond* inscribed in various accounts of what *ought* to be, is never actually a *world beyond*. What appears as the most radical challenge to the status quo produced by the heroic philosopher king is always conditioned and shaped by available socially produced and enacted meaning. At some level, therefore, the *ought* is always inscribed in the *is*. The political philosopher, as author, is authoritative only in the response of an audience able to recognize (re-cognize, re-think) the thought with which they are presented as something that is already thought, explicitly or implicitly, in available legal, institutional, or logical vocabularies. When political philosophy is thought about in this way, as the rethinking or recognition of what *is*, then it becomes both more and less ambitious as a project. It becomes less ambitious in that it abandons the idea that the exercise of reason in abstraction will, by itself, provide a persuasive model of the good life. It becomes more ambitious, because it is self-consciously making the claim to definitively conceptualize or elicit the universal meaning of a particular, contingently developed set of social, economic, and political forms.

Hegel's way of thinking about political philosophy provides a route to the immanent critique of his work, because it implies the ongoing contextualization of the universal inherent in, or emergent from, historical particularity. If political philosophy is a child of its time, then there can be no guarantees that its meaning will be recognized, or that its meaning will remain consistent, as its audience changes. Hegel's logic and philosophy of history require that the terms of his writing and our reading are brought together, a process that opens up all kinds of spaces for interpretation, but which certainly precludes an unquestioning reception of his understanding of the meaning of freedom in history.[8]

The reading of Hegel's comprehension of the state that follows is a Hegelian one to the extent that it takes Hegel's historicism seriously. In doing so it seeks neither to rescue Hegel as a route toward a contemporary theory of justice, nor to dismiss Hegel as the spokesman for an imperialist and racist modernity. The aim is rather to trace the resonances between twentieth- and twenty-first-century experiences of the state and Hegel's interpretation of its meaning. That there are resonances, I will argue, in no way vindicates Hegel's prescriptive claims for the state and world order, it speaks, rather, to the dilemmas of political organization around the idea of individual and collective freedom that we share with Hegel's time.

2   The Terms of Ethical Life

The first two parts of *PR* are designed to demonstrate how the realms of abstract right and morality fail as adequate instantiations of what they claim to be their idea, of spirit as self-determination. Neither of them provides a satisfactory conceptualization of the source and nature of modern legal, social, and political institutional forms. Instead they are more like the tip of the iceberg of contemporary ethical life, partial and potentially misleading. As the argument of *PR* unfolds, abstract right and morality are shown to be shaped and conditioned by the institutions of family, civil society, and the state. It is not only that individual right and conscience require certain kinds of socially embedded institutions and practices to work, it is that without those institutions and practices the notions of individual right and conscience would not be comprehensible. The self-understanding of individuals as property owners or moral beings is immanently connected to their self-understanding as sons, members of civil society, citizens. And of these elements of modern self-understanding, it is the idea of the state that emerges as being of overwhelming significance. Without the state not only abstract right and morality but also family and civil society cannot be thought in terms of freedom (*PR* §257, p. 275).

Hegel followed a familiar pathway in the political thought of his time in arguing for the necessary connection between individual freedom and particular forms of legal and political authority. The difference in his account is that, rather than positing a state of nature in which the need for political institutions and authority are derived from individual freedom in the abstract, Hegel took his starting point from the meaning of individual freedom inherent in what he identified as distinctively modern social and economic practices. Within this context the family and the realm of production and trade (civil society)⁹ are, in their different but complementary ways, fundamentally concerned with the reproduction of a particular kind of free individuality, the self with the capacity to choose, to own, to take legal and moral responsibility, to contract. What Hegel seeks to show is that neither family nor civil society could reproduce this free individual without invoking what is beyond the realm of free individuality itself.

> Any discussion of freedom must begin not with individuality [*Einzelheit*] or the individual self-consciousness, but only with the essence of self-consciousness; for whether human beings know it or not, this essence realizes itself as a self-sufficient power of which single individuals [*die einzelnen Individuen*] are only moments. (*PR* §258 Addition (G), p. 279)

In seeking to comprehend the state in *PR*, Hegel is aiming to extrapolate the most adequate conceptualization of the conditions that enable the production and sustenance of free individuality. His aim is neither purely descriptive nor purely prescriptive. He isn't describing how actual states work, or identifying any actual state with the ideal. He is, however, building up an ideal type of the modern state, which he claims is the "actualization of freedom." Only this idea of the state is commensurate with the requirements of a self-understanding of spirit as self-determination. Because only in this idea of the state is the dependence of particular freedom on universal conditions explicitly, consciously recognized.

> The state is not a work of art; it exists in the world, and hence in the sphere of arbitrariness, contingency and error, and bad behaviour may disfigure it in many respects. But the ugliest man, the criminal, the invalid, or the cripple is still a living human being; the affirmative aspect – life – survives [*besteht*] in spite of such deficiencies, and it is with this affirmative aspect that we are here concerned. (*PR* §258 Addition (G), p. 279)

When Hegel asks the affirmative question of what makes a state a state, he is asking a question that he acknowledges is historically specific, the equivalent to, and in his view more fundamental version of, the modern question of what makes a human being a human being. In essence, the answers to both questions are the same, what makes a state a state and a human being a human being is their explicit identification with self-determination (*PR* §260 Addition (H, G), p. 283). In the case of the human being, this self-awareness is captured more and less adequately in the different forms of self-understanding articulated in abstract right, morality, family life, work, and citizenship. In the case of the state, this self-awareness resides in the recognition, by individual and collective actors, of themselves (self-determination) in the state's institutional configuration, internally and externally (*PR* §261, pp. 284–285). If the state is necessary to sustain spirit as self-determination within the family and civil society, then it cannot be understood in terms other than those of freedom. Otherwise, self-determination would collapse into determination, and the claim of modernity to instantiate the meaning of spirit adequately would fail.

In discussing the state, in this ideal-typical sense, therefore, Hegel is laying out how it is that the free individual could recognize his or her freedom in the practices and institutions that make free individuality possible. It turns out that there are two key ways in which this is possible: first, through the explicit recognition of the multiple ways in which the state provides the conditions for free individuality; second, through the substantial, positive identification of the individual with the state. Throughout his discussion Hegel employs both organic and educational metaphors. On the one hand, the state is a holistic entity, which lives only in the elements that make it up; on the other hand, it is the culmination of an educative, civilizing process. The organic metaphor expresses the dependency of free individuality on institutions of sovereignty, law, and government (*PR* §263 Addition (H), p. 286). The educational metaphor expresses the individual's (citizen's and reader's) explicit realization of the state as the ultimate instantiation of free being (*PR* §264, p. 287; §274, p. 312). In order for the state to work in the terms of self-determination, individual actors not only have to grasp their reliance on the state but also have to positively embrace this reliance as essential to their own self-understanding. In effect, Hegel's anatomization of the internal and external constitution of the ideal-typical state traces out this double-sided process. We see it at work in his exposition of the relation between state and civil society and in his discussion of interstate relations and world history.

In his account of civil society, the sphere of private contractual relations, Hegel repeatedly demonstrates how civil society would be unsustainable without various kinds of state institutions and interventions. Left to its own devices, the tendency of civil society is to collapse into chaos and conflict, producing dangerous extremes of wealth and poverty and creating surplus populations, who form into an anarchic, uneducated rabble (*PR* §244, pp. 266–267). In order to sustain the free individuality of civil society and market relations, the state plays a crucial role as the provider, supervisor, manager, and guarantor of education, law, the administration of justice, processes of colonization, police and welfare authorities, and the corporate institutions that collectively organize civil society activities. The unsustain-ability of a society organized in practice on the self-understanding of free individuality is nowhere more clearly demonstrated than in that society's need for mechanisms of welfare, justice, and security. It needs welfare because of the danger posed to particular freedom by class conflict (*PR* §235–245, pp. 261–268). It needs justice and security because a self-understanding of freedom as individual choice provides no criteria for distinguishing between harmful and harmless choices, including choices that undermine or threaten the free individuality of others. Justice and security enable mediation between different choosers and prevent the collapse of relations of particularity into the arbitrary imposition of one will onto another, they *secure* the possibility of freedom. Precisely because there are no criteria inherent in the self-understanding of civil society as the sphere of particular free will, security has to be introduced and administered from elsewhere, by the state (*PR* §234, p. 261).

For Hegel, welfare, justice, and policing are not unfortunate constraints on free individuality but conditions for its exercise. It is only, however, when free individuality itself recognizes welfare, justice, and policing as immanent to its own self-understanding as free, that social and political arrangements genuinely articulate the principle of self-determination. The idea of the state necessitates that the state be actively embraced by its members as an extension of themselves. This latter move, which is more or less advanced in actual states, is accomplished in different contexts in Hegel's account of the idea of the state. It happens in the internalization of economic and social roles through education (*PR* §187, pp. 224–226; §239, p. 264), in the identification of individuals with the corporations and estates whose role is institutionalized within the formal constitution of the state (*PR* §250–254, pp. 270–274), and, ultimately, through the citizen's identification with the state as an independent, self-moving whole (*PR* §268, p. 288–289; §272 Addition (H), p. 307; §274, p. 312). It is in this latter respect, in patriotism and the possibility of dying and killing in war that the identity of particular and universal freedom is most clearly expressed, and it is in this context that the world-historical role of the state emerges (*PR* §330–340, pp. 366–371).

As with Hegel's discussion of civil society in relation to the state, his account of the relation between the internal and external constitution of the state is simultaneously a story about organic interdependence and education. The existence of the state as an actor in relation to other actors within an international sphere conditions the complex webs of recognition that allow the internal workings of the state to be understood in terms of self-determination. The external aspect of the state helps to produce the identification of individual self-consciousness with the state by literally linking the survival of one to the other. As Hegel acknowledges, "current emergencies" feed into the degree of mediation necessary to sustain the elements of ethical life. And war, in particular, plays a crucial part in reinforcing citizens' sense of the interconnection between their particular freedom and state sovereignty (*PR* §324, p. 361; §327, p. 364). This process educates both citizen and reader into understanding how the self-awareness of the state as self-determination has implications beyond the finite form of a particular political order. The action of states in the international sphere is the education of spirit. In international relations, in the realms of commerce, colonization, and war, different forms of spirit's self-understanding conflict with one another (*PR* §340, p. 371). This culminates, notoriously, in the predominance of the self-understanding of spirit as self-determination that Hegel traces in his own age and attributes to the legacies of Roman law and Protestantism (*PR* §358, p. 379).

> The present has cast off its barbarism and unjust [*unrechtlich*] arbitrariness, and truth has cast off its otherworldliness and contingent force, so that the true reconciliation, which reveals the *state* as the image and actuality of reason, has become objective. (*PR* §360, p. 380)

Hegel's discussion of the terms of ethical life concludes with a schematic philosophy of history, in which the principle that he discerns as distinctive of modernity is claimed to be the ultimate lesson for his readers. His own capacity to learn and articulate this lesson was, as he acknowledged, immanent to the historical movement he claimed to discern; it was the political project of his time. For Hegel, the task of structuring social and political existence in terms of freedom was both complex and dangerous. In his view, partial understandings that remained stuck with the idea of free individuality, without comprehending its conditions, could lead to ruinous outcomes, as in the French Revolutionary Terror or in the destructive anarchy of a civil society without regulation. In place of a thoroughly individualist account of the modern state, Hegel, it appears, gives us one in which sociality comes before individuality, and the non-contractual enables and conditions the contractual realm. It is for this reason that it is tempting to read Hegel's work as a kind of corrective to individualism and libertarianism in political philosophy. To do this, however, requires setting up an *opposition* between individualism and social, which is somewhat misleading in the context of Hegel's argument. As I have tried to suggest in the discussion above, Hegel's key concern in *PR* is to show how it is possible for the state to be understood as self-determination. In other words, he is interested not so much in the tension between individual and collective freedom as in the possibility of the identification of the two. What does it take for free individuality to recognize itself as free in the ways in which it is educated, nurtured, coerced, killed, or enabled to kill, by the practices and institutions that simultaneously underpin its (free individuality's) existence? Simply put, it requires a lot of work, and Hegel's philosophy of right attempts to show us how that work could be accomplished.

3   The Hard Work of Freedom

Contemporary Hegel scholarship continues to debate exactly what it is that Hegel is telling us in his account of how the state can be identified with the work of freedom. At one extreme of modernist readings of Hegel's work, Winfield (2001) argues that Hegel's state is the work of freedom because its institutions are genuinely free, and free individuality can see the principle of its own existence directly reflected in those institutions.[10] For him, Hegel's philosophy of right captures the essence of the principles of modernity, which are rationally comprehensible (even if historically delivered) and are of universal application. The institutions described in the *PR*, on Winfield's account, which he interprets as those of a liberal democratic, market society, economy, and polity, are a "uniquely valid form of civilization" that incorporate "the timeless normativity of freedom" (2001: 92, 107). The modern (Hegelian) state is peculiarly legitimate because its legitimacy is immanent to it, rather than derived from externally given foundations. The recognition of this normativity depends upon historical circumstances but it is not in any sense relative to those circumstances (2001: 92).

   Winfield sustains his reading of Hegel, and of the modern state, by drawing a clear distinction between the contingent, particular realms of history and practice (which may be pathological in a variety of respects) and their universal and necessary implications. To the extent that the actual history of the modern state and economy has involved the coercion and oppression of individuals and communities, it has failed to live up to its idea. Hegel's account of the impossibility of drawing a clear line between what is and is not the state's business, and Hegel's account of the self-consciousness of superiority embedded in the "advanced" states of his time are disconnected from any actual totalitarian or imperialist practices. In examining the relation between modernity and either totalitarianism or imperialism, therefore, Winfield argues that the former contradicts both of the latter, and any historical relation between them is a matter of contingency. On his account, the principles of modernity (self-determination) are incompatible with totalitarianism, racism, or the external imposition of modern principles on others (Winfield 2001: 102). Hegel's philosophies of right and of history offer an account of the spontaneous emergence of the historical conditions that enable the recognition of spirit as self-determination. For this reason, Winfield reads the discussion of colonialism in *PR* as being about the universalization of principles of right through trade, and the concluding account of history as an inclusive story of modernization (107). From this point of view neither the complex range of ways in which the internal constitution of Hegel's state is held together, nor Hegel's treatment of the "Germanic" realm as the culmination of historical development signify any *necessary* link between the self-understanding in terms of freedom of individuals and collectivities, and self-understandings that are exclusive and hierarchical:

> because modernity's institutions of freedom do not depend on any particular culture for their legitimacy, they are inherently capable of global, not to mention, intergalactic, realization. (Winfield 2001: 93)

Winfield's (2001: 93) reading of Hegel's modernism is countered by postcolonial interpretations offered by commentators such as Bernasconi, Hoffmeier, and Serequeberhan. According to these readers, Hegel's political thought affirms (and even celebrates) that the self-awareness of the state as self-determination is sustained by its self-conscious superiority to other forms of individual and collective self-consciousness. In Hegel's philosophy of history, they argue, non-European peoples and forms of political community are defined as either underdeveloped or incapable of development in the direction of self-consciousness as freedom. As Bernasconi points out, Hegel's treatment of Africa in his philosophy of history did not simply reflect scholarly understandings of his day; it drew selectively on available evidence in order to place Africa at the beginning of history, but without the capacity to develop more fully in terms of spirit as self-determination (1998: 52, 62). Hoffmeier argues that Hegel's attitude to the indigenous communities of the Americas was even more dismissive, effectively excluding them even from the beginning of history (2001: 35). Serequeberhan argues that Hegel's philosophy of history is both reinforced by and reinforces those aspects of his argument in *PR* when he addresses issues of colonialism and imperialism (1989: 315). For all of these thinkers, Hegel not only makes the link between the modern state and both racism and imperialism explicit, but also justifies these phenomena as necessary to the development of the modern state.[11]

And yet, as Hegel's defenders point out, many of Hegel's claims in *PR* and elsewhere seem incompatible with racism and imperialism. One line of argument in defense of Hegel focuses on the substantive refutation of the charges, looking for places in his work where Hegel explicitly condemns, or appears to condemn, slavery, colonialism, and racism, as for instance in the passage in *PR* stating that in the modern state the individual is recognized as an individual, not in terms of a particular ethnic or religious identity.[12] A second line of argument uses Hegel against himself, seeking to show how his logic and philosophy of history work against the kinds of prejudices he displays in his comments about other peoples and cultures and about the role of imperialism, colonialism, war, and conquest in the progress of spirit that culminates in the most "advanced" states.[13] In all of these cases, the aim is to render what is uncomfortable to contemporary ears in Hegel's work contingent in relation to his broader argument. As with Winfield's reading of Hegel, these defensive readings depend on being able to draw a clear line between the meaning of self-determination as Hegel articulates it, and the contingencies of history in which the emergence of the modern state as the only recognized form of political community happened to be bound up with exclusive and hierarchical self-understandings.

The opposition between modernist defenders of Hegel and the postcolonial critics appears to be mutually exclusive, in the sense that if the postcolonial reading is accurate then the modernist reading must be wrong, or vice versa. Here, however, I want to suggest that there may be a different way of reading this standoff. Along with the postcolonial critique of Hegel's argument, other critiques have developed which are more closely focused on Hegel's account of the internal workings of his state. Durst suggests that

Hegel's argument operates as an account of, and apology for, disciplinary power. He interprets Hegelian *Vernunft* as a "productivist form of functional reason," in which a focus on the well-being of individual subjects renders them into instruments for the reinforcement of state power (Durst 2001: 230, 231, 239). In Durst's view Hegel's neglect of the importance of communicative reason (in a Habermasian sense) in the public sphere, means that his state is in danger of the kinds of panopticism criticized by Foucault in *Discipline and Punish*. At the same time, however, Durst argues that the rationale for Hegel's focus on "societal techniques" through which individuals can be integrated into state institutions is rooted in his desire to institutionalize respect for free individuality. It is precisely disciplinary mechanisms that, in strengthening the state, enable the recognition of others as individuals rather than in terms of religious or ethnic identities:

> although I have argued that Hegel's philosophy of ethical life may tend to render the happiness of the individual into a political factor for the reinforcement of the modern state, it is just such a strong state rooted in the ethical life of a nation that has the inner ability to practice what Hegel refers to as toleration. (Durst 2001: 241)

For Durst, this is a "paradoxical" conclusion. But it is paradoxical only if one accepts the view of Winfield and other modernist defenders of Hegel, that what counts as the work of freedom must fit with a particular set of criteria a priori, rather than be extrapolated from, and then recommitted to, historical contingency. The notion that there is a formal logical contradiction between the self-awareness of individual freedom and the processes through which that self-awareness is produced and guaranteed has different implications for Hegel than it does for his contemporary liberal defenders. For the latter, it drives a wedge between logic and history, and sets up the self-awareness of individual freedom (what freedom *really* means) as the source of critique of actual social and political practices. For Hegel, in contrast, the conditions of free individuality become part of what freedom means, and set the philosopher the double-sided task of grasping the nature of those conditions and working out how it is that they may be embraced as the meaning of freedom. Although Durst uses Foucault *against* Hegel, his concluding observations undermine this opposition; instead Hegel becomes someone who prefigured Foucault's insights into the roles of sovereign, disciplinary, and biopolitical power in the modern state.

Kimberly Hutchings

Rather than taking sides between the modernist and postcolonial readings of Hegel, I suggest that the *Hegelian* solution to this dilemma is to get to grips with the truth inherent in both, but also to understand how the partiality of both readings stands in the way of grasping the contemporary interest of Hegel's thought. Modernist readings of Hegel are true because he *was* engaged with articulating social and political life in terms of the principle of freedom. Many of his specific prescriptions embody practices embedded in modern, liberal, and social democratic states of individual right, family life, market society, representative government, rule of law, state sovereignty, and so on. And even those aspects of his state architecture that seem particularly anachronistic or absurd, from his account of the monarch's role to his institutionalization of the "estates," can be made sense of in terms of reconciling tensions between individual and collective existence that are specific to modern social and economic forms.

Postcolonial readings of Hegel are true because he *did* explicitly link the story of emergent modernity to a bigger story, in which European states are claimed to have captured the meaning of history, and other times, places, and cultures are positioned in a normative hierarchy that clearly legitimates claims to European superiority. Hegel was a child of his time (and place), he was by no means sure that the recognition of spirit as self-determination would continue to be the explicit principle for ordering political community. Nevertheless, he wanted it to be so, and in reading his time in the way that he did, he clearly endorsed the denigration of other ways of thinking about social and political order, and legitimized past and present victories of, in his terms, civilization over barbarism.

Modernist and postcolonial readings of Hegel are both true, but they are also both partial. In both cases, the readings rest on drawing a line between logic, history, and practice that Hegel does not draw. From the modernist perspective, the *idea* of freedom makes it impossible that Hegel could be simultaneously according state control, racism, and imperialism a role in the sustaining of freedom. To the extent that he did so, he is therefore making a mistake. From the postcolonial perspective, Hegel endorses the necessary link between modernity, racism, and imperialism and is therefore contradicting modernity's claim to instantiate the *idea* of freedom. He is wrong, or if he is right about modernity, then modernity is wrong, because the *idea* of freedom contradicts the *ideas* of hierarchy, coercion, and exclusion inherent in racism and imperialism. But in reading Hegel *normatively*, both readings miss the fact that Hegel's *idea* of freedom is not a static universal but the self-conscious recognition of practices as free that emerges out of actual, contingent social relations, and shifts and develops as it is put to work in actual, contingent social relations. This is a not a world of logical contradictions, but a world of experience, in which thinking six impossible things before breakfast may turn out to be a practical requirement for living with oneself.

4   Conclusion

In *PR*, Hegel gives us his particular view of the work of freedom, that is to say, of the ways in which freedom can be institutionalized and recognized in political community. His particular view is interesting not primarily because of its specific normative implications but because of the ways in which it points us toward the range of conditions that enable free individuality to find itself at home with itself in the state. This is not to say that Hegel gives us the definitive account of that range of conditions, nor is it to suggest that all states must take on a totalitarian and/or imperialist form. Hegel's own account of how the work of freedom can be done mixes liberal, conservative, social democratic, and republican elements in the internal constitution of the state, and presents a pluralist international society as the direction in which states, as external actors, are heading. The point from Hegel's account of the state as the work of freedom that continues to resonate with contemporary experience is that we cannot understand this work by remaining, as Hegel would put it, in the realm of "empty, one-sided ratiocination." In order to understand how political life may be practiced as freedom we have to get a grip on the processes through which we produce and sustain it. And we have to give up on the idea that any practice of freedom is going to float free of dangerous implications.

At the beginning of the chapter, I suggested that Hegel's thought retains its interest as much for the ways in which it opens itself up to immanent critique as for its explicit content. This openness to immanent critique follows from the fact that in telling us that philosophy is a child of its time, Hegel recognizes that his own perception of history in terms of freedom is itself historically contingent. This may invite more and less radical responses from contemporary readers (whenever they were/are contemporary). A less radical response accepts the parameters of Hegel's reading of his time in terms of freedom and looks for ways in which his account of the work of freedom can be perfected, perhaps through a different kind of state constitution or a more culturally sensitive account of interstate relations. A more radical response raises the question for Hegel that Hegel raises in relation to other times and places: What was it about his time and place that led him to read history in terms of the self-determination of spirit, and what are the limits of this way of reading history in relation either to his own time or to ours? As the postcolonial critics point out, Hegel's articulation of the idea of freedom depends on the identification of his time and place with the world-historical present. It could be argued that this move is skewed in two respects. First, it involves a peculiar elevation of *one* principle (freedom) as the key to both western modernity and history at large; second, it blocks the possibility of thinking Hegel's time from alternative perspectives. The elevating of the principle of freedom is possible only through a unilinear reading of history in general, and modernity specifically. On this account, other histories and other modernities become beyond comprehension in their own terms. But this follows only if we universalize Hegel's thought in a way that runs contrary to his own account of the nature of his work. Thinking history or the state in terms of the hard work of freedom may still be an illuminating exercise in many respects, but it is not necessarily the permanent fate of political philosophy.

Notes

1. Hegel 1991: *PR* §272 Addition (H), p. 307 (hereafter *PR*). I follow the practice of citing the paragraph/addition number, in addition to the page numbers of the English text, so that the reader can more easily consult the German original.
2. The revisionist reading of Hegel's social and political thought in Anglophone scholarship began in the 1970s with books such as Pelczynski 1971, Avineri 1972, Taylor 1979, and has continued since, e.g. Smith 1989; Wood 1990; Dallmayr 1993; Franco 1999; Neuhouser 2000.
3. See exchange between McCarney and Bernasconi 2003.
4. For example, Smith 1989; Wood 1990; Franco 1999.
5. See Brooks 2007.
6. See chapter on Hegel's *Philosophy of Right* in Pinkard 2000: 469–494.
7. See Shilliam 2009.
8. My reading of the relation between logic, history, and practice in Hegel's thought takes its cue from the work of scholars such as Burbidge (2007) and Pippin (2008). For a more detailed account of my interpretation of the links between Hegel's philosophies of thought and spirit, see Hutchings 2006.
9. *PR* §158–180, pp. 199–218; §182–256, pp. 221–274.

10. Winfield represents a particularly strong version of a modernist reading of Hegel, which is premised on a view of Hegel's systematic philosophy as genuinely foundationless.
11. Bernasconi 1998: 59; Serequeberhan 1989: 317.
12. See McCarney, "Hegel's Racism? A Response to Bernasconi," in McCarney and Bernasconi 2003: 33.
13. McCarney, in McCarney and Bernasconi 2003: 34.

References

Avineri, S. (1972) *Hegel's Theory of the Modern State*. Cambridge: Cambridge University Press.

Bernasconi, R. (1998) "Hegel at the Court of the Ashanti." In S. Barnett, ed., *Hegel after Derrida*. London: Routledge, pp. 41–63.

Brooks, T. (2007) *Hegel's Political Philosophy: A Systematic Reading of the Philosophy of Right*. Edinburgh: Edinburgh University Press.

Burbidge, J. (2007) *Hegel's Systematic Contingency*. Basingstoke: Palgrave Macmillan.

Chanter, T. (2010) "Antigone's Liminality: Hegel's Racial Purification of Tragedy and the Naturalization of Slavery." In K. Hutchings and T. Pulkkinen, eds., *Hegel's Philosophy and Feminist Thought: Beyond Antigone?* Basingstoke: Palgrave Macmillan.

Dallmayr, F. (1993) *Hegel, Modernity, and Politics*. Newbury Park, CA: Sage.

Durst, D. C. (2001) "The End(s) of the State in Hegel's *Philosophy of Right*." In R. Williams, ed., *Beyond Liberalism and Communitarianism: Studies in Hegel's Philosophy of Right*. Albany: SUNY Press, pp. 229–247.

Franco, P. (1999) *Hegel's Philosophy of Freedom*. New Haven: Yale University Press.

Hegel, G. W. F. (1991) *Elements of the Philosophy of Right*, ed. A. Wood, trans. H. B. Nisbet. Cambridge: Cambridge University Press. [Abbreviated PR in the text.]

Hoffmeier, M. H. (2001) "Hegel, Race and Genocide." *Southern Journal of Philosophy* (Supplement) 39: 35–62.

Hutchings, K. (2006) "Hegel, Ethics and the Logic of Universality." In K. Deligiorgi, ed., BT Hegel: New Directions. Chesham: Acumen, pp. 105–123.

Inayatullah, N., and Blaney, D. L. (forthcoming) "Shed No Tears: Wealth, Race and Death in Hegel's Necro-Philosophy." In R. Vij, ed., *Hegel and International Relations*. Basingstoke: Palgrave Macmillan.

McCarney, J., and Bernasconi, R. (2003) "Hegel's Racism?" *Radical Philosophy* 119: 32–37.

Neuhouser, F. (2000) *Foundations of Hegel's Social Theory*. Cambridge, MA: Harvard University Press.

Pelczynski, Z. A., ed. (1971) *Hegel's Political Philosophy: Problems and Perspectives.* Cambridge: Cambridge University Press.

Pinkard, T. (2000) *Hegel: A Biography.* Cambridge: Cambridge University Press.

Pippin, R. B. (2008) *Hegel's Practical Philosophy: Rational Agency as Ethical Life.* Cambridge: Cambridge University Press.

Serequeberhan, T. (1989) "The Idea of Colonialism." *International Philosophical Quarterly* 29: 301–318.

Shilliam, R. (2009) "Hegel's Revolution of Philosophy." In *German Thought and International Relations: The Rise and Fall of a Liberal Project.* Basingstoke: Palgrave Macmillan, pp. 88–118.

Smith, S. (1989) *Hegel's Critique of Liberalism: Rights in Context.* Chicago: University of Chicago Press.

Taylor, C. (1979) *Hegel and Modern Society.* Cambridge: Cambridge University Press.

Winfield, R. D. (2001) "Postcolonialism and Right." In R. R. Williams, ed., *Beyond Liberalism and Communitarianism: Studies in Hegel's "Philosophy of Right."* Albany: SUNY Press, pp. 91–109.

Wood, A. (1990) *Hegel's Ethical Thought.* Cambridge: Cambridge University Press.

6

Gender, the Family, and the Organic State in Hegel's Political Thought

Alison Stone

1 Women's Place in the Hegelian State

For Hegel, woman's place is in the family:

> Man [der Mann] . . . has his actual substantial life in the state, in science, etc., and otherwise in work and struggle . . . so that it is only through his division that he fights his way to self-sufficient unity with himself. In the family, he has a peaceful intuition of this unity, and an emotive and subjective ethical life. Woman, however, has her substantial vocation in the family, and her ethical disposition consists in this *piety*. (*PR* §166, p. 206)

Here in his discussion of the family in the *Philosophy of Right*, Hegel effectively denies equality to women in a number of respects. Women are not to undertake paid work in the public sphere; rather, in each family the husband is the head of household who is "primarily responsible for external acquisition and for caring for the family's needs" (§171, p. 209). As each new generation comes to maturity, only sons leave their families to enter civil society. Although women (daughters) do have enough civil personality to enter into marriages, the nature of the marriage "contract" – which is no ordinary kind of contract but one that "begin[s] from the point of view of contract . . . *in order to supersede it*" (§163, p. 203; emphasis original) – is that the two marriage partners renounce their independent legal personalities to form a common unit. The husband, however, is the rightful representative of this unit: "The family as a legal person in relation to others must be represented by the husband as its head" (§171, p. 209) – so that in fact it is

Hegel's Philosophy of Right: Essays on Ethics, Politics, and Law, First Edition.
Edited by Thom Brooks.
© 2012 Blackwell Publishing Ltd. Published 2012 by Blackwell Publishing Ltd.

only women who renounce legal autonomy upon marrying, whilst men retain it under their new guise as heads of household. Consequently, wives also relinquish their maiden names; and although family property is owned in common, only the husband administers it (Hegel 1996: §82, pp. 150–151). Finally, not being rightful participants in civil society, women are not rightly to participate in political activities or processes either, since for Hegel political participation is properly mediated through participation in economic and civil activity.

Hegel is not simply prescribing how gender roles ought to be divided but describing the kind of family he saw taking shape in nineteenth-century Europe: the nuclear heterosexual family as a domain not of production but of intimate personal relations, structured by what Carole Pateman (1988) calls the "patriarchal marriage contract." This peculiar kind of contract effectively recognizes women's freedom (presupposed in their freedoms to marry and to choose their spouse) only to take that freedom away again by slotting women – and men – into roles preassigned according to sex. These are the roles respectively of (male) head of household versus that of (female) care-giver primarily occupied with the needs of others, especially children. This kind of family structure persists to varying degrees today, at least as an ideal. But, as many feminists have shown, this structure has inherent deficiencies. The economic and psychological dependency in which it places women makes them vulnerable to various forms of abuse, while the whole structure is arguably premised on women's economic exploitation insofar as their care-giving work is unpaid and largely unvalued and unrecognized.

Hegel admits that things can go wrong within the patriarchal family – for instance, he notes that the husband's right to manage the family property can conflict with its common ownership. Moreover, he recognizes that this possibility is built into the structure of the family – although for him this is not because that structure is patriarchal, but because, in his words, "the ethical disposition of the family is still immediate and exposed to particularization and contingency" (*PR* §171, p. 209). That is, family members are disposed to embrace and act on behalf of their common good on the basis of their immediate feelings of mutual love. Hence, if love dies, spouses (in practice, husbands) may lose the motivation to serve the family's common good and may lapse into pursuing their self-interest at other family members' expense. Still, although the patriarchal family is not flawless in Hegel's view, on the whole he deems it rational, because the "immediate unity" of its members which the family embodies – their direct identification with their common good based in immediate loving feeling – is one essential aspect of modern social life, despite the potential problems that can result from this immediacy. Hegel, then, is not offering a value-neutral description of the gender division of labor as it was crystallizing in modern Europe, but a normative redescription of that emerging division, a redescription in which this division and the family structure bound up with it form essential aspects of reason's progressive self-actualization in the modern social world.

Hegel's account of the family is one of the parts of the *Philosophy of Right* least discussed by commentators – not surprisingly, because commentators understandably tend to look for what is true and insightful in Hegel's work, and prima facie his account of the family is neither true nor insightful but merely a "remnant of his era" (Halper 2001: 817). Yet the fact remains that Hegel saw the nuclear family as one of the three fundamental spheres of modern society and as rightly structured by a rigid, hierarchical, division of sex roles. He saw no legitimate room for "non-traditional" family arrangements: unmarried couples, single-parent families, homosexual families all fail to conform to rational family structure (see Brooks 2007: 70–75). Unappealing as these views are today (to many of us, anyway), we cannot fully understand Hegel's *Philosophy of Right* without confronting his view of the family and sex roles. Having said this, feminist and feminist-informed interpreters have debated whether the division of sex roles that Hegel describes as rational really should count as rational by the standards of his own philosophy. Perhaps, despite what Hegel actually says, "the logic of his system should have led him to conclusions very close to recognizing women's equal rights in social, economic, and political spheres," as Jean-Philippe Deranty puts it (2000: 145; for similar views see Mills 1996; Ravven 1988). On this view, Hegel's own ideal of individual freedom, and his support for (what he regards as) the Christian principle that all human beings are free, imply that all individuals of both sexes should be able to realize their freedom; Hegel simply failed to pursue this implication because he succumbed to the prejudices of his time.

In partial agreement with this interpretation, I will argue that Hegel's view of women is indeed in tension with one particular implication of his political philosophy: that all citizens should be able to participate in *every* key sphere of modern society – family, civil society, and state – because each sphere gives them access to an essential aspect of modern social membership. This latter idea follows from Hegel's organic conception of the state, according to which family, civil society, and government are the necessary articulations of politically ordered society as a whole, so that participation in all three spheres, and self-identification as a member of every one of these spheres, is essential to social membership and to feeling and being at home in modern society. However, this same organic conception of the state implies that each social sphere must have its proper class of representatives, with the family represented by women. Thus Hegel's organic conception of the state does not simply point toward gender equality, but has egalitarian and anti-egalitarian implications which are in some tension with one another, and where Hegel on the whole – especially in regard to women – pursues the latter. I argue, then, that Hegel's view of women is not merely a contingent result of prejudice on his part, but follows from a core element of his political philosophy, namely his organic conception of the state. But this does not mean that Hegel's philosophy is simply irremediably sexist and must be left behind, since that philosophy – and indeed the very same element within it, the organic view of the state – also has inherent egalitarian implications.

In connecting Hegel's patriarchal views on women to his organic conception of the state, I may seem to be lending support to the many previous critics of that conception, of whom Karl Popper is perhaps the most (in)famous. The worry is that the organic conception of the state is proto-totalitarian, allocating individuals to fixed "stations" within the social whole and so denying them liberty and equality. I do not endorse this criticism; rather, Hegel's organic conception points both toward *and* away from equality (particularly but not only in respect of gender). Moreover, these tensions are internal not to the organic *concept* of the state as such but to Hegel's specific *conception* of the political organism on the model of the animal organism. In his *Philosophy of Nature*, Hegel affirms the superiority of animal to plant nature on the grounds that it is only in animal organisms that all parts are fully subordinated to the whole. In contrast, he maintains that in plant organisms each part directly reproduces or contains the whole within itself, rather than being decisively subordinated to playing one specific role within the whole. If we reverse Hegel's natural hierarchy and take plant nature as our model, then we can reimagine political society in more thoroughly egalitarian – and gender-egalitarian – terms than Hegel does. I will explore this by turning to the political use that the early German Romantics made of the plant model.

My aim, then, is neither to discredit the organic concept of the state nor to suggest that Hegel's particular organic conception should automatically be dismissed. Instead, I wish to open up discussion about the political meanings and merits of different organic conceptions, which are not necessarily illiberal. Moreover, by reflecting on this issue we can illuminate one way in which Hegel's political thought is systematically connected to his philosophy of nature – something almost entirely neglected in Hegel scholarship.

2 The Organic State and Individual Freedom

Critics of Hegel, such as Popper in *The Open Society*, have seen him as the arch-proponent of an organic and totalitarian state. Supposedly, he values the freedom only of the state as a whole and not of individuals, whom he subordinates to the state, allocating to each individual a fixed place in a range of "stations" chosen by the state according to its needs. At the same time Hegel allegedly misdescribes individuals as attaining freedom through this subordination, on the grounds that this subordination makes individuals into the parts of an organic political whole, a whole that is free qua organic, and from which freedom flows down into the parts – so that individuals become free just by taking up their social stations. The doctrine of the organic state is, then, supposedly merely the mystifying wrapping around a totalitarian core. (I take it that this is the core of Popper's complaint against Hegel – to the extent that one can discern a coherent argument in his invective. See Popper 1945: vol. 2, esp. pp. 31–45.)

That the totalitarian picture of Hegel is wrong has been abundantly shown by scores of interpreters, who have established that individual freedom – in multiple aspects – is one of the fundamental values on which Hegel's political philosophy is based. The *rechtliche Staat*, for Hegel, is one that realizes individual freedom. Yet so much emphasis recently has fallen on Hegel's liberal commitment to individual freedom that the ways in which he does nonetheless regard the rational state as organic – something manifested in the abundant references to the state as organism which pepper the *Philosophy of Right*[1] – have come to be largely ignored. In turn, some scholars, including Frederick Neuhouser (2003) and Nathan Ross (2008), have begun to correct this,[2] arguing that Hegel conceives of the organic state in a way that is compatible with his commitment to individual freedom.[3]

How, then, does Hegel reconcile these commitments? Very schematically: Hegel begins the *Philosophy of Right* by taking free will to be the ability to choose which to pursue from the set of one's individual desires or of the available courses of action (*PR* §11, p. 45). The condition of an individual's exercising this ability, for Hegel, is that they own private property – enjoying rights over a range of material objects in respect to which they can embody and realize their freedom. But property-ownership is possible only if different individuals recognize and respect one another's property (§71, p. 102). This mutual recognition and respect amongst property-owners can reliably be achieved only if they respect one another not merely when it benefits them to do so but out of genuine respect for the rights of others. That is, individual freedom in Hegel's first sense – which Neuhouser calls "personal freedom" – requires that individuals be moral subjects, capable of recognizing and acting on moral principles and obligations: personal freedom requires the further *moral* freedom to legislate moral principles to oneself (Neuhouser 2008: 205–206). However, the latter will not constitute a form of freedom if it is experienced as mere subjection to moral law: moral *freedom* can be such only if it is reconciled with personal freedom, that is, in case individuals desire to do what morality demands. This requires that they undergo a moral education, by virtue of living amongst appropriate social institutions which cultivate their emotional and practical dispositions to align with moral requirements (§153, p. 196) – so that individuals want what is in the common good as well as their own individual goods.

These educative institutions, which make up *Sittlichkeit*, are the family, civil society, and the strictly political state – what Michael Wolff calls the "constitutionally organized set of political powers" to legislate, execute, and decide (2007: 298). The family educates us to renounce our exclusively individual interests entirely and to embrace the whole family's common good; the family does this by drawing out the rational, universal, dimensions that are embodied in individuals' immediate feelings of love. Civil society continues the educative work by leading citizens to embrace the common purposes pursued by legal and public authorities and by the corporations – although generally these are still seen as common in a deficient sense, either as being common merely to all individuals as single agents or as being common only to those with a shared economic vocation. The state completes the educative work by bringing us to embrace the common good in the genuine sense and by regulating and organizing the family and civil society so that they lead us toward and not away from this embrace of the common good. In this respect the state overarches family and civil society so as to become politically organized society as a whole. Thus nested within one another, these three spheres educate us to want what morality requires and they thereby provide the conditions of our individual (moral and personal) freedom.

However, this reconstruction presents *Sittlichkeit* as merely instrumental for individual freedom. But, for Hegel, securing the conditions for individual freedom *transforms* the kinds of freedom that individuals enjoy and appreciate. It gives them a further freedom: to participate in, and to reproduce through their own activity, social institutions that flow out of and reflect the particular identities that they have acquired *as* members of those institutions, that is, as family members, *Bürger*, and citizens. Personal and moral freedom are possible only within this new form of freedom. But what makes this a form of *freedom* at all? As Michael Hardimon (1994: ch. 3) has shown, in a society that enabled individuals to be free only as individuals, what Hegel regards as a fundamental need of individuals would remain unfulfilled, namely their need to feel (as well as to be) at home in the social world. For this, individuals need to be able to participate in social institutions, to act according to the roles available within those institutions, and to affirm these roles as both constituting and expressing their own self-identities, rather than experiencing them as externally constraining or burdensome. This form of freedom – "subjective social freedom," as Neuhouser calls it (2008: 214) – is a fundamental part of freedom, of being self-determining rather than acting from externally imposed constraints.

Now, Hegel further maintains that the rational state as a whole must *itself* be free and self-determining, and that for this it must be organically structured. How does he reach these seemingly bizarre conclusions? For him, the overall purpose of political society is to reconcile people's sense of having individual interests (of individual difference) with commitment to the collective good and the good of others (a sense of unity with others or of universality). This is the internal end or *telos* of political society. But to fulfill its purpose, the social order must be differentiated into family, civil society, and the political powers that overarch and organize these, because each of these *differentiae* corresponds to or embodies a distinct "moment" of the individual–universal spectrum the extremes of which are to be reconciled. The family embodies and fosters "immediate unity" between individuals; civil society embodies and fosters individual "difference"; and the political state reconciles the two by embodying and fostering "mediated unity" between individuals (Neuhouser 2003: 133; this terminology derives from Taylor 1975). Why are exactly *these* three moments those through which the reconciliation of the poles must be achieved? Because Hegel's general method of overcoming oppositions, or of reconciling their poles, is not to deny the existence of the opposed poles but to show that each pole requires the other as the necessary condition of its own existence, so that the two prove to be united within a broader structure that encompasses them both. Thus, for the individual/universal opposition to be resolved, there must be a sphere embodying sheer universality (the family, in which all commitment to isolated individual interests is abandoned), another sphere embodying sheer difference (the apparent free-for-all of civil society), and a third sphere reconciling and overarching the previous two.

Politically organized society thus differentiates itself into distinct subsystems in accordance with its intrinsic purpose. As Charles Taylor puts it, this state articulates itself according to a necessary plan (1975: 438). It self-determines. In so doing, it simultaneously organizes itself organically. An organism is an entity that has its own purposes – chiefly self-preservation, development, and reproduction – and that articulates itself into specialized subsystems which interlock so that they fulfill these purposes (*EM* §381A, pp. 9–10). An organism is self-determining because it unfolds into a coherent system in accordance with its *own*, inbuilt, purpose or plan. And so Hegel declares that: "As living spirit, the state exists only as an organized whole, differentiated into particular functions which proceed from the single concept ... of the rational will and continually produce it as their result" (§539, p. 265).

In describing the state as an organized whole, Hegel is not simply taking the organism to furnish a handy metaphor for the state. He believes that the rightly organized state *really has* the structure of an organism: self-differentiation into articulations each serving a function within the whole. "The state *is* an organism, that is the development of the Idea in its differences" (*PR* §269A, p. 290; emphasis added; on the non-metaphorical status of Hegel's organic language, see also Wolff 2007: 312). This idea that states can really be organisms may seem strange, but it relies on Hegel's particular understanding of organisms as self-organizing systems (which descends from Kant's third *Critique*, especially his conception at §65 of that work of a *Naturzweck* – a purposively organized natural system).

These metaphysical beliefs of Hegel's feed into his political philosophy, but they do not contradict his support for individual freedom. Rather, for Hegel, the organic state acts from the purpose of reconciling individual freedom (in its various forms) with social membership, so that a commitment to individual freedom is built into this state – even as it incorporates individual freedom into social freedom, the freedom to be a social member and to be at home in society. This incorporation is intended to preserve individual freedom whilst also satisfying our need for reconciliation with the social world. But we might still wonder whether this scheme allows for individual freedom to be fully realized. This question arises particularly in relation to Hegel's treatment of women.

3 Tensions in the Organic Model: For and Against Sex Equality

On the face of it, the organic conception of society seems to imply that everyone ought to be permitted to participate in all three spheres of modern *Sittlichkeit*, because each sphere gives its participants access to an essential aspect of membership in a modern society. Neuhouser spells this implication out very clearly:

> the idea of [an organic] social world not only specifies the necessary internal structure of the three basic institutions . . . but also gives an account of the different kinds of *identities* required of individuals if they are to participate freely in such institutions. Focusing on the latter point suggests that Hegel's demonstration of the [organic] structure of *Sittlichkeit* includes the claim that the modern social world is rational (in part) because it allows its members to develop and express different, complementary types of identities, each of which is indispensable to realizing the complete range of relations to others (and to self) that are . . . worthy of achieving. On this view, then, to lack membership in any of the three basic institutions would be to miss out on an important part of what it is to be a fully realized (individual) self. (2003: 140)

Apparently, then, the organic view of society entails that women *and* men alike ought to be able to participate fully in family, civil society, and state.

Admittedly, merely formally opening civil society and state up to women is not enough to ensure that they can really participate in these realms as fully as men, as has become apparent in our own time. If within the family women remain the presumptive care-givers while men remain the presumptive breadwinners, then women's care-giving role will continue informally to limit their possibilities for participation in paid work and politics, and will impose on women a double burden of care-giving and paid work. A necessary condition of real sex equality is a complete redistribution of care-giving work. And we might think that it is another logical consequence of Hegel's organic conception that this redistribution ought to take place. For if each individual ought to be able to participate fully in all spheres of social life, then men ought, as well as having access to civil society and state, also to participate in the family just as fully as women: that is, men ought to embrace the communal spirit of family life as a vocation (although not the only one) and so to undertake an equal share of domestic responsibilities. More precisely, as Edward Halper (2001) explains: as Hegel divides up the roles of husband and wife, husbands will the family unity primarily as a "universal" – as an individual case of marriage in its general concept, understood to be rational and necessary – while wives will that unity primarily as an "individual," that is, they will this particular instance of marriage (albeit implicitly as an instance of the general type). Each party also wills the material activities necessary to sustain the marriage under the particular mode in which they will it: thus wives do the material work of caring for the constituent members of the family, while husbands act on behalf of the family unit (*as* a unit) within the wider world. But if in fact Hegel's organic vision implies that each party ought to have access to both dimensions of participation in family life, then both wives and husbands ought to will and materially support the family in both respects.

Hegel, of course, draws no such inference. On one view, this is just because the prejudices he inherited from his time prevented him from thinking through the sex-egalitarian implications of his own ideas. Deranty defends this view. He emphasizes that, according to Hegel, women are free individuals and all persons are fundamentally equal. Yet, Deranty objects, Hegel illogically restricts women's freedom, dividing sex roles on the basis of (1) biology – when on his own terms society ought to be structured in accordance with the concept, not nature – and (2) experience, empirical acquaintance with the patriarchal division of gender roles (Deranty 2000: 155) – when on Hegel's own terms society ought to be structured by reason, not by sheer empirical givens.

Perhaps, then, his organic conception should have directed Hegel to support sex equality. Yet other considerations suggest (*pace* Deranty for whom Hegel's sex division of roles is illogical by his own criteria) that the organic conception leads Hegel to support this sex division. As Allen Wood puts it, for Hegel "differentiated institutions require a social differentiation among individuals. Each principle must have its proper representative and guardian" (1990: 244). Each organic social function (unity, difference, mediated unity) requires its specialized sphere or institution; and each sphere or institution requires a particular class of individuals to be permanently based in and responsible for its material and spiritual maintenance. After all, each of an organism's purposive functions is realized by a specific subsystem within it – digestion by the digestive system, sexual reproduction by the reproductive system, and so on. And each functional subsystem is embodied in a particular range of organs: the stomach, bowels, etc. within the digestive system; the gonads, genitals, etc. within the reproductive system. Certain material parts of the organism are taken over by the purposes of the organism as a whole, and shaped in their very material configuration so that they serve those purposes. What would otherwise be formless, undifferentiated matter becomes a range of functionally organized, highly differentiated, and specialized organs. Similarly, then, Hegel supposes that each social sphere must be maintained by a dedicated set of people who serve as its "organs" or functionaries: what would otherwise be a formless, undifferentiated mass of individuals (a mere aggregate) is subdivided into distinct classes of specialized functionaries each with a determinate social role. Thus Hegel writes that:

> The actual Idea is the spirit which divides itself up into the two ideal spheres of its concept – the family and civil society – as its finite mode ... In so doing, it allocates the material of its finite actuality, that is individuals as a *mass*, to these two spheres. (*PR* §262, p. 285)

Charles Taylor (1975: ch. 16) identifies the same principle at work in much of the *Philosophy of Right*, such as Hegel's subdivision of civil society into the agricultural, business, and civil service classes (which replicates within civil society the broader division into unity, difference, and mediated unity). In choosing a line of work, each individual takes up a position within the complex whole, rather than falsely pretending to be able to realize the whole totality directly within themselves. Similarly Hegel introduces subdivisions into the political state, and within its estates assembly he has the representatives of the business class appointed by the corporations, thus opposing both universal suffrage and direct democracy. Appointment is through the corporations so that representatives can play their political role as members of an articulated economic structure, not as sheer individuals; and so that those who appoint them can also do so qua participants in corporations, in terms of their economic roles and identities, not as sheer individual atoms. As for the agricultural class, they are represented only by the unappointed landed aristocracy. Consequently, Hegel says, "in our modern states, the citizens have only a limited share in the universal business of the state" (*PR* §255A, p. 273). Just as women represent the family and may not advance beyond it, most *Bürger* and all of the peasantry represent civil society and may not advance beyond it to the political level as such. The organic model now appears to support a series of hierarchical social stratifications – of which women's confinement to the family is merely an instance. Far from being illogical, then, that confinement now seems to be an eminently logical consequence of Hegel's organic approach.

We may still think that Hegel's particular argument for women's place in the family makes illegitimate reference to mere nature. For presumably the reason why women and not men are deemed to be the rightful representatives of the family sphere is because of women's reproductive biology and functions. But matters are more complex than this. In a rational state, the division in gender roles does not result merely from biological sex difference as such but from the state's elevation of that biological difference into the basis of a functional differentiation between citizens, a functional differentiation which, as we've seen, is itself rationally necessary so as to raise the citizens to the status of being members of an organic whole rather than leaving them as a heap of atoms. Thus, Hegel writes:

> The *natural* determinacy of the two sexes acquires an *intellectual* and *ethical* significance by virtue of its rationality. This significance is determined by the difference into which the ethical substantiality, as the concept in itself, divides itself up in order that its vitality may thereby achieve a concrete unity. (§165, p. 206)

The "ethical substance" of the rational state needs to achieve a unity at once concrete and vital – that is, organic. This requires that this state "divide itself up" into two functional roles corresponding to family versus civil society. In turn, each role must be assumed by a determinate set of representatives. Here natural sex difference, which would otherwise have merely contingent practical consequences but no intrinsic ethical significance, comes into play as a basis on which to assign roles. This role difference gives ethical meaning – sociopolitical purpose – to natural sex difference, converting what would otherwise be its merely practical consequences into rational functions of the state. Accordingly, Hegel speaks of women's female (*weibliche*) nature becoming the basis of the sociopolitical identity of woman as wife and mother (*Frau*). Women's biological nature does not *cause* them to become wives and mothers (so, *pace* Deranty, Hegel does not wrongly biologize spirit). Rather, women's nature "acquires" (*erhält*), or "receives" (§165, p. 206), the new significance of a domestic role when that nature is enfolded by the purposes of the state.[4]

Overall, then, the organic conception of society points both toward equality, including sex equality, *and* against it, toward the rightfulness of social hierarchies, where it is generally the latter implication that Hegel pursued.[5] I now want to argue that the source of this tension in Hegel's thought is not his organic concept of the state per se but his particular *conception* of it.

4   Animal State, Vegetal State: Hegel versus Early German Romanticism

Hegel's confinement of women to the family, as we've seen, follows from his principle that each social sphere requires a specific class of people to represent it – just as each functional subsystem within an organism requires a specific set of organs to embody it. Functional specialization of this kind is for Hegel intrinsic to the structure of organisms, political or natural. If it is intrinsic to organisms, though, it achieves full realization only in *animal* organisms – which for Hegel are the highest form of organic life, surpassing the other two forms, the earth (mineral life) and plants (vegetable life).

What makes animal life so excellent? Hegel does not actually see the earth as properly alive at all; he calls it "self-alienated life." As for the plant, he complains that here "the objective organism and its subjectivity are still immediately identical" (*EN* §343, p. 303). The plant

> is not as yet ... the articulated system of its members ... It unfolds its parts;
> but since these members are essentially the whole subject, there is no further
> differentiation of the plant; leaves, root, stem, are themselves only indivi-
> duals. Since the reality which the plant produces ... is completely identical to
> it, it does not develop authentic members [*Glieder*[6]]. (*EN* §337A, 276)

The whole of the plant is directly contained in each of its parts. That is, the entire set of functions specified by the whole is in principle performed by each part. It may seem that the parts of plants are functionally differentiated: leaves absorb light, roots absorb moisture, stems distribute water and sap, etc. But each part can, if cut from the whole, take on any of the other functions and undergo a transformation in its material structure to support this. Branches, for instance, can be cut off and planted to become roots from which new plants grow. In an animal, in contrast, the whole organism so completely masters its manifold parts and adapts their materiality to its purposes that those parts become materially incapable of taking on another function if removed from the whole. As Hegel likes to say (following Aristotle), a hand cut from a body ceases to be a hand. The hand cannot regenerate a new body from within itself, so thoroughly has it been made into the material of its function. But the parts of plants are not so mastered by the unity of the whole plant as to serve as organs of one and only one function. Instead, each part contains within itself the potential to perform any number of functions, even if circumstances dictate that one of these functions predominates in it at some given time. Because plants exhibit a level of functional specialization, they meet Hegel's criterion for being organic, but their manifold parts are not completely subordinated to their general functions as they should be according to the concept of an organism. For this reason, Hegel complains that plants grow by simple addition of more and more identical parts – identical, in principle, because each alike contains the same potential for the same set of functions. Plants grow not by qualitative development but mere quantitative proliferation.[7]

Evidently, underpinning Hegel's conception of the political organism is the idea that its organic form is animal, not vegetal. But what might a state be like that was modeled on the plant instead? Presumably, in such a state, each individual would have to contain within themselves at least the potential for participating in every social sphere, and which sphere they specialized in – and to what extent they specialized in it – would be a matter of contingency and might change over time. But to contain these multiple potentials, individuals would have in addition to their specializations to have some level of access to all spheres. *All* social spheres would be realized in each individual to some extent at least.

This intriguing possibility of a "vegetal state" is not as whimsical as it might seem. We can explore it further with reference to the political writings of the early German Romantics. They share Hegel's commitment to an organic state – but for them, the model of the organism is the plant rather than the animal. In fact this privileging of the plant applies across all areas of their work (see Miller 2001). Friedrich Schlegel remarks in 1799 that: "The highest, most complete life would be nothing other than *pure vegetating*" (1991: 66). He also states that "The *world* as a whole, and originally, is a plant" (1958–: vol. 18, 151) – by which he meant that the universe is a self-differentiating organic whole whose manner of self-differentiation is that of the plant: this whole develops endlessly, never reaching a point of closure, but forever progressing to higher and higher levels of organization. The same plant model underpins the fragmentary literary form beloved of the Romantics, a form that reflects their belief that a philosophical system can exist only as a sequence of interconnected fragments. Yet despite their interconnection, each fragment is a whole unto itself: "A fragment . . . has to be entirely isolated from the surrounding world and be complete in itself like a porcupine" (Schlegel 1991: 189). This is because each fragment contains within itself the potential to become each of the others: it contains all the others *in nuce* and thus crystallizes the entire system within itself – again like each part of a plant as Hegel saw it. Thus, Schlegel – who here as elsewhere may be taken as representative of Jena Romantic thought more broadly – conceives the plant in similar terms to Hegel, but valorizes it positively because of its fragmentation and open-ended development. This reassessment of the plant is bound up with early Romantic political thinking about the ideal of an organic state.

This Romantic ideal has often been seen as politically reactionary. But in their youth the Romantics ardently embraced the ideals of the French Revolution and, despite growing reservations in view of the Terror, they continued throughout the 1790s to support the Revolution's basic principles (see Beiser 1996: xiv). This specifically *early* German Romantic political thinking is my focus here. Admittedly, none of the Romantics developed their political thinking to the level of systematicity and sophistication we find in Hegel. Their political ideas are expressed largely in fragmentary and exploratory form. Even so, instructive contrast with Hegel is possible.

The Romantics opposed the so-called "machine-state," the paternalist, enlightened absolutist state which took its purpose to be the provision of security and the satisfaction of individuals' material needs (a view of the state upheld by influential theorists of the time, such as Christian Wolff; see Ross 2008: 12). But in opposing this kind of state the Romantics did not, generally, oppose the state per se. Some did: Wilhelm von Humboldt's opposition to the machine-state led him to advocate what we now call a minimal state (see Humboldt 1969); and the author of the "Earliest System-Programme of German Idealism" – variously identified as Hölderlin, Schelling, or the young Hegel – declares that: "We must . . . go beyond the state! For every state must treat free human beings as if they were cogs in a machine; but that it should not do; therefore it should *cease* to exist" (Beiser 1996: 4; emphasis original). On the whole, though, the Romantics proposed instead a different, organic, kind of state,[8] which does not dominate other spheres of social life from the outside but instead permeates and animates them from within. The organic state must therefore self-differentiate into these manifold social spheres; and within each sphere, political participation and common will arise immanently, "elevating us" (as Schleiermacher puts it) to embrace the unity of the state as a whole. Civil life is not to be set free from the state, but to become the organ *of* the self-differentiating state, so that politics and orientation to the common good pervade all areas of daily life, leaving no footholds for atomistic individualism. For individuals to be fully free – rather than being dominated by the state as an external limitation on their activity – they need to be able to find the state to be their home, flowing out of their own activities and identities; this requires that political participation run through the entirety of social life. The Romantics saw this ideal as that of a "true republicanism," in which there is a "general participation in the state" (Beiser 1996: 47).

To see how these thoughts relate to the Romantic privileging of the plant model, we can turn to Novalis's controversial 1798 essay "Faith and Love; or, The King and Queen." On first reading, Novalis here seems to be proposing a renewal of a (highly idealized) feudal monarchy – the essay was occasioned by and appeared to celebrate the coronation of the new Prussian king Friedrich Wilhelm III and his wife. But, as Novalis indicates in his prefatory comments on cryptic language, he is covertly using the idealized royal couple whom he eulogizes here as a symbol of a possible future organic state, which might be monarchical, aristocratic, or democratic, but where the key issue is not its "indifferent form" but its organic or "republican" essence (see Novalis 1960–1988: vol. 2, 503). Moreover, Novalis covertly situates this kind of state as something the coming of which has been made possible by the French Revolution (see O'Brien 1995: 169–171). The idealized royal couple provides a model of felt commitment to the common good, a model that permeates and inspires all of society, Novalis suggests: "It is a great mistake of our states that one sees so little of the state. The state should be visible everywhere, and every person should be marked as its citizen. Can not badges and uniforms be introduced everywhere?" (Beiser 1996: 40) Although these remarks by Novalis have been criticized as proto-totalitarian, they are surely meant to be a humorous illustration of the idea that attachment to the common good is not to be separate from but to run through all dimensions of social life. The idea, then, is not that most people are to participate in political affairs only indirectly via economic life, but that through economic life everyone is to become educated to become an active participant in politics and the state too, as irreducible to but permeating civil society. The vegetal model is at work: each member – each individual agent – is directly to contain, and to realize to at least some degree, the potential for political activity as well as for economic activity (after making the above claims, Novalis compares this ideal state to "a new plant"). These radical ideas, however, are disguised, not to say distorted, by Novalis's monarchical symbol, since the monarchy that he envisages makes no structures available to enable people's active political participation (and so we have to question Novalis's claim that the "form" of the republican state is a matter of indifference).

The vegetal model also shapes Novalis's thinking about women and the family in this essay, although, again, a tension emerges between its radical implications and its distorted conservative presentation. Novalis sees the family, too, as a sphere which is to give rise directly to political partic- ipation: each household is modeled on that of the royal couple whose household is organized by commitment to the common good, and, Novalis writes:

> by such means one could ennoble daily life through the king and queen as the ancients once did with their gods. Then there was a genuine religiosity through the constant mixture of the divine in daily life. Now a genuine patriotism can emerge through the constant interweaving of the royal couple in domestic and public life. (Beiser 1996: 44)

If the family is to be a sphere through which individuals can be directly raised into political activity and identification with the common good, then equally the state – as symbolized by the royal couple – has to have its *own*, internal, domestic aspect that descends into and arises out of family life. This is the queen's domain: the domestic life of the entire nation, encompassing the education of women and children, pastoral care for "the sick and poor," and matters of sex and personal morality. For Novalis, then, there must be a king *and queen* – as his essay title indicates – because the organic political sphere must expand into a domestic aspect so that participation in domestic life, especially by women, can reciprocally rise to political participation. Evidently, in making these claims, Novalis accepts women's domestic vocation. On the other hand, when he suggests that all women are to emulate the queen, hence – non-cryptically – to participate in the (pastoral side of the) life of the state, he implicitly suggests that women ought to be full participants in the state and that their domestic role is to feed into this.

Women's domestic role is not to be merely private or privatizing but to expand into broader social concerns. Rather than seeing women's domestic role as excluding them from the state, as Hegel does, Novalis sees this role as compatible with women's participation in the state insofar as that state, as an organism, intrinsically differentiates itself into a pastoral side.

However, cutting short this potentially radical idea, Novalis suggests that the state's pastoral side is not actually political after all: "The queen has indeed no political sphere of influence, but she does have a domestic one" (Beiser 1996: 42). Yet her supposedly merely domestic pastoral realm *is* part of the state, on his own account: it is an intrinsic self-differentiation within the organic state. In denying that the queen's – and by extension all women's – roles are political, Novalis contradicts his own organic conception of the state. Whereas Hegel's exclusion of women from politics has roots in his organic conception and so does not merely reflect the prejudices of his time, Novalis's exclusion of women from politics contradicts his organic view and thus *does* reflect merely the prejudices of his era.

Because of his vegetal model, Novalis suggests that each individual is to be raised into direct political activity by their participation in either economic or family life. However, we can now see that he divides participation in those last two spheres by sex: family life and pastoral political work for women, for men civil life and direct participation in government. On this point again Novalis fails to pursue his own vegetal model of the state consistently. Since under that model each individual is to be raised through their everyday activities and self-identifications to "*general* participation in the state," as Novalis puts it, each individual should have full access to both family and economic activity and identities and to the forms of political activity and self-identification arising from each. When pursued consistently, the vegetal model pushes toward sex equality.

From Hegel's standpoint, a vegetal state would be defective. It would involve a merely immediate union of individual citizens with the state as a whole, rather than their mediated union by way of nested hierarchies. Yet that latter form of union is in some tension with Hegel's own idea of social membership which also flows from his organic conception of the state. We could resolve this tension in Hegel's thought by rethinking the organic state along vegetal rather than animal lines. Even if the resulting kind of state would contain more immediacy than Hegel would have liked, offsetting this is the fact that this kind of state would enable all individuals to achieve full social membership and thus would be more fully their home.

Notes

1. See for instance PR §200R, p. 234; §267, p. 288; §269, p. 290; §279, pp. 316–321.
2. Franz Grégoire (1996) also emphasizes that Hegel understands the state as organic in a sense that includes individual autonomy. Likewise, Charles Taylor (1975) stresses Hegel's organicism within his reading of Hegel as a specifically communitarian liberal, while Michael Wolff (2007) argues that Hegel's organic conception of the state has not only political but also epistemological roots in his idea of *Wissenschaft* (science/systematic knowledge) as the understanding of methodically self-unfolding wholes. Another recent (brief) re-examination of Hegel's organicism is Lambier 2008.
3. To be precise, Ross argues this only apropos of Hegel's Jena political writings (the *Natural Law* essay and the *System of Ethical Life*), in which, he maintains, Hegel argues that the most genuinely organic state integrates into itself the mechanism of civil society, which it regulates and organizes; such a state thus includes bourgeois freedoms, rather than excludes them as did the ancient Greek *polis*. But Ross argues that in the *Philosophy of Right* Hegel adopts a different view of the state as an "absolute mechanism" (a concept derived from Hegel's *Logic* where it primarily applies to the solar system): a set of mechanisms which regulates civil society. This, it seems to me, incorrectly reduces the Hegelian state to what Hegel describes as its "ethical root" within civil society (*PR* §255, p. 272), namely that sphere's regulatory and legal institutions plus the corporations.
4. I examine at greater length how Hegel thinks about nature and spirit in relation to gender division, and how he understands women's biological nature, in Stone 2010.
5. Neuhouser argues, however, that over time Hegel increasingly favored "the right of all (male) individuals to participate in social life as a family member, as the practitioner of a socially productive occupation, and as a citizen all at once" as a condition of full social membership (2003: 141–142). That is, Hegel understood organicism more and more in egalitarian terms, and so, Neuhouser suggests, the fact that Hegel nonetheless remained supportive of the patriarchal family shows that this support was merely an accidental consequence of sexism and was not held on philosophical grounds. But we could equally argue the reverse: that Hegel remained supportive of patriarchy indicates that he did not consistently go over to construing organicism in egalitarian terms. Moreover, there need be no conflict for Hegel between the ideas that most male individuals are limited to civil society *and* that they participate in social life both as *Bürger* and as citizens – for they achieve a limited, but still real, level of participation as citizens *just by* participating in the corporate life of civil society (through which they contribute to appointing representatives to the estates assembly).

6. *Glied* is Hegel's term for a limb or organ as an articulation within a fully realized organic system.
7. Hegel is drawing extensively on Goethe's 1790 *Metamorphosis of Plants*. Goethe identified how the parts of plants could assume one another's functions and thus metamorphose into one another, and he identified this as the principle of plant growth. Thus, he argued that the universal, common principle in a plant is not unitary form or structure but metamorphosis itself, as process, of which the different parts are more or less transitory manifestations. However, Goethe evaluates this metamorphic character of plants positively, whereas Hegel regards it as indicative of their inferiority to animals. See Miller 2001, esp. pp. 53–56.
8. Thus Schleiermacher inveighs against views like Humboldt's: "Whoever thus regards the most splendid work of art of humanity [the state], which elevates it to the highest level of its being, as merely . . . an indispensable mechanism . . ., must feel as only a restriction that which is designed to secure him the highest degree of life" (Beiser 1996: 192). (The artwork counts here as paradigm of a self-determining organic whole.)

Abbreviations

PR   *Elements of the Philosophy of Right*, trans. H. B. Nisbet. Cambridge University Press, 1991.
EM   *Philosophy of Mind*, trans. W. Wallace. Oxford: Clarendon Press, 1971.
EN   *Philosophy of Nature*, trans. A. V. Miller. Oxford: Clarendon Press, 1970.

Translations have occasionally been amended without special notice in light of Hegel 1969–1972.

References

Beiser, Frederick, ed. (1996) *The Early Political Writings of the German Romantics.* Cambridge: Cambridge University Press.
Brooks, Thom (2007) *Hegel's Political Philosophy: A Systematic Reading of the Philosophy of Right*. Edinburgh: Edinburgh University Press.
Deranty, Jean-Philippe (2000) "The 'Son of Civil Society': Tensions in Hegel's Account of Womanhood." *Philosophical Forum* 31(2): 145–162.
Grégoire, Franz (1996) "Is the Hegelian State Totalitarian?" In Jon Stewart, ed., *The Hegel Myths and Legends*. Evanston, IL: Northwestern University Press.

Halper, Edward (2001) "Hegel's Family Values." *Review of Metaphysics* 54:815–858.

Hardimon, Michael (1994) *Hegel's Social Philosophy: The Project of Reconciliation.* Cambridge: Cambridge University Press.

Hegel, G. W. F. (1969–1972) *Werke in zwanzig Bänden,* ed. Eva Moldenhauer and Karl Markus Michel. Frankfurt: Suhrkamp.

Hegel, G. W. F. (1996) *Lectures on Natural Right and Political Science: The First Philosophy of Right, Heidelberg 1817–1819, with Additions from the Lectures of 1818–1819,* trans. J. M. Stewart and P. C. Hodgson. Berkeley: University of California Press.

Humboldt, Wilhelm von, (1969) *The Limits of State Action,* ed. J. W. Burrow. Cambridge: Cambridge University Press.

Lambier, Joshua (2008) "The Organismic State against Itself: Schelling, Hegel, and the Life of Right." *European Romantic Review* 19(2): 131–137.

Miller, Elaine (2001) *The Vegetative Soul.* Albany, NY: SUNY Press.

Mills, Patricia J. (1996) "Hegel's Antigone." In Patricia J. Mills, ed., *Feminist Interpretations of G. W. F. Hegel.* University Park: Pennsylvania State University Press, pp. 59–88.

Neuhouser, Frederick (2003) *Foundations of Hegel's Social Theory: Actualizing Freedom.* Cambridge, MA: Harvard University Press.

Neuhouser, Frederick (2008) "Hegel's Social Philosophy." In Frederick Beiser, ed., *The Cambridge Companion to Hegel and Nineteenth-Century Philosophy.* Cambridge: Cambridge University Press.

O'Brien, William Arctander (1995) *Novalis: Signs of Revolution.* Durham, NC: Duke University Press.

Novalis (1960–1988) *Schriften: Die Werke von Friedrich von Hardenberg,* 6 vols., ed. Richard Samuel et al. Stuttgart: Kohlhammer.

Pateman, Carole (1988) *The Sexual Contract.* Cambridge: Polity Press.

Popper, Karl (1945) *The Open Society and its Enemies,* vol. 2: *Hegel and Marx.* London: Routledge.

Ravven, Heidi (1988) "Has Hegel Anything to Say to Feminists?" *The Owl of Minerva* 19(2): 149–168.

Ross, Nathan (2008) *On Mechanism in Hegel's Social and Political Philosophy.* London: Routledge.

Schlegel, Friedrich (1958–) *Kritische Friedrich Schlegel Ausgabe,* ed. Ernst Behler et al. Paderborn: Ferdinand Schöningh.

Schlegel, Friedrich (1991) *Lucinde and the Fragments,* trans. Peter Firchow. Minneapolis: University of Minnesota Press.

Stone, Alison (2010) "Matter and Form: Hegel, Organicism, and the Difference between Women and Men." In Kimberly Hutchings and Tuija Pulkkinen, eds., *Hegel's Philosophy and Feminist Thought: Beyond Antigone?* Basingstoke: Palgrave Macmillan.

Taylor, Charles (1975) *Hegel.* Cambridge: Cambridge University Press.

Wolff, Michael (2007) "Hegel's Organicist Theory of the State: On the Concept and Method of Hegel's 'Science of the State'" [1974]. In Robert B. Pippin and Otfried Hoffe, eds., *Hegel on Ethics and Politics*, trans. Nicholas Walker. Cambridge: Cambridge University Press.

Wood, Allen (1990) *Hegel's Ethical Thought*. Cambridge: Cambridge University Press.

Part III
Law

7

Natural Law Internalism

Thom Brooks

1 Introduction

G. W. F. Hegel developed a new understanding of natural law that departs
from both traditional and more contemporary accounts. Natural lawyers
defend standards that are external to the law in order to survey the merits of
law. Call these accounts theories of natural law *externalism*. Hegel offers a
very different account where we survey the merits of law through a standard
that is internal to law. This essay will explain Hegel's natural law *internalism*
and whether it marks an advance on existing natural law accounts. I will
argue that Hegel offers us a novel understanding of natural law that is
compelling, but ultimately unstable and problematic.[1]

2 Classical Natural Law

Perhaps the best statement of classical natural law can be found in *De Re
Publica* by Cicero:

> True law is right reason in agreement with nature; it is of universal appli-
> cation, unchanging and everlasting; it summons to duty by its commands,
> and averts from wrongdoing by its prohibitions. And it does not lay its
> commands or prohibitions upon good men in vain, though neither have any
> effect on the wicked. It is a sin to try to alter this law, nor is it allowable to
> attempt to repeal any part of it, and it is impossible to abolish it entirely . . .
> there will not be different laws at Rome and at Athens, or different laws now

Hegel's Philosophy of Right: Essays on Ethics, Politics, and Law, First Edition.
Edited by Thom Brooks.
© 2012 Blackwell Publishing Ltd. Published 2012 by Blackwell Publishing Ltd.

and in the future, but one eternal and unchangeable law will be valid for all nations and all times, and there will be one master and ruler, that is, God, over us all, for he is the author of this law, its promulgator, and its enforcing judge. Whoever is disobedient is fleeing from himself and denying his human nature, and by reasons of this very fact he will suffer the worst penalties, even if he escapes what is commonly considered punishments. (Bix 1996: 224)

There are several elements in this statement that are representative of classical natural law. First, natural lawyers make a distinction between "law" and "true law." Not all laws share equal standing. This is because not all laws are "true," which is to say that some laws are *more* law than others. We determine how close a law is to true law from the perspective of a particular point of view, namely, the standpoint of justice. The more our laws cohere with and embody the standpoint of justice, the more true our laws. Laws that are inconsistent with the standard of justice are not merely morally corrupt and unjust: they are not law, properly speaking. Thus, classical natural lawyers adhered to the maxim of *lex iniusta non est lex* ("an unjust law is not law"). Our laws may embody varying degrees of justice and injustice. Laws become more valid (and, therefore, more "true") the closer they approximate justice. Conversely, laws lose their moral authority the more they approximate injustice. Laws which are consistent with a standpoint of justice are more law (and true) than laws that are inconsistent with this standard. Indeed, laws that are inconsistent may not serve as "law" at all.

What serves as our standpoint of justice clearly plays a central role in the natural law account. This standard may take different forms. For example, the standard of justice employed may be theological in nature and claim that our view of justice should approximate the perspective of God's will. Natural lawyers, such as Cicero, argue that God is "the author" of natural law and we ought to draft our laws so that they are not inconsistent with the design of the divine (Freeman 1994: 130).[2] The authority of law then rests upon the existence of God. Justice is not merely something God might agree with, but something prescribed for all of us.

A different natural law conception of the standard of justice is based on reason. Following H. L. A. Hart, we might define natural law thus: "that there are certain principles of human conduct, awaiting discovery by human reason, with which man-made law must confirm if it is to be valid" (1994: 186). This perspective claims that the source of natural law is reason. We can employ our power of effective reasoning to determine the necessary features of our conception of justice independently of theological considerations.

God may accept the view of natural law we would want to defend, but our view is not dependent upon God's acceptance. Such a perspective is also found in the passage by Cicero above. For example, he says true law is "right reason." This idea is not unique and many natural lawyers since, such as Mark Murphy, accept that "natural law theorists claim that, necessarily, law is a rational standard for conduct" (2005: 15).

A further feature of classical natural is that often "true law" is understood to be universally and eternally true. For example, Cicero argues that "true law . . . is of universal application, unchanging and everlasting" (quoted in Freeman 1994: 130). If God is the author of what serves as human justice, then what God prescribes does bind us all. However, if our natural reason is the source of natural law, then its conception of justice is what binds us all instead. Either way, the normative source for justice as true law holds firm: thus, God's will and natural reason are not thought to alter over time. The only thing that does change is the relation between our laws and this standard of justice.

Finally, we should recognize that the standard of justice is *external* to our assessment of law (see Spaak 2003). The measure we use to assess law is an independent standard of justice. Such a conception of natural law is of a *natural law externalism*. We consider our law using external standards of justice that help us assess how "just" (or how "true") our laws are with a view to further reformation and amendment. Those laws most commensurable with our standard of justice are most "true"; conversely, those laws least commensurable are most invalid. We apply this external criteria in our normative assessment of law.

Classical natural law externalism then might be said to adhere roughly to five different criteria in its classic formulation:

1. We can distinguish between "law" and "true law."
2. We can make this distinction by the standard of a standpoint of justice.
3. Law is more "true" the closer it coheres with a standpoint of justice.
4. The standpoint of justice is external and applied in our normative assessment of law.
5. "True" law is universally and eternally true.[3]

We shall now turn our attention to a consideration of modern conceptions of natural law. While modern conceptions differ in some important respects from the classical conception, both share in being externalist conceptions.

3   Modern Natural Law

Before turning to Hegel's understanding of natural law, we should first recognize that modern natural lawyers offer substantive changes to the Ciceronian conception of natural law, although modern natural lawyers share in their endorsing natural law externalism. Modern natural lawyers share much in common with classic natural lawyers, although the former are more skeptical about whether any understanding of law is eternally "true" in any substantive sense. Instead of speaking about "true law," modern natural lawyers are more concerned with spelling out the conditions that might satisfy the establishment of a just legal system. Disagreement here centers on what conditions should be met, with most grounding their analyses in the use of reason, as noted above.

One example is found in the work of John Finnis. He argues that there are seven basic forms of the human good, including knowledge, play, and sociability (see Finnis 1980: 85–90). These forms may be discerned via practical reflection upon what basic forms of the good we might possess. We consider what these goods are and this helps structure his natural law theory: "they lay down for us the outlines of everyone one could reasonably want to do, to have, and to be" (1980: 97). Thus, we determine basic forms of the good first and then apply them in our consideration of law and legal systems.

A second example of natural law externalism is found in the work of Lon Fuller, although this may be controversial at least initially. After all, Fuller defends what he calls "the inner morality of law" (1969: 42). Such a view of law would seem to suggest that his natural law theory is a version of natural law internalism with a focus on the inner life of law rather than standards external to law that we apply. However, this is not the case.

Fuller highlights eight principles that any legal system ought to satisfy (see 1969: 39–49). These principles include our ensuring to "make the law known, make it coherent and clear . . . etc." (1969: 42). Fuller says that a "total failure in any one of these eight directions does not simply result in a bad system of law; it results in something that is not properly called a legal system at all" (1969: 39). The internal morality of law does not emanate and develop from within the law itself, but externally according to standards of reason and in response to circumstances. For example, Fuller gives an illustration of visiting a former Minister of Justice in Poland. The Minister had recounted how his government had endeavored to make the law clear and well known to citizens.

However, Fuller says: "It was discovered ... that making the laws readily understandable to the citizen carried a hidden cost in that it rendered their application by the courts more capricious and less predictable" (1969: 45). We balance adhering as best we can to our moral principles in light of the changing circumstances within which we work. The project is one of applying principles to the law that we determine independently of the law. For Fuller, we can determine the inner morality of law before we determine the laws themselves (see 1969: 33–39). This is further evidence that Fuller's inner morality of law is a version of natural law externalism. The inner morality concerns the moral principles that any legal system ought to cohere with, although these principles are brought to our analysis of law rather than located from within law. Indeed, Fuller also refers to his natural law theory as "a procedural version of natural law" (1969: 97).

This brief analysis of modern natural law theories is not meant to be comprehensive, but strongly suggestive. My aim has been to argue that, despite whatever differences we may find between classic natural lawyers and modern natural lawyers, many of them adhere to some version of natural law externalism. Each theorist offers different understandings of how we might determine the criteria for the normative assessment of law, but all make this assessment in order to apply it to their study of law. These are theories of natural law externalism. I have also demonstrated that even Fuller's internal morality of law fits comfortably within the natural law externalism family.

We will now turn our attention at last to Hegel's natural law theory. Our aim will now be to understand the important break his theory offers from natural law accounts that have been offered both before and since in order to highlight the distinctive and new understanding of *natural law internalism* his theory offers us. Let us turn to this now.

4 Hegel's Natural Law Internalism

Hegel's legal philosophy is widely understood as a natural law account.[4] My claim is not that previous interpreters have been mistaken in understanding his theory in this way. Instead, my claim is that previous interpreters have failed to acknowledge the distinctly *new* conception of natural law offered by Hegel. Thus, the commonplace consensus on Hegel's natural law theory is mistaken in believing that it is part of the natural law externalist family with which it has been associated.[5] I will attempt to make this case in this section.

Hegel's conception of legal philosophy clearly sits within the natural law tradition, albeit with a twist. This conception recognizes a strong link between law and morality.[6] An account of justice is required for a proper understanding of law: "To the Ideal of Freedom, Law and Morality are indispensably requisite" (Hegel 1956: 41). Law and morality are independent of one another; instead, they are interdependent with each other. Moreover, Hegel has a developmental conception of law in that law is thought to be more "actual" the more it embodies a specific form of normativity. Law is understood to be more valid when it best coheres with morality. For example, Hegel argues that "what is law [*Gesetz*] may differ in content from what is right in itself [*an sich Recht*]" (*PR* §212). Thus, slavery may be *both* legally valid *and* unjust (see Hegel 1995: §8R; 1956: 99). Law more greatly coheres with justice when law becomes an improved "realization" (*Verwirklichung*)" of "Right" (*Recht*) when law better embodies "Right" (Hegel 1971: §529).

Hegel regularly plays upon the ambiguity of the German for law using both *Recht* and *Gesetz*, albeit not interchangeably. Hegel often refers to either law or a statute as *Gesetz* while using *Recht* for true law or justice. These different ways of referring to law come together where Hegel claims that "actual legal relationships presuppose laws founded on right [*Rechtsgesetz*] as something valid in and for itself" (1995: §109). The difference between *Gesetz* and *Rechtsgesetz* is that only the latter is fully commensurate with justice. All other varieties of positive law (*Gesetz*) embody lesser forms of legal justice (*Recht*).

Hegel argues that our understanding of law is centered upon the law itself. He says that "what is *legal* [*gesetzmäßig*] is . . . the source of cognition of what is *right* [*Recht*], or more precisely, of what is *lawful* [*Rechtens*]" (*PR* §212R). Our assessment of law does not begin with a normative standard already in hand that we might apply to the law. On the contrary, we merely begin with the law as it is. Our normative standard arises from within the law itself: what is right (*Recht*) is instantiated from within what is lawful (*Rechtens*) (see *PR* §3R). Hegel says: "Law is part of the existing state of things, with Spirit implicit in it" (1956: 268). His view of law is an account of "the present and the actual, not the setting up of a world beyond which exists God knows where" (*PR* 20). Hegel accepts that law becomes more true (or actual) the better it coheres with a standard of justice. What is novel is that this standard does not exist independently of the law, but it is derived from our careful study of the law.

For Hegel, we should understand the internal development of law. Robert Stern captures this sense of internal development well where he says:

we can use here an "internal" notion of rationality, whereby it is rational to change from one outlook or theory to another *not* because the latter possesses the transcendental predicate of "truth" or "absolute validity," but rather because it represents a resolution of the problems, incoherences, anomalies, inconsistencies and limitations of the *previous* scheme or theory, and so constitutes an advance on it, in relative but not absolute terms. (Stern 1994: 151)

The progressive, immanent development of law might be best understood as the resolution of inconsistencies and anomalies within the law. For Hegel, a legal system may appear to be little more than "a collection without principle, whose inconsistencies and confusion require the most acute perception to rescue it as far as possible from its contradictions" (1999: 11). Nevertheless, the law can seek to resolve its own contradictions from within its own resources (see *PR* §216). Hegel says:

the progress from that which forms the beginning is to be regarded as only a further determination of it, hence that which forms the starting point of the development *remains* at the base of all that follows and does not vanish from it. (Hegel 1969: 71)

We develop our progressive comprehension of law from within the law's own normative content (see *PR* §31).

The development of law is a dynamic process. Hegel argues that "the scope of the law [*Gesetz*] ought on the one hand to be that of a complete and self-contained whole, but on the other hand, there is a constant need for new legal determinations [*gesetzlicher Bestimmungen*]" (*PR* §216, see §3R). He says further:

an advance of the analytic intellect, which discovers new distinctions, which again make new decisions necessary. To provisions of this sort one may give the name of *new* decisions or *new* laws [*Gesetze*]; but in proportion to the gradual advance in specialization the interest and value of these provisions declines. They fall within the already subsisting "substantial," general laws, like improvements on a floor or a door, within the house – which though something *new*, are not a new *house*. (1971: §529)

That which is *new* in any determination of law's normative content is only law's previously unrecognized content. For Hegel, law is a seamless web: we must endeavor to articulate the implicit, but thus far unrecognized, legal determinations from law's resources found in its normative content.

Our understanding of law becomes more rich the more these determinations are made explicit. Hegel's task is to help show us how we ought to think about the laws that govern us. Our law progressively coheres with justice the more we are able to fill apparent gaps in the law and to resolve law's own internal contradictions.

This task of gap filling and contradiction breaking in law's seamless web is the project of *codification*. For example, Hegel assumes that no community will be able to construct a timeless and unproblematic legal code on a first attempt. Legal codes are everywhere incomplete and unfinished collections, albeit some more incomplete than others (*PR* §211R). This task is "the work of centuries" and not to be achieved overnight (*PR* §274A). For Hegel, justice has its "existence [*Dasein*] in the form of law [*Gesetzes*]" rather than in "particular volitions and opinions" (*PR* §219). Law helps us all gain a "cognition of what is *right* [*Recht*], or more precisely, of what is *lawful* [*Rechtens*]" (*PR* §212R; emphases original). It is "a perennial approximation to perfection [*Volkommenheit das Perennieren der Annäherung*]" (*PR* §216R). This is not a reason to abandon law as a means of giving embodied substance to the law, but rather a necessary feature of any legal system that should be recognized (see *PR* §216).

5   Natural Law Internalism or Externalism?

We have now uncovered two different families of legal theories within the natural law tradition. The dominant family that exemplifies much of what we identify as "natural law theory" is natural law externalism. There is great variety within this large camp, but a common similarity: all member theories identify a normative criterion external to law and employ it in their assessments of law and legal systems. There is no one method by which such a criterion is determined, but all such natural law theories are theories that apply the use of some standard in their legal evaluations.

However, we have identified a previously unknown family of approaches that understand "natural law theory" in a different way. This family claims that the normative criterion by which we might assess and evaluate law and legal systems is to be found within the laws themselves, and is not external to them. This family is natural law internalism. Hegel's legal philosophy is perhaps the first example of natural law internalism, although there are other more recent examples as well.[7]

There are then two families of law within the natural law tradition: natural law externalism and natural law internalism. We might now ask which we should prefer. Of course, there are prospects and problems for each. Natural law externalism has been found compelling for many reasons. One reason is that we might believe that our laws are crudely designed rules by which to regulate society, often created piecemeal over time. Many of us might speak of law as a system of justice: after all, legal systems may include persons serving as "Justice Minister" or "Justice" (e.g. "Justice Thurgood Marshall"). We take part in court trials hoping that justice may be done and seen to be done. This view of justice rests on understandings of what justice entails, as well as how our laws may fall short of this normative standard. However otherwise problematic, it is easy to see the appeal of natural law theories for many citizens.

There are many important criticisms we might raise as well, although these may differ depending upon which conception of natural law we focus upon. One criticism is that morality and law are conceptually distinct: law does not have its status because it shares in some significant relation with morality. A second criticism is that natural lawyers too readily engage in moral criticism rather than legal argument.

Hegel's natural law internalism has much that we may find compelling about it. One is its addressing this common criticism of natural law. Hegel does not argue that external moral standards should bear on our evaluation of law, but rather the moral standards internal to the law itself. It is concerned with the common law's "making the law pure." Our focus is on the law itself and the normative principles that may be internal to it. This focus might best speak to the concerns of legal positivism because natural law internalism likewise centers its attention on the law itself rather than on elements outside the law.

Nevertheless, natural law internalism is also problematic. One problem is that natural law internalists have the problem of misidentifying internal legal principles. In short, their problem is that it is at best unclear if the natural law internalist finds what he is looking for only in the absence of an independent criterion. This worry can be spelled out in the following way. For example, our comprehension of justice must focus on the community's shared sense of justice and not on mere personal convictions: following our personal convictions would lead to our legal understanding becoming tainted (see *PR* §309). The community's shared view of justice is crucial to understand how Hegel views the progressive development of law toward justice. The movement of law to justice is away from a purely individualistic and non-communitarian conception of Right (see *PR* §§144, 260). Likewise, Hegel argues that judges should ensure that their own personal views should not interfere with their legal decisions for fear their decisions would be rendered "arbitrary" (*Willkür*) (*PR* §211A). Therefore, courts should seek to comprehend justice "in the particular case, without the subjective feeling [*Empfindung*] of *particular* interest" (*PR* §219).

But how do we ensure that a particular understanding of justice is internal to the law waiting to be discovered and is not a conjuration of our imagination? Proper safeguards seem unclear. Hegel does offer some guidance on how we might discern the development of Spirit in the world, but such a view rests on contentious positions on metaphysics and other matters that many try to steer clear of, not least, his defenders (see Wood 1990: 4–6). Natural law internalism may represent a new understanding of natural law jurisprudence, but it suffers from this epistemological problem of our ability to discern justice within law with safety.[8]

6   Conclusion

Previous interpreters have been correct to identify Hegel's legal philosophy as part of the natural law tradition. What has been overlooked is the way in which his legal philosophy offers a genuinely novel reinvention of natural law. We now understand natural law in a new light with the great majority of natural law theorists adopting some form of natural law externalism whereby a moral standard is determined externally to law and applied. Hegel's natural law internalism determines its moral standard from within the law itself. This view has the benefit of more closely satisfying legal positivist concerns that natural lawyers too often focus their attention beyond law. However, natural law internalism suffers from the problem that it is difficult to know whether the moral standards we identify are genuinely internal to law or we are finding what we were looking for in advance.

Hegel's understanding of law may have much to teach us about the tradition of natural law and the ways in which we might fundamentally reconsider how a theory may be part of this tradition, even if this view of law is ultimately too problematic for us to accept.

Notes

1. This essay corrects my previous interpretations of Hegel's legal philosophy (see Brooks 2005, 2007a, 2007b). My earlier view was that Hegel's view of law rested somewhere in between natural law and legal positivism. I no longer hold this

view. My claim now is that Hegel's position is not between the two, but offers a new understanding of how we might conceive natural law theory. This claim will be spelled out in what follows. Inspiration for viewing Hegel's legal philosophy as advancing a version of natural law internalism is inspired by Derrick Darby's (2004) discussion of rights as divided between rights internalism and rights externalism.

2. This perspective is similarly shared by Augustine and Thomas Aquinas: see Augustine 1998; Finnis 1998; Aquinas 2002.
3. These five features appear in many classical natural law theories, but my claim is not that they hold in all such theories. My primary aim here is to demonstrate that, whatever other differences may remain, all should be understood as versions of natural law externalism.
4. Hegel scholars who claim he offers a theory of natural law include Rommen (1964: 116); Paton (1972: 114–115); Brod (1992: 38, 79); Pinkard (1994: 177); Burns (1996); Weinrib (1996: 338); Thompson (2001: 42); and Knowles (2002: 128).
5. Examples of previous commentators who have claimed that Hegel's legal philosophy belonged to legal traditions such as natural law, the historical school of jurisprudence, Marxist legal theory, postmodern critical theory, or even transcendental idealist legal theory include del Vecchio (1952: 123, 125–129); Paton (1972: 114–115); Dias (1985: 384–385); Freeman (1994: 783–785, 838–840, 853); Salter and Shaw (1994); Hoffheimer (1995); Curzon (1996: 179, 212); and Douzinas (2002).
6. On the relation between law and morality more generally, see Brooks 2004.
7. One such example concerns an interpretation of Ronald Dworkin's legal theory; see Brooks 2007a.
8. This is to say nothing of the further problem of how clearly we might identify the developmental nature of "Spirit" (*Geist*) present within our laws.

References

All references to Hegel (1970, 1971, 1991, 1995) are by section (§), noting "R" for Remark and "A" for Addition where appropriate. All other references are to page numbers. Furthermore, all English quotations of Hegel 1970 are to Hegel 1991 (abbreviated *PR*) unless otherwise noted.

Aquinas, Thomas (2002) *Political Writings*, ed. R. W. Dyson. Cambridge: Cambridge University Press.
Augustine (1998) *The City of God against the Pagans*, ed. R. W. Dyson. Cambridge: Cambridge University Press.
Bix, Brian (1996) "Natural Law Theory." In Dennis Patterson, ed., *A Companion to Philosophy of Law and Legal Theory*. Oxford: Blackwell, pp. 223–240.

Brod, Harry (1992) *Hegel's Philosophy of Politics: Idealism, Identity, and Modernity*. Boulder, CO: Westview.

Brooks, Thom (2003) "Does Philosophy Deserve a Place at the Supreme Court?" *Rutgers Law Record* 27: 1–35 Reprinted in Brooks 2012.

Brooks, Thom (2004) "On the Relation between Law and Morality." *Associations: Journal for Legal and Social Theory* 8: 135–139.

Brooks, Thom (2005) "Hegel's Ambiguous Contribution to Legal Theory." *Res Publica* 11: 85–94.

Brooks, Thom (2007a) "Between Natural Law and Legal Positivism: Dworkin and Hegel on Legal Theory." *Georgia State University Law Review* 23: 513–560.

Brooks, Thom (2007b) *Hegel's Political Philosophy: A Systematic Reading of the Philosophy of Right*. Edinburgh: Edinburgh University Press.

Brooks, Thom, ed., (2012) *Rawls and Law*. Aldershot: Ashgate.

Burns, Tony (1996) *Natural Law and Political Ideology in the Philosophy of Hegel*. Aldershot: Avebury.

Curzon, L. B. (1996) *Jurisprudence*, 3rd edn. Q&A Series. London: Cavendish.

Darby, Derrick (2004) "Rights Externalism." *Philosophy and Phenomenological Research* 68: 620–634.

del Vecchio, Giorgio (1952) *Philosophy of Law*, 8th edn., trans. Thomas Owen Martin. Washington, DC: Catholic University of America Press.

Dias, R. W. M. (1985) *Jurisprudence*, 5th edn. London: Butterworths.

Douzinas, Costas (2002) "Identity, Recognition, Rights, or, What can Hegel Teach Us about Human Rights?" *Journal of Law and Society* 29: 379–405.

Finnis, John (1980) *Natural Law and Natural Rights*. Oxford: Oxford University Press.

Finnis, John (1998) *Aquinas: Moral, Political, and Legal Theory*. Oxford: Oxford University Press.

Freeman, M. D. A., ed. (1994) *Lloyd's Introduction to Jurisprudence*, 6th edn. London: Sweet & Maxwell.

Fuller, Lon L. (1969) *The Morality of Law*, rev. edn. New Haven: Yale University Press.

Hart, H. L. A. (1994) *The Concept of Law*, 2nd edn. Oxford: Oxford University Press.

Hegel, G. W. F. (1956) *The Philosophy of History*, trans. J. Sibree. New York: Dover.

Hegel, G. W. F. (1969) *Hegel's Science of Logic*, trans. A. V. Miller. Atlantic Highlands, NJ: Humanities Press.

Hegel, G. W. F. (1970) *Grundlinien der Philosophie des Rechts*, vol. 7, ed. Eva Moldenhauer and Karl Markus Michel. Frankfurt: Suhrkamp.

Hegel, G. W. F. (1971) *Hegel's Philosophy of Mind [Geist]: Being Part Three of the "Encyclopaedia of the Philosophical Sciences"* [1830], trans. A. V. Miller. Oxford: Clarendon Press.

Hegel, G. W. F. (1991) *Elements of the Philosophy of Right*, ed. Allen W. Wood, trans. H. B. Nisbet. Cambridge: Cambridge University Press. (Abbreviated *PR*.).

Hegel, G. W. F. (1995) *Lectures on Natural Right and Political Science: The First Philosophy of Right, Heidelberg 1817–1818, with Additions from the Lectures of 1818–1819*, trans. J. Michael Stewart and Peter C. Hodgson. Berkeley: University of California Press.

Hegel, G. W. F. (1999) "The German Constitution." In *Political Writings*, ed. Laurence Dickey and H. B. Nisbet. Cambridge: Cambridge University Press, pp. 6–101.

Hoffheimer, Michael H. (1995) "Hegel's First Philosophy of Law." *Tennessee Law Review* 62: 823–874.

Knowles, Dudley (2002) *Hegel and the Philosophy of Right*. London: Routledge.

Murphy, Mark C. (2005) "Natural Law Theory." In Martin P. Golding and William A. Edmondson, eds., *The Blackwell Guide to the Philosophy of Law and Legal Theory*. Oxford: Blackwell, pp. 15–28.

Paton, George Whitecross (1972) *A Textbook of Jurisprudence*, 4th edn., ed. G. W. Paton and David P. Derham. Oxford: Clarendon Press.

Pinkard, Terry (1994) "Constitutionalism, Politics and the Common Life." In H. Tristam Engelhardt, Jr., and Terry Pinkard, eds., *Hegel Reconsidered: Beyond Metaphysics and the Authoritarian State*. Dordrecht: Kluwer, pp. 163–186.

Rommen, H. A. (1964) "In Defense of Natural Law." In Sidney Hook, ed., *Law and Philosophy*. New York: New York University Press, pp. 105–121.

Salter, Michael, and Shaw, Julia A. (1994) "Towards a Critical Theory of Constitutional Law: Hegel's Contribution." *Journal of Law and Society* 21: 464–486.

Spaak, Torben (2003) "Legal Positivism, Law's Normativity, and the Normative Force of Legal Justification." *Ratio Juris* 16: 469–485.

Stern, Robert (1994) "MacIntyre and Historicism." In John Horton and Susan Mendus, eds., *After MacIntyre: Critical Perspectives on the World of Alasdair MacIntyre*. Cambridge: Polity Press, pp. 146–160.

Thompson, Kevin (2001) "Institutional Normativity." In Robert R. Williams, ed., *Beyond Liberalism and Communitarianism*. Albany, NY: SUNY Press, pp. 41–65.

Weinrib, Ernest J. (1996) "Legal Formalism." In Dennis Patterson, ed., *A Companion to Philosophy of Law and Legal Theory*. Oxford: Blackwell, pp. 332–342.

Wood, Allen W. (1990) *Hegel's Ethical Thought*. Cambridge: Cambridge University Press.

8

Hegel on the Relation between Law and Justice

Alan Brudner

1 Introduction

Nowhere in his writings on legal philosophy does Hegel systematically address the central question of analytical jurisprudence: whether the concept of law does or does not entail the justice of law.[1] Worse, his fragmentary remarks on the subject seem to assert contradictory positions. In his only explicit references to the issue, Hegel appears to take the side of the natural lawyer. Thus in the *Philosophy of Right* he writes: "That force and tyranny may be an element in law is accidental to law and has nothing to do with its nature" (Hegel 1967: para. 3). Less ambiguously, he states that "positive law has obligatory force as Right only by virtue of [the] identity between its implicit and posited character" (Hegel 1955, para. 212; my translation). If by "implicit character" (*Ansichseins*) Hegel means inherent or essential nature, then the sentence seems straightforwardly to state the natural lawyer's view that law's essential nature is Right and that a positive law discordant with Right has no obligatory force. Moreover, if law is a species of command distinguished by its entailing some kind of obligation to obey, then Hegel appears to be saying that a law discordant with Right is not a law. This would be an extreme version of the natural lawyer's insistence on the connection between law and justice. *Lex injusta non est lex.*

However, this cannot be Hegel's complete view, for he also says that "there may be a discrepancy between the content of a law and the principle of rightness" (Hegel 1967: para. 212). The principle of rightness, he tells us, is that "each individual [must] be respected and treated by the other as a free

Hegel's Philosophy of Right: Essays on Ethics, Politics, and Law, First Edition.
Edited by Thom Brooks.
© 2012 Blackwell Publishing Ltd. Published 2012 by Blackwell Publishing Ltd.

being" (Hegel 1986: 22). Hegel could not have thought that a law's discrepancy with this principle always annuls it as law, for he wrote that slavery, though wrong, was nonetheless appropriate to a primitive stage of human development at which the individual lacks awareness of its selfhood or free agency (Hegel 1967: para. 57). At that juncture, he says, "wrong has validity" (Hegel 1967: addition to para. 57).[2]

There are other examples. Much of Roman law, Hegel believes, was unjust in the extreme, and yet he does not deny it the designation "law"; nor does he deny that Roman laws permitting creditors to kill defaulting debtors and treating children as their father's property had "legal authority" (Hegel 1967: paras. 3, 175). Indeed, he implies the opposite, for he states that "legal authority" is the guiding principle of an autonomous "science of positive law," suggesting that the concept of legal authority is itself autonomous vis-à-vis the concept of Right, which proposition is just the signature thesis of legal positivism (Hegel 1967: para. 3). Hegel does not collapse positive jurisprudence into philosophy of law; rather, he concedes it an independent existence, and its specific difference from legal philosophy, he says, is that it takes for its object "authoritative law, all the laws that have validity in a state, and that have validity by virtue of being posited ... whether [their] content is rational and intrinsically just or ... extremely irrational, unjust ... and given by authority of external force" (Hegel 2002: 315). The object of legal philosophy, by contrast, is law that conforms to the concept of Right. For positive jurisprudence, Hegel says, "what is, is law," whereas for philosophy "only what is reasonable, what suits the concept is law" (Hegel 2002: 315).[3]

No doubt, the ambiguity in Hegel's stance would resolve itself if we could say that he regards the viewpoint of legal philosophy as correct and that of positive jurisprudence as incorrect. But alas, we cannot. The propositions "What is, is law" and "Only what is reasonable ... is law" seem contradictory, and yet Hegel nowhere argues that the philosophical viewpoint has it right while that of positive jurisprudence is mistaken. On the contrary, he suggests that both are right. Positive law may have "the form of being valid in a particular state" and yet be invalid from the standpoint of the legal philosopher because of its unjust content (Hegel 1967: para. 3). To have the "form of being valid" is not, in Hegel's view, to have a superficial appearance of validity, for he argues that the content of Right has the same form when it is concretized in positive law and enforced by the state. Thus to say that a law may have the form of being valid and yet be incongruent with Right is to say that an unjust law can have legal validity. Yet how can this conclusion be squared with Hegel's statement that "positive law has obligatory force as Right only by virtue of [the] identity between its implicit and posited character"? No doubt the statements are made from different viewpoints – one jurisprudential, the other philosophical – but how can both viewpoints be right?

It might be suggested along Benthamite lines that both viewpoints can be right because they ground separate disciplines having different objects. Positive jurisprudence, one might argue, orients itself by what is legally authoritative as a matter of fact, whereas the philosophy of law deals with what ought to be authoritative as a moral ideal. Problems arise only when the two disciplines overreach, one claiming that only the just is legally authoritative (Aquinas), the other that the legally authoritative is also morally obligatory (Hobbes). The first claim leads to anarchy, the second to moral quietism. Only if the "is" and the "ought" orient separate disciplines are legal authority and moral criticism of law co-possible.

Yet Hegel would certainly decline an offer of help from that way of reconciling the opposing viewpoints. He does not think that jurisprudence stands to the philosophy of law as positive description stands to moral prescription. That much is clear from his famous denial that his philosophy of law deals with what merely ought to be as distinct from what is already implicitly realized, as well as from his statement that the Right not only ought to, but must and indeed does, become effective in positive law: what is reasonable is also real (Hegel 1967: preface and para. 3). Thus the philosophy of law too deals with what is, because it holds that what is is inherently reasonable and indeed that *only* what is reasonable *is* without qualification – without admixture of non-being or finitude. But Hegel also denies that identifying what *is* law with what suits the concept or nature of law as an embodiment of Right entails either moral quietism or anarchy. It does not entail moral quietism because there may be a gap between law as it exists empirically and law as it exists "actually" or in its perfected nature, and this shortfall may be criticized. It does not entail anarchy because the Right held up by philosophy as unqualifiedly authoritative is the object of public science, not private opinion (Hegel 2002: 315–316). As against opinion, Hegel thinks, the Right has the same exclusionary authority as Hobbes's sovereign.

That said, Hegel nevertheless acknowledges that, although Right is no mere ideal, although it entails legal authority and must become effective through positive law, still, legal authority can exist without Right. Legal authority is a generic idea that can be specified both in the authority of legal determinations of Right and in the authority of laws evincing "violence and repression" or "the ineptitude of legislators" (Hegel 1995: 51). Its generic idea, we might say, is coercive power exercised by (or in the name of) an agent (who might be a natural or a notional person) who, for whatever reason (be it fear, blind trust, rational advantage, or insight into logical necessity), is accepted as commander, so that an order issued by this agent is obeyed just because the commander issued it and regardless of whether one understands why he issued it or agrees that the balance of considerations favors it (Hegel 2002: 315). That legal authority is a generic idea embracing both just and unjust instances explains why there can be a positive science of jurisprudence independent of the philosophy of law. Positive jurisprudence always orients itself by legal authority in the generic sense, whether or not legal authority actualizes Right, whereas the philosophy of law is specifically concerned with Right and its determinations.

Accordingly, Hegel quite clearly eschews the extreme natural law thesis that *lex injusta non est lex*. Yet he also opposes the legal positivist thesis that the concepts of law and justice are analytically disjoint, for from his philosophic viewpoint he states that only a law congruent with the principle of rightness has obligatory force. The question for discussion in this essay is: how can both positions be true? How can it be true at once that a positive law has obligatory force only in virtue of its congruity with Right and that there can be legal authority independent of the authority of Right attaching to just and unjust laws alike?

In what follows I try to answer this question by elaborating from Hegel's legal philosophy an account of the relation between law and justice. Because this account is not explicit in Hegel's texts, I have to construct a Hegelian position on the issue dividing natural lawyers and legal positivists from a variety of Hegelian sources. Not surprisingly, that position will synthesize the opposing views. The "notion" of authority in the sense of its ideal nature or perfection is constitutional authority under the concept of Right; but the logical process of the notion's realization through imperfect stages is part of the Idea of authority, for the notion would not itself be objectively authoritative without that process. Therefore, authority is neither identical with just authority nor disconnected from it. Whatever authority unjust rulers possess they possess by virtue of their partaking in some degree of the ideal form of authority, a discussion of which follows.

2   The Ideal Form of Mutual Recognition

The point of departure for an exposition of Hegel's account of authority is his idea of mutual recognition, a discussion of which appears in the section of the *Phenomenology of Spirit* dealing with the irruption of self-consciousness from nature (Hegel 1977: 104–119). Hegel presents an ideal form of recognition as well as a series of stages through which the form is imperfectly but progressively manifested. The ideal form consists in a certain kind of relationship between two free agents, both of whom claim end-status on the basis of a capacity to renounce every aim given by nature, self-preservation included. The relation is one of mutual subordination wherein the claim of each to end-status is objectively confirmed through the free recognition of the other. Instead of seeking to prove its claim by subjugating the other and making the other a means to its end-status, each makes itself a means for the other (recognizes the other's end-status) and yet is preserved and confirmed as an end in this deference to the other by virtue of the other's reciprocally deferring to it. Because the validation of a claim of end-status can come only from an independent other equal in status to the claimant, each must respect the other's independence for the sake of its own objectively realized worth; and each is confirmed as an end in bowing to the other by virtue of the reciprocity of the transaction. The ideal form of recognition, accordingly, is a relation of mutual subordination between two worth-claiming selves, each of whom recognizes the other's end-status for the sake of the realization of its own (Hegel 1977: 109–110).

Right and duty are products of this relationship. A claim of end-status is a claim to others' respect for one's end-status, but a claim is just a claim. To be confirmable as an objective right to respect, the claim must be capable of being spontaneously recognized without loss to its independence by the agent to whom the claim is addressed. Accordingly, only those claims of end-status capable of being recognized without self-effacement by other agents are valid claims, and only valid claims of right are rights others have a duty to respect. Duty is correlative to right, and both issue from an ideal transaction evincing the mutual recognition of worth-claiming agents.

The ideal's realization does not, however, occur all at once. It proceeds by stages through which the free agent progressively learns what the conditions of its realized end-status are. And this education of the agent to the conditions of its realized dignity is simultaneously the validation of the ideal form of recognition as the sole framework of valid worth claims. At first, validation is sought through the agent's solitary negation of the independence of things by means of an acquisition and consumption still driven by biological appetite (Hegel 1977: 109). The inadequacy of this unilateral and appetitive mode of confirmation leads to the awareness that validation can come only from the recognition of one's freedom by another free agent; and so we proceed by well-known steps through a fight to the death by rival claimants to absolute worth, to slavery and domination, to the mutual recognition of equals in a Roman world of private property relations grasped in the Stoic thought of natural law (Hegel 1977: 111–123).

What is important in this for our purposes is the following. First, each stage of the development manifests the form of ideal recognition in a defective but partial way; second, since the ideal form of recognition is itself validated as the structure of valid worth claims only through this process of learning, the process is itself essential to the form's validity as the form of right and duty. This means that each stage of the process generates as much of the full or perfected form of right and duty as the limited understanding informing the stage allows. Each stage realizes part of the conditions (negation of the independence of things, risk of life for honor, recognition by a living other, recognition by an equal) necessary and sufficient for a fully validated claim of worth. As a consequence, once a worth-claim emerges from the biosphere, there is no stark dichotomy between relationships of brute power devoid of normativity on the one hand, and relationships of perfect right and duty on the other. Rather, there is a logical continuum, each stage of which evinces a mixture of power and right that is purer than its predecessor, culminating in a clear solution in which arbitrary power is fully dissolved.

In the progress depicted in the *Phenomenology*, the end driving the movement is the isolated self's claim of end-status, and the goal of the development is the perfect validation of that claim. However, we should be able to construct a similar kind of progression if we take as the thing to be validated, not a right-claim of the private individual, but an authority-claim of a putative ruler. The question would then be: what are the stages by which a claim of authority by a would-be ruler is progressively validated? Each stage would satisfy a necessary condition of valid authority and so would constitute a partial authority, but only the stages together would constitute the necessary and jointly sufficient conditions of valid authority. Moreover, each stage would realize a potential for validating an authority-claim incubated at the previous stage and, in doing so, would create a new potential for the next stage to fulfill. Hegel himself never gave an account of authority's career – at least not explicitly. Nevertheless, we can construct one from his scattered remarks about the state of nature, about despotism and slavery, about rule through general and knowable laws, and about the rule of public reason.

3   Hegel's State of Nature

The concept of a state of nature plays a minor role in Hegel's political philosophy. This is so because Hegel is not a social contract thinker who, like Locke and Kant, thinks that human beings have rights outside of political society and that political authority is justified only as protecting or actualizing these already minted (or nearly minted) rights.[4] For Hegel, individual rights are embedded within a political community that recognizes the independent dignity of the monadic agent for the sake of its own confirmation as the agent's end; and so the political community sufficient for dignity is the *telos* of the human individual, not an artifact instituted by morally self-sufficient atoms.

Nevertheless, Hegel does speak occasionally about a state of nature. In *The Philosophical Propaedeutic* he writes that the state of nature is a condition of "violence and nonjustice for the precise reason that men in this state act toward each other according to their natures" (1986: 33). In the *Philosophy of History*, he writes that the state of nature is a condition of "untamed natural impulses, of inhuman deeds and feelings" (1956: 41). In the *Philosophy of Right*, he calls it a "state of affairs where mere force prevails" and where the "natural will" has free rein (1967: para. 93). The natural will is discussed in the Introduction to the *Philosophy of Right*. It is the will that is free only in form because the content of its choices is derived from impulses and inclinations the will simply finds within itself (Hegel 1967: paras. 10–20). The natural condition is one in which "the mental is plunged in the natural . . . [a condition] of savagery and unfreedom, while freedom itself is to be found only in the reflection of mind into itself, in mind's distinction from nature" (Hegel 1967: para. 194). In his Heidelberg lectures, Hegel reportedly said: "rather is it the case that a state that could be described as a state of nature would be one wherein there were no such things as right and wrong because spirit had not yet attained to the thought of its freedom (and it is only with this thought that right and wrong begin)" (Hegel 1995: 53).

From this we can glean the following. In a state of nature, there is no possibility of right and wrong. But this not (as Hobbes thought) because each person has a natural right to do with other persons what it pleases; nor is it (as Locke and Kant thought) because, though each person's right is limited by another's, each is judge of whether an action is right or wrong. Rather, no rights or wrongs exist in a state of nature because there are no *persons* in that state whom one could wrong. No one lays claims to a dignified status that others must respect or could disrespect. This is because no human animal has yet attained a consciousness of its free agency; everyone is sunk in biological existence. Accordingly, each simply aims at the satisfaction of appetites he finds within himself, exercises force to obtain satisfaction when he believes this would be advantageous, and resists or suffers the force of others, exactly as other animals do.

The state of nature is thus pre-moral. It stands to norms as prehistory stands to history. It is not necessarily a state of ongoing violence, for it may be that individuals regard themselves as too equal to fight safely. But it is a constant state of incipient violence, because aggression is always an eligible means of achieving one's ends; there is no norm against it. Though savage, therefore, the state of nature can be considered from one point of view as a state of innocence, because there is no consciousness of a norm in whose light human beings could be judged or feel themselves inadequate. From another viewpoint, however, the natural state may be considered a state of evil, because human beings in that state are not the free beings they are potentially and ought to become (Hegel 1967: para. 18). "Freedom," Hegel writes," as the ideal of that which is original and natural, does not exist as original and natural" (1956: 40).

For Hegel, accordingly, the state of nature is not a thought experiment as opposed to an actual anthropological condition. It is not a modern Western society of right-claiming persons abstracted from a sovereign authority and assumed to be the natural condition of humanity. Rather, it is a prehistoric condition in which human relations are driven by biological need and in which an understanding of right and wrong has not yet emerged – a kind of childhood of the human race (Hegel 2002: 304). Because there are no norms, there are no stable ethical relationships. There are families but their bond is the natural feeling that also exists in other animals and that is inherently fleeting and changeable (Hegel 1956: 42, 59).

Though an anthropological condition, however, Hegel's state of nature is unlike Rousseau's idealized picture thereof, in that it is not a condition of primitive autonomy in which human beings have simple needs they can satisfy on their own and which it is their misfortune to have lost. Natural impulses may be moderate or immoderate depending on individual temperament. Since there is no opposed will to curb them, they will seek the maximum satisfaction circumstances permit (Hegel 1967: paras. 17, 20). They will also find outlet in barbarous practices – cannibalism, for example – because the natural will has no sense of a cardinal distinction between human beings and other animals. Accordingly, Hegel rejects the idea that appetites become immoderate only through the vices of pride and vanity acquired in civil society. Indeed, he even denies that the desires spawned by *amour propre* are unambiguously lamentable. For Hegel, the sophisticated mental wants engendered by society and depreciated by Rousseau are wants generated by freedom, signifying humanity's liberation from physical necessity (Hegel 1967: para. 194).

As Hegel's conception of the natural state differs from that of his predecessors, so too does his view of the state of nature's characteristic deficiency. What is uniquely defective about the natural state is not that each is insecure in his life, liberty, and possessions (this may also be true of some political regimes); nor is it that rights are unreal because each is judge of right and wrong and there is no public guarantee of enforcement. The defect is rather that the natural state is devoid of the consciousness of free will that is an inherent property of the natural will – of the will sunk in nature – and that makes normativity possible. The consciousness of free choice (self-consciousness) first brings a normative firmament into being, for it is the consciousness of an end – selfhood – standing outside the laws and ends of the biosphere, an end that is universal to *homo sapiens* and that can therefore issue "oughts" to the natural will. Since, moreover, human beings are destined by their capacity for free choice to live in a norm-governed condition, the only duty they have in a state of nature is to leave it (Hegel 1971: para. 502).[5]

What does it mean for Hegel to leave the state of nature? It does not mean to surrender one's natural liberty to judge wrong and to enforce one's proprietary and contractual rights to a sovereign judicature and executive; for that view reads into nature an implicitly juridical relation between free agents already juxtaposed to nature. Rather, human beings leave the state of nature when a claim of authority to rule erupts from the sphere of factual power relations and when the "hero" who makes this claim succeeds in getting others to acknowledge it (Hegel 1967: para. 93 and addition). The would-be ruler is a hero for no other reason than that he introduces into an erstwhile moral desert a normative claim – a claim to

authority or rightful rule. That the normative claim might be a rational-
ization of an urge to power is of no moment, for the important thing is that
the hero's private purposes accord with what human ethical development
requires; to reduce the hero's normative revolution to his psychological
motivations is to take the standpoint of the envious valet (Hegel 1956:
31–32).

The irruption of a claim of authority from the state of nature is no
miracle. For the natural will already implicitly involves, by virtue of its
freedom from external determination, a potential for renouncing biological
ends and for acting purely for the sake of demonstrating one's indifference
to them. This potential in turn reveals an end not given by nature – namely,
the self who can renounce biological ends and make radical freedom its goal.
And the existence of an end transcendent of nature makes rule over nature
possible. The hero is someone who realizes the natural will's potential for
disentangling itself from biological drives, who thus becomes conscious of
his own end-status, and who thus claims a right that others acknowledge
him as the end of their biological lives. Moreover, argues Hegel, the
authority-claimant has a "right of heroes" to subdue others to his rule
because his force now serves a claim of authority for a non-natural end
rather than the satisfaction of natural appetite; and so it effects an exodus
from the moral wasteland of the state of nature.[6] Still, this is not a Kantian
right of heroes to coerce others into a rightful condition. Rather, the hero's
force is sufficiently justified by its bringing into being a relationship of
authority and obedience, for there can be no condition of justice unless there
is first a condition of normativity (Hegel 1956: 39). Thus, the hero who
inaugurates a normative world is justified in his force even if the authority he
exercises is unbounded.

Let us examine more closely the basis of the hero's claim of right to rule
others. Historically, the criterion is indeterminate. In ancient Greece, says
Hegel, the first rulers claimed authority from "superiority in riches,
possessions, martial accoutrements, personal bravery, pre-eminence in
insight and wisdom, and lastly, in descent and ancestry" (1956: 229).
Logically or systematically, however, the basis of the first ruler's title to rule
is specific: it is his uncompromising commitment to the freedom from
natural ends as manifested in his willingness to fight to the death to win
others' recognition of his end-status – that is to say, in his readiness to die
for the non-natural end of glory (Hegel 1977: 113–115). His willingness to
stake all for the sake of others' recognition of his distinction is what
underlies the hero's claim to rule, and those who yield to his force do so

because they prefer life in subjection to a ruler to risking death for pre-eminence.

In yielding, however, the defeated do not simply give way for the time being to physically overpowering force. Rather, they acknowledge the ruler's claim to rule on the basis of his having achieved a liberation from nature that they have not accomplished, yet sense is their own inner potential, something they ought to accomplish. We can say that the subject accepts the hero's rule out of awe for his valor. He, not they, has shown the radical freedom of which humanity is capable. But then theirs is a voluntary submission to an ideal that partakes of the pure form of recognition and that therefore gives a partial validation to the ruler's claim to rule. An authority, albeit a rudimentary one, has come into being.

4   *De Facto* Authority

The normative condition inaugurated by the hero's subordination of others to his rule may be called a condition of *de facto* authority. It is a condition of authority because, as we have seen, it realizes a claim of authority through the voluntary acceptance by the ruled of the hero's spiritual title to rule.[7] It is a condition of *de facto* authority because the ruler's claim of authority is validated by an ongoing factual obedience to his commands and nothing more. It is not validated by autonomous acceptance, because the hero's subjects are not autonomous agents acting from self-authored ends. They are natural wills following their appetites. True, their submission is voluntary, for (whether they know it or not) they have freedom of choice, and they chose to submit out of admiration for the hero; indeed, this is why their acceptance partakes minimally of the ideal form of recognition conferring a particle of authority on the ruler. Nevertheless, their acceptance is not that of beings aware of their capacity to set ends for themselves, and so it is the acceptance, not of autonomous subjects, but of subjects sunk in natural life.

At this point, therefore, the relation between ruler and ruled is one between despot and slave. The despot is not necessarily a tyrant who rules solely in his private self-interest; he may rule also for the benefit of his slaves. The distinguishing mark of this stage of authority, however, is that, while the ruled recognize the freedom and end-status of the ruler, the ruler recognizes no end-status in the ruled, and so there is no normative stature in the ruled capable of limiting the ruler's rule. Consequently, the ruler cannot wrong those subject to his authority; that is what makes him a despot. Moreover, the fact that no norm exists to restrain the despot's liberty means that the moral void or barbarism of the state of nature – the state of mere factual power – persists almost unmitigated in a condition of *de facto* authority. The ruler may do as he pleases with the subject; the subject may resist the ruler's force as soon as it is prepared to risk death for freedom. The vast room left for unaccountable power is the obverse of the thinness of the normativity of *de facto* authority.

Nevertheless, there is a particle of authority in the relation between despot and slave. It consists in the slave's duty to obey the despot until he develops an awareness of his own capacity to set ends for himself and can thus disobey on the principled ground of his unfitness for slavery (Hegel 1967: para. 57). He may not disobey merely to satisfy an impulse of the natural will. Moreover, this temporary duty to obey holds even if the despot is a tyrant. This is so because the despot's particle of authority issues from a voluntary recognition of a claim of authority under a non-natural end, not from the ruler's partial virtue or from his claim of authority under a partial conception of a common good. That is to say, there is normativity here just because the despot–slave relation minimally partakes of the form of mutual recognition.[8] One human being claims a right to rule others based on his unique liberation from nature and attracts their admiration by displaying valor. In that he attracts rather than overpowers, he defers to their volition. The addressees of the authority-claim voluntarily accept it because they acknowledge that an autonomous self is entitled to rule beings governed by biological drives. Acceptance of the claim by volitional beings of that sort gives the claim a meager kind of validation, and so the despot has a weak authority irrespective of whether he rules solely in his own interest or for the benefit of the ruled. His orders therefore also have a particle of authority irrespective of their content.

A despot rules over slaves through ad hoc decrees expressing his (benevolent or selfish) whims and settles their disputes through ad hoc judgments ungoverned by rules. He owes no duty to his subjects to rule through general laws, for the latter presuppose a subject with enough sense of its agency to interpret the ruler's generalities and thoughtfully apply them to its own conduct; and yet the slave has no such sense of its agency. Not having manifested a capacity for authoring ends, subjects are not wronged by being ruled according to ends entirely external to them. But that is what rule by ad hoc orders is. Such orders call for mindless compliance in the service of another's ends (even if they are another's opinion of one's own good), for there is no space for appropriating the

command through interpretation, hence none for thoughtfully participating in their implementation. Hegel tells us that rule through general
and knowable laws is a "right of self-consciousness," for it is a procedural
condition of the subject's imposing the law on itself (Hegel 1967: paras.
215, 132). But a subject capable of acknowledging the rule of someone
who does not acknowledge its own end-setting capacity has no self-
consciousness that could bear the right.

The condition of *de facto* authority is the worst manifestation of the
form of mutual recognition; hence it generates the weakest possible form
of authority. It is indeed a manifestation because, not only does the subject
voluntarily accept the ruler's claim to rule, but the ruler *wins* acceptance
through heroism rather than simply abducting and confining by force.
Thus deference to agency is mutual. Nevertheless, it is the worst manifestation because a claim of authority can be independently validated by
the addressee only if the addressee is an agent with ends of its own and
whose independent agency is respected by the claimant. It cannot be
satisfactorily validated by one who passively adopts given ends and who
does not identify itself as a free agent, for such a being cannot deliver an
independent validation.

Further, whatever particle of authority the despot has is dependent on the
slave's continuing perception of him as a hero superior in ethical achievement to himself as well as on the slave's own immersion in natural appetites.
Yet neither is stable. Once the hero warrior settles down to rule, he cannot
but revert to a life of pleasure because, there being no end-status in his
subjects to constrain his liberty, there is no law to do so, and so there is
no available content for his choices but the satisfaction of desire (Hegel
1956: 18). So the despot as warrior (Augustus) becomes the despot as
libertine (Caligula). This means that the despot cannot sustain the heroism
that attracted the subject's awe, which alone validated his claim to rule.
Because, moreover, the slave accepts the despot's rule only from a fear of
risking his life for freedom, the ruler's validation is entirely contingent on
the slave's continuing aversion to risk, and so too, therefore, is the slave's
duty to obey. But a duty to obey that is contingent on the duty-bearer's
remaining in a thing-like condition in which it ought not to remain is hardly
a duty at all. It is a duty qualified by the subjective condition that the
subject choose to remain in a state inconsistent with its human potential.
Correlatively, resistance is permitted on the weak condition that it assert the
subject's free personality. Once resistance of that type is shown, authority
collapses into merely factual power.

5   *De Jure* Authority

De facto authority contains the seeds of its supersession in a kind of authority more adequate to the idea of a valid authority. In *de facto* authority we have the idea that a necessary condition of valid authority is acceptance by a subject who could have chosen not to accept it. An authority-claim is valid only insofar as it is validated by the addressee through voluntary acceptance of the claim. This means that authority requires not only a deference of the subject to the authority, but also a deference of the authority-claimant to the volition of those he needs to validate his claim. The despot satisfied this condition. His deference consisted in his having abjured unilateral subjugation through the sheer physical overpowering of a weaker rival or through low-risk strategies relying on deceit and cunning and in his having instead won voluntary acceptance by displaying valor.

Still, recognition was lopsided. The slave recognized the end-generating (purposive) agency of the despot – his capacity to act from ends he sets for himself – but the despot recognized no purposive agency in the slave that could independently validate his authority-claim and set bounds to his liberty to do as he pleased. This was shown in the despot's rule by ad hoc orders, obedience to which can only be mindless and mechanical. In despotic authority, accordingly, we saw only the germ of the ruler's deference to the subject's agency. We saw a deference to the subject's volition but not to its autonomy, for the good reason that the subject had not yet displayed a capacity for acting from self-authored ends. Hence the validation the despot received for his authority claim was not a validation from a genuine other – from an agent with aims of its own – and this imperfect validation was mirrored in the slave's weak duty to obey. The slave was permitted to withdraw obedience as soon as he perceived a softness in the despot or sensed that he could act from purposes of his own.

Nevertheless, the potential for a better validation of the ruler's authority was incubated within despotic authority itself. By voluntarily accepting the rule of someone whose heroism he esteemed, the slave manifested a potential for acting from ends not given by nature, for his admiration for the ruler's autonomy showed that autonomy was also nascent in him. He admired the hero as his own ego-ideal – as the actualization of what was still only implicit in him. Were the potential not in him, he could not have admired an exemplar to the point of acknowledging its right to rule him. Moreover, the slave's service for his ego-ideal actualized his potential for purposive agency, for he no longer worked to satisfy his immediate appetites but rather to serve an ego-ideal – exactly what the ruler did in heroic battle (Hegel 1977: 118). Within despotic authority, accordingly, there develops a purposive agency in the subject to which the ruler can defer; and this potential for a more satisfying validation of authority through the autonomous acceptance of the ruled is actualized in *de jure* rule.

De jure authority perfects the potential for autonomous acceptance germinally contained in the slave's voluntary acceptance of *de facto* authority. *De jure* authority is a species of *de facto* authority distinguished by the ruler's ruling through fixed, general, published, and comprehensible laws rather than through ad hoc decrees. Here Hegel's model is Justinian, whom he praises for distilling and codifying the basic principles of Roman law (Hegel 1967: para. 215). In ruling through general and published directives, the ruler defers to his subjects' purposive agency, for he now leaves room for their thoughtful self-execution of his commands. Directives published in general but clear terms and having only prospective force allow the subjects to interpret the command and to judge whether their planned conduct is permitted or forbidden by the rule. As a result, subjects act not simply in obedience to the ruler's external ends but to the ruler's ends as interpreted and appropriated by subjects and self-applied to their own conduct. In this way, subjects actively participate in the ruler's executive power, and the ruler obtains a more satisfying validation of his claim of authority. That claim is now validated by a thoughtful obedience rather than a mindless one.

Correlative to a more satisfactory validation of authority, moreover, is a stronger duty to obey. The slave's duty was conditional on a subjective condition, namely, his contingent choice against risk, and so it could hardly be called a duty at all. As soon as he was ready to rise up, his duty ended. By contrast, the subject ruled by laws has a qualified *binding* duty to obey because his duty is conditional, not on what *he* chooses, but on the ruler's satisfying an objective condition for a verifiable authority claim. The ruler must rule through fixed, general, and knowable laws. Provided he does so, the subject must obey unless resistance is for the purpose of instituting a further objective condition of valid authority. Accordingly, normativity has thickened on both sides of the relationship. Not only does the subject have a qualified duty to obey a ruler who observes the procedural constraints of legality; the ruler can now wrong his subjects by ruling outside of general and published laws and by applying force to them in the absence of a proven breach of law (Hegel 1967: paras. 215, 222–224). No doubt the pleasure of the prince is still the source of law. Nevertheless, the requirement of ruling through law itself restrains princely license, for passions he would unhesitatingly slake in secret and against particular individuals might yield to fear of consequences if they could be pursued only publicly and generally.[9]

Here again the content of the ruler's laws is irrelevant to the ruler's *de jure* authority. The prince who rules through laws serving his selfish interests has an authority stronger than the benevolent despot just because his rule is accepted by autonomous subjects rather than by slaves. His *de jure* authority is simply a product of the grade of mutual recognition achieved in ruling through laws that subjects can interpret and apply to their own conduct; it has nothing to do with whether he rules tyrannically in his own interest or virtuously in his subjects' interest. A philosopher king who ruled for the common good through ad hoc decrees would not have an iota of right to be obeyed by persons, whereas a tyrant who ruled in his own interest through fixed, general, and knowable laws applied by subjects to their own conduct would have a partial authority (qualified by a right of resistance for the exclusive purpose of instituting a further condition of authority), and his subjects would have a duty correlative to that grade of authority.

If the ruler possessed only of *de facto* authority is a despot, the ruler possessed of *de jure* authority and nothing more is an absolute monarch (Hegel 1956: 44). Unlike the despot's, his relationship with his subjects evinces a kind of *arche*, for he rules not by momentary caprice but in accordance with fixed laws. Yet he is necessarily an autocrat, for rule that is *de jure* and nothing more evinces only a weak reciprocity between ruler and ruled and not even a germ of equality between them. The ruler rules through laws without having to serve the interests of the ruled; the ruled are subject to rule by law but cannot call the ruler to account for legislating against their welfare. Under merely *de jure* authority, accordingly, the relationship between ruler and ruled is still hierarchical. No doubt, the absolute rule of a few over many (or of many over few) is also hierarchical, but in this case the authority relationship within the ruling body would exhibit a reciprocity we have not yet attained. So, insofar as authority is *de jure* and nothing more, it is the authority of a monarch who, though he can wrong his subjects by ruling by extempory decree or by confining them without legal process, cannot wrong them by anything he legislates.

Thus far a Hegelian account of what may be called the internal morality of authority has revealed the procedural aspects of legality – generality, publicity, clarity, *nulla poena sine lege* – as part of that morality. But observe the contrast between the Hegelian account of authority's internal morality and that of Lon Fuller. Fuller explains the aspects of legality as being necessary for effective rule – for the subject's being able to comply with the ruler's commands so as to achieve the latter's purpose of subjecting the conduct of a multitude to the governance of rules (Fuller 1969: 33–39, 96–97).[10] As a consequence, his account of authority's internal morality (if one may call prudential imperatives rules of morality) stops at its procedural morality, for rule constrained by legality may be effective in securing compliance without serving the common good; at least Fuller makes no argument to the contrary. By contrast, the Hegelian account of authority's internal morality treats procedural legality as a necessary condition of a confirmable authority claim and hence of a duty to obey the claimant. Legality is necessary as that without which acceptance of the authority-claim by the addressee would not be an autonomous acceptance capable of validating it. On this account, authority's internal morality drives beyond procedure to substance, because, while the procedural elements of legality are necessary conditions of a confirmable authority-claim, they are insufficient, as we will now see.

Under *de jure* authority, there is a duty to obey general and knowable laws, but that duty is qualified by a permission to resist the ruler for the sole purpose of instituting a further condition of valid authority. What is this condition?

In ruling through general laws, the ruler defers to the autonomous agency of those who defer to his authority, and so there is a germ of reciprocity in the relation between ruler and ruled. But there is no developed reciprocity because, while the ruled deferred to the ruler's legislative say-so, the ruler paid no deference in his legislation to the subject's reason for deferring. For subjects who themselves act from non-given ends, that reason is no longer awe of another's emancipation from nature but rather the ends they autonomously project and whose secure satisfaction requires coercive authority under laws. The ruler acknowledged a duty to rule by general laws on pain of the subject's being absolved of a duty to obey (and his authority-claim becoming unreal); but he did not acknowledge a constitutional duty to legislate exclusively for the sake of the interest the ruled had in acknowledging his authority. For the ruler who is *de jure* and nothing more, any such duty is one of virtue, the sanction of which is bad conscience or ill fame. It is not a constitutional duty on whose performance the subject's duty to obey is conditional. So, while the subject owes a duty relative to the ruler's *de jure* authority to serve the ruler's interest in ruling, the ruler owes no reciprocal duty to serve the interest the subject has in accepting his rule.

Provided he does so under general laws, the ruler may enrich himself at his subjects' expense without constitutional penalty.

The want of full reciprocity under *de jure* authority constitutes an imperfection in the validation the prince receives for his authority claim. This is so because authentic validation must be uncoerced validation. Yet, where compliance with threat-backed law is the only mode of validating the ruler's authority-claim, that claim is never validated because compliance is coerced. No one would think that a parliament whose members feared reprisal from the ruler if they did not unanimously approve his rule could give a meaningful vote of confidence in the ruler. But that is the position of subjects under the *de jure* rule of an absolute monarch. Thoughtful or not, their compliance with the monarch's laws cannot constitute an objective validation of his authority-claim, because the ruler threatens them with dire consequences if they do not comply. And because the authority claim receives no uncoerced validation, subjects have no unqualified duty to obey a ruler who is *de jure* and nothing more. They may resist for the sake of a better authority.

The defect in *de jure* authority shows what a better authority is. It shows that the validation of an authority-claim must be the product of an interaction between ruler and ruled that is prior to the everyday interaction consisting of the promulgation of, and compliance with, laws and that is free of the coercion involved in that interaction. That is to say, validation and resultant duty must be the product of a constituent act (which may be a hypothetical founding act or a historical covenant, as Magna Carta was) whereby subjects freely authorize the ruler to make laws for them and to punish them for disobedience. Moreover, such a constituent act must take the form of a reciprocal covenant through which subjects authorize the ruler in return for the ruler's pledge to rule solely for the sake of the subjects' interest in submitting to his rule. This is so because, as we have seen, only another end can validate a claim of end-status. Authorization of rule by someone who treats himself solely as a means to the ruler's ends is not the independent authorization the ruler requires. It is once again the authorization of a servile being incapable of delivering an objective validation.

However, the subjects of absolute monarchy no longer treat themselves solely as objects for another. They are autonomous agents who act from ends they set for themselves and whose potential for doing so was perfected through compliance with general laws they could interpret and apply to their own conduct. Absolute monarchy has thus schooled the kind of subjects the ruler requires for an authentic validation of his authority claim.

Beings who treat themselves as ends will authorize a ruler only if his rule is exclusively for the sake of their common interest in submitting to another's rule. And the ruler will accept this condition because it is the condition of his authority-claim's being validated by an independent end and hence of the subject's strong duty to obey. For validation to count, the subject's submission to the ruler's say-so must be met by the ruler's submission to the reason for the subject's submission, whatever that reason is. Matthew the Apostle encapsulates the transition to the new order thus: "Ye know that the princes of the Gentiles exercise dominion over them, and they that are great exercise authority upon them. But it shall not be so among you: but whosoever will be great among you, let him be your minister; and whosoever will be chief among you, let him be your servant" (Matthew 20: 25). Princes as servants, subjects as masters. This marks the transition from merely *de jure* to legitimate authority.

6 Legitimate Authority

Legitimate authority is that species of *de jure* authority distinguished by a fully developed reciprocity in the relation between ruler and ruled. Legitimate authority perfects the germ of reciprocity incipient in *de jure* authority in that it is the product of an uncoerced covenant (whether hypothetical or real) between ruler and ruled whereby subjects freely acknowledge the ruler's authority on condition that the ruler acknowledge a duty to serve his subjects' common purpose for accepting his rule. Each is thus both end and means for the other. In this fully reciprocal relationship, there is also an equality between ruler and ruled, though only in germ. Both are equally ends for the other, but the ruler is so far under no duty to share his legislative power with the subject.

Where authority is legitimate and nothing more, the common interest the ruler is duty-bound to serve is non-specific. The subject is the author of particular ends, some of which many others share because they share a way of life or because the achievement of some ends – security of life, limb, and possessions, for example – is generally a precondition for everyone's achieving idiosyncratic ends. Where authority is merely legitimate, these shared material values are the only available source of a common interest for the sake of whose promotion the subjects submit to a ruler. Thus St. Augustine defines a republic as "an assemblage of reasonable beings bound together by common agreement as to the objects of their love"

(Augustine 1950: 19. 24). They may love wealth, security, national honor, racial superiority, or whatever. Authority is legitimate if, and only if, the subjects freely submit to a ruler on condition that the ruler acknowledge a duty to promote the values the subjects commonly prize and for the sake of which they submit.

Also indeterminate is the composition of the group to whom the ruler is accountable. The subjects who share an interest requiring submission to a common authority for its satisfaction and who are conceived to have covenanted with the ruler may be all those subject to the ruler or a part of all. They may define themselves in any way they choose. If they are a part, rule is legitimate as between the parties to the covenant but only *de jure* as between the ruler and those excluded from the covenant. Legitimate rule is thus compatible with the tyrannical (self-interested) rule by the parties to the covenant over those excluded – for example, by those of noble birth over commoners, property-owners over the propertyless, the propertyless over the propertied, or by one ethnic group over another. Accordingly, while normativity has thickened relative to merely *de jure* authority, it is still thin relative to just authority. A legitimate ruler may promote the interest of the part that authorizes him, and those subject to his rule do not necessarily have a duty to obey of the same strength. The dominated part may resist for the purpose of making their particular interests count for the ruler, whereas the domineering group may resist a dutiful ruler on the more onerous condition that their resistance aim at a revolution of a kind to be discussed shortly.

Under legitimate rule, the duty to obey is stronger relative to that under merely *de jure* rule. This is so because we have here for the first time an authority-claim that is autonomously validated by an independent end. The ruler is duty-bound to serve the shared interests of at least some of his subjects as the condition of their being able to deliver an independent validation. Because recognition is finally symmetrical, validation is authentic; and so the covenanting subject has an obligation to obey on condition that the ruler keep his pledge to rule through laws having nothing in view but the benefit of those with whom he covenanted.

In that sense, a strong duty to obey a ruler's laws is conditional on his laws having a certain content. But observe that the content need not be that of justice. It suffices for legitimacy and for the obligation relative thereto that the content of laws be the shared values for the sake of which a self-defined group submits to a common ruler. And those values may be not only indifferent from the standpoint of justice but also antithetical to justice.

They may be an interest in feudal privilege, in secure possession against the destitute, in despoliation of the rich by the poor, in religious orthodoxy against reformers, or in racial purity against the different. No doubt those excluded from the covenant have a weaker obligation to obey relative to *de jure* authority, one qualified by a right of resistance to compel a *de jure* ruler to take account of their welfare. But the members of the in-group have an obligation to obey their legitimate ruler qualified only by a right of revolution for the sake of constitutional rule under a public reason all agents could accept.[11]

Because ruler and ruled are now means and ends for each other, the form of government belonging to legitimate authority cannot be autocracy. Those for the sake of whose common interest the ruler is duty-bound to rule (whether some or all) must exercise (at least) a power of oversight and deposition to enforce the covenant. If, moreover, their reason for accepting rule is security of body and possession, they must reserve a power of consent to taxation and be able to call the ruler to account for extra-legal uses of force. So the form of government belonging to authority that is legitimate and nothing more is a mixture of monarchy (which can be an elective presidency or leadership as well as a hereditary kingship) and republicanism, though the republican element need not be democratic and need have no share in government beyond advice and oversight.[12]

If legitimate authority were fully valid authority, legal positivists would be right and natural lawyers would be wrong. There could then be laws carrying (for some) an unqualified jurisprudential obligation to obey even though the laws were contrary to justice as serving the exclusive interest of a part. There might be a moral permission to disobey, but the morality invoked would be external to the jurisprudential morality of authority and would therefore carry anarchical implications.

However, legitimate authority is not the climax of authority's career. While a constituent covenant between ruler and ruled is a necessary condition of valid authority, it is not sufficient, for it is also necessary that the covenant be of a particular type – that the interest for the sake of which subjects submit to a ruler be a specific interest. This is so because the independent validation for an authority-claim produced by all but one type of covenant is inherently unstable. Covenants between ruler and ruled that are unimpeachable as to their voluntariness and reciprocal benefit can reproduce *within the covenanting group itself* a condition of despotism over slaves in which the ruler fails to obtain recognition from independent ends. This means that legitimate authority can be criticized from within the jurisprudential morality of authority itself, without invoking the (so far) external standard of justice.

The gap between legitimate and valid authority is exemplified in the social contract described by Hobbes (1957: ch. 17). Under that covenant, in-dividuals surrender all their powers of independent self-rule to a common sovereign on condition that the sovereign serve their fundamental interest in felicity by securing civil peace. As Hobbes argues, the sovereign's rule is legitimate because conditionally authorized by its subjects in return for the conditions of "commodious living" (1957: 84). But because individuals traded their moral independence and self-rule for felicity, the sovereign is an unlimited ruler who, as long as he keeps the peace, cannot wrong his subjects by any official action; for when they alienated their powers of self-government to him, they authorized all such actions (1957: 112, 115–116). Accordingly, this is a covenant through which the ruler loses the indepen-dent subject it needs to validate its authority.

Hitler's authority over racially acceptable Germans was another example. This authority was legitimate vis-à-vis Aryan Germans, for they freely authorized Hitler's rule for the purpose of promoting their interest in national honor and racial dominance. Moreover, his authority was treated as conditional on his success, as the plots against his life once defeat became certain (not because of his crimes) attest. Though legitimate, however, Hitler's authority was also despotic *vis-à-vis the legitimating group*, in that Aryan Germans surrendered their moral independence to his absolute dictatorship, so that he could not wrong them by a purely personal rule according to his mercurial moods. They too alienated the independence that can alone yield an objective validation to the ruler's authority claim.

Hegel provides his own analysis of an interaction between ruler and ruled that, while producing legitimate authority, fails to produce valid authority. It is the interaction between monarch and courtier depicted in the *Phe-nomenology* (Hegel 1977: 313–315). The courtier recognizes the monarch's claim of authority through obsequious flattery and loyal service. In return, the monarch serves the courtier's interest in wealth and patronage. The monarch's authority is legitimate because conditional on his serving the venality of those who realize his authority; and yet it is not valid because, in abasing himself before the monarch for the sake of wealth, the courtier creates an unlimited ruler who once again cannot wrong his subjects. Since the monarch finds no validation in servile flattery, the duty to obey him ceases as soon as the courtier is ready to rebel against his humiliation, just as in the case of the slave.

Alan Brudner

We can generalize from these examples in the following way. To the extent that the constituent covenant between ruler and ruled involves a trading of the subject's independent self-rule for the satisfaction of some material interest, it reinstates a despot–slave relation incapable of generating a valid authority to which obedience is owed. This means that a further condition of valid authority is a specific kind of covenant through which, in surrendering its powers of independent self-rule to the ruler, the subject remains (as Rousseau says) as independent as before. But this is possible only if the common interest for the sake of which subjects authorize authority is independence itself.[13]

7 Constitutional Authority

Accordingly, we come to a species of legitimate rule that is distinguished by the subject's acknowledging a public authority on condition that the authority protect and respect its civil independence and right of self-rule. However, the only authority to which a subject can surrender without loss of self-rule is the authority of a public reason in whose legislative power the reasonable subject can participate and of which the ruler is only a minister and representative. By a public reason I mean a reason for submitting to rule that is universally and necessarily shared by beings possessed of a capacity for free choice and a potential for authoring ends. Such a reason is their interest in securing the institutional conditions for exercising the capacity and developing the potential. Because it is only to the authority of a public reason that a subject can submit without losing the independence needed to validate authority, no natural person can have an absolutely valid authority over others. Only incumbents of offices executing the legal determinations of public reason and answerable to public reason through courts and democratic legislatures may do so. In this way, constitutional rule under public reason realizes the equality between ruler and ruled implicit in the reciprocity of legitimate authority. Everyone is equally ruler because the public reason that is sovereign is everyone's reasonable will; and everyone is equally subject to the authority of public reason. For Hegel as for Rousseau and Kant, public reason is freedom, and Right consists of the laws that protect and promote it (Hegel 1967: para. 4).

It follows that the only authority relation conformable to the ideal form of mutual recognition is the relation between public reason and the individual person. Thus only the political authority of public reason is valid without qualification, and the subject has an unqualified duty to obey only those laws of a constitutional regime that have been confirmed by courts or democratic assemblies as instantiating public reason. This is what Hegel means when he says that "positive law has binding force as Right only in virtue of the identity between its implicit and posited character." He means that just laws alone have *unqualified* binding force. There is no further reason internal to the nature of authority to which one could appeal as justification for disobeying a command certified as consistent with the *Rechtsstaat.*

Observe, however, that just laws are the only laws binding without qualification for reasons internal to the juridical logic of recognition, not because unjust laws are immoral and so non-binding for the moral conscience. They are indeed binding to a degree relative to the grade of authority under which they are issued, though the moral conscience is free to criticize them. Because conscience is bound to accept authority in whatever degree it objectively (that is, measured by a standard of ideal recognition independent of morality) exists, Hegel's identification of absolutely valid laws with just laws avoids the anarchical implications legal positivists ascribe to natural law theory generally.

Observe, further, that authority's career intersects with Right only at its zenith and only after it has accumulated other conditions – namely, the procedural aspects of legality as well as legitimation by an implicit covenant with the ruled enforced through institutions of accountability. *De jure* and even legitimate authority (along with their correlative obligations) can exist without Right – that is, even though the authority serves the interest of a part; and a natural person who rules virtuously in accordance with Right through ad hoc orders rules justly but with the weakest of authorities: as soon as their autonomous agency dawns on his subjects, they may resist his authority for the purpose of compelling him to give them laws. If a natural person rules virtuously through laws but without being institutionally responsible to the ruled, he rules justly but not legitimately, and so the subject does no wrong in resisting his authority for the purpose of gaining institutions ensuring accountability. For Hegel, accordingly, that authority is alone valid without qualification which satisfies all the architectural necessities of authority, of which justice is only the capstone.

It follows that legal positivists are right to distinguish law and legal obligation from justice. But they are wrong to assert an absolute separation, for the legal obligation to obey a ruler's commands under despotic, merely *de jure*, and merely legitimate regimes derives from the varying degrees to which these regimes participate in the ideal form of mutual recognition; and so the obligation derives from the varying degrees to which regimes approximate the best embodiment of that form in rule through general laws approved by courts and democratic legislatures as determinations of public reason. Hence the obligation to obey rulers under imperfect regimes is qualified by a permission to resist for the purpose of compelling reforms that allow for a fuller participation in the ideal form. Only constitutional regimes under the authority of public reason can claim an absolute authority to which resistance is impermissible. So, while there can be unjust laws and legal obligations to obey them, unjust laws are laws only in a qualified sense, and the obligation to obey them is relative to the particle of authority they possess; disobedience is permissible for the sake of a stronger authority. The extreme natural law thesis is thus also both right and wrong. It is right to assert a connection between law and justice but wrong to deny authority outright to unjust laws and regimes.

Because legal authority of some degree exists in all the regimes we discussed, there can be an autonomous science of positive law geared to authority in a generic sense common to despotic, merely *de jure*, merely legitimate, and constitutional regimes. The meta-theorists of this discipline debate over what the generic sense of legal authority is. They search, not for the archetype or ideal notion of authority in which all types participate, but for the minimum condition of authority, a kind of lowest common denominator definition. Is authority the bare capacity to secure habitual obedience to commands? Does it exist if and only if there is voluntary acceptance of a meta-rule for identifying the commands of a legal system? Is it an exclusionary reason for acting prudentially followed for the sake of happiness or of realizing better the norms applying to conduct independently of authority? Hegel's philosophy of law claims no superior wisdom regarding such matters, and so it leaves the issue for the best specimens of analytical reasoning to resolve. But while Hegel's legal philosophy leaves room for an autonomous science of positive law geared to authority in the abstract, it still claims the title of master legal discipline; for its object is the absolutely authoritative regime by virtue of their participation in which other regimes have the authority they have.

Authority's development from despotism to constitutionalism is no more than its maturation from childhood to early adulthood. It is still far from the ripeness of old age. This is so because, while valid authority is constitutional rule under the public reason of freedom, there are several conceptions of freedom, each of which is capable of informing its own constitutional order. These conceptions respectively organize the three parts of Hegel's *Philosophy of Right*, which may be said to presuppose the entire preceding development culminating in the sovereignty of *some* conception of freedom. Thus, negative liberty informs "Abstract Right"; positive freedom organizes the part called "Morality"; while freedom in community presides over "Customary Ethics." Each conception of freedom disintegrates as a public reason precisely in being realized in an effective constitutional order; yet each is preserved as a constituent element of a comprehensive conception that alone satisfies the concept of a public reason. We can say, then, that the absolutely authoritative regime (obligation to which is unconditional) is constitutional rule under the conception of freedom that is alone adequate to the concept of a public reason. For Hegel, that conception is *Geist*.

8   Conclusion

I'll conclude by drawing out one concrete implication of the relation between law and justice as understood by Hegel. It concerns the dispute between legal positivists and natural lawyers over the nature of punishments meted out to those who committed atrocities under the authorization of laws valid in a jurisdiction at the time they were committed. Were these punishments inflicted under retroactive laws? Was justice done at the expense of legality?

The extreme version of the natural law thesis says "no," because the so-called laws authorizing the crimes were not really laws, and reasonable beings ought to have known this. The legal positivist says "yes," although the evil of imposing a retroactive punishment was perhaps outweighed by the good it did. The natural lawyer, according to legal positivism, covers up the evil and so fails to consider the moral cost of denouncing a greater evil (Hart 1961: 206–207).

The Hegelian account of law's relation to justice takes a view of this issue that is more nuanced than that of either the natural lawyer or the positivist. Someone who executes the unjust law of a merely *de jure* or legitimate authority executes law and conforms to the obligation relative to that type of authority. Still, if he is later convicted under the law of a constitutional democratic republic, he cannot complain of punishment under a retroactive law; for the obligation of obedience he invokes in his defense existed only by virtue of his regime's participation in the ideal form of authority, whose perfect embodiment is constitutional rule under a public reason all free agents could accept. The ideal form of authority is thus already implicit in the particle of authority a merely *de jure* or legitimate regime can claim and upon which the defendant relies; it is not an *ex post facto* imposition. Since, moreover, there is a logical continuum connecting the authority the defendant obeyed and the authority that convicts him, he cannot claim unfair surprise; the reasonable agent knows the connection. Accordingly, the accused cannot invoke his regime's authority in defense without summoning against himself the authority of the constitutional regime under which he is punished.

Notes

1. This essay develops ideas I sketched in Brudner 2004: 39–49.
2. In the *Propaedeutic*, Hegel says that laws permitting slavery are "only" positive laws "which are opposed to Reason or absolute Right." Nonetheless, they are laws (see Hegel 1986: 23).
3. I have substituted "law" for "Right" as a translation of *Recht* in order to avoid tautology.
4. For Hegel's critique of social contract theory, see his 1967: paras. 75, 100, 258.
5. See Hegel 1986: 33; 2002: 53.
6. So Hegel says that the hero's right is the "higher right of the Idea against Nature" (1967: addition to para. 93).
7. This seems to agree with Hart's idea that a rule of recognition accepted from the internal viewpoint of the subject is what inaugurates a legal order; see Hart 1961: 86–88. But Hart thought that everything more than this was external to legal authority and belonged to morality. We'll see, however, that the internal normativity of legal authority is much thicker than this.
8. In minimally partaking of the form of recognition, slavery lies at the border of the normless state of nature and a developing normative environment. Thus Hegel says: "Slavery occurs in man's transition from the state of nature to genuinely ethical conditions; it occurs in a world where a wrong is still right. At that stage wrong has validity and so is necessarily in place" (1967: addition to para. 57). And in the *Philosophy of History* he writes: "The origin of a state involves imperious lordship on the one hand, instinctive submission on the other. But even obedience – lordly power and the fear inspired by a ruler – in itself implies some degree of voluntary connection" (1956: 46). Thus, slavery is not part of the state of nature; it is the first step out of it, because the despot

claims a *right* to rule by virtue of his manifesting freedom, and the slave acquiesces in that claim out of awe for the despot. And that, however minimal, is an example of the form of recognition.

9. An argument made by Fuller (1969: 155–159).

10. Sometimes, it is true, Fuller explains the procedural requirements of legality as conditions of reciprocity between ruler and ruled; see e.g. Fuller 1969: 20–21, 61, 207–210. But as Jennifer Nadler (2008) argues, this move renders the restriction of law's morality to procedural morality unstable, for reciprocity is hardly observed if the ruler despoils his subjects according to law. See also Allan 2001: 52–87.

11. This qualification is explained further on. Of course, those excluded from the covenant may also resist for the purpose of instituting the rule of public reason. But those for whose sake the prince rules may resist the prince (though he abide by the covenant) *only* for this purpose.

12. Several variations are consistent with this form. For example, the republican body might assume the legislative power and leave the executive power to a king or president. In that case, if the republican body comprises all subjects or their representatives, the government is democratic; if a few, it is oligarchic. If a single individual has the legislative power and the republican body only advises and deposes, the government is a limited monarchy.

13. How is the validation of authority through an implicit covenant to recognize authority for the sake of the subject's independence consistent with Hegel's criticism of social contract theory? What Hegel criticizes is the political theory according to which morally self-sufficient atoms in a stateless condition constitute public authority for the purpose of protecting their pre-political rights. One may reject this theory and still hold that it is through an implied covenant (or mutual recognition) between authority and subject that individual agents fulfill their essential nature as members of a political community whose laws are laws of freedom. On this account, the covenant, whether hypothetical or real, occurs *within* a developing legal and political system (see Hegel 1967: para. 258).

References

Allan, T. R. S. (2001) *Constitutional Justice*. Oxford: Oxford University Press.

Augustine, St. (1950) *The City of God*, trans. M. Dods. New York: Random House.

Brudner, Alan (2004) *Constitutional Goods*. Oxford: Oxford University Press.

Fuller, Lon L. (1969) *The Morality of Law*. New Haven: Yale University Press.

Hart, H. L. A. (1961) *The Concept of Law*. Oxford: Clarendon Press.

Hegel, G. W. F. (1955) *Grundlinien der Philosophie des Rechts*, ed. Johannes Hoffmeister. Hamburg: Meiner.

Hegel, G. W. F. (1956) *The Philosophy of History,* trans. J. Sibree. New York: Dover.
Hegel, G. W. F. (1967) *Hegel's Philosophy of Right,* trans. T. M. Knox. Oxford: Oxford University Press.
Hegel, G. W. F. (1971) *Philosophy of Mind,* trans. W. Wallace and A. V. Miller. Oxford: Oxford University Press.
Hegel, G. W. F. (1977) *Hegel's Phenomenology of Spirit,* trans. A. V. Miller. Oxford: Oxford University Press.
Hegel, G. W. F. (1986) *The Philosophical Propaedeutic,* trans. A. V. Miller. Oxford: Blackwell.
Hegel, G. W. F. (1995) *Lectures on Natural Right and Political Science,* trans. J. Michael Stewart and Peter C. Hodgson. Berkeley: University of California Press.
Hegel, G. W. F. (2002) *Miscellaneous Writings of G. W. F. Hegel,* ed. Jon Stewart. Evanston, IL: Northwestern University Press.
Hobbes, Thomas (1957) *Leviathan,* ed. Michael Oakeshott. Oxford: Blackwell.
Nadler, Jennifer (2008) "Hart, Fuller and the Connection between Law and Justice." *Law and Philosophy* 27(1): 1–34.

Index

Absolute Idea, 9, 93
  see also the Concept
Absolute Spirit, 9
Abstract Right, 9, 11, 20–3, 26–7, 29–32,
  39, 44, 108–15, 119, 126, 129,
  131, 205
  see also Ethical Life; Morality
Act-Description Problem, 60–3
administration of justice, 108, 112, 120,
  132
  see also civil society; Ethical Life; family;
  police
Ameriks, Karl, 54–5
Anderson, Jami, 107
antinomies, 67
arbitrary will, 19, 110
  see also free will
Arendt, Hannah, 65
Augustine, 177, 198–9
autonomy, 44, 51, 68, 91, 94, 144, 161,
  187, 193
Avineri, Shlomo, 140

Baier, Annette, 94
Baron, Marcia, 25, 40
Beiser, Frederick, 157–60, 162
Bernasconi, Robert, 125, 135, 140–1
Bosanquet, Bernard, 117–18
Bradley, F. H., 93, 117

Brandom, Robert, 16, 40
Brentano, Franz, 90
British Idealism, 1, 121
  see also Bosanquet, Bernard; Bradley, F.
  H.; Green, Thomas Hill;
  MacKenzie, J. S.; Ritchie, D. G.;
  Seth, James
Brooks, Thom, 3–4, 66, 117, 120–1, 140,
  145, 176–7
Brudner, Alan, 4–5, 206
Burbidge, John, 140

Christian/Christianity, 15, 96, 145, 157
Cicero, 167–70
citizen/citizens, 4, 23, 125, 129, 131–3,
  145, 148–9, 153–4, 158, 160–1,
  170–1, 175
civil society, 36, 112–15, 121, 124, 126,
  129–33, 143–5, 148–54, 159, 161,
  188
  see also administration of justice;
  Ethical Life; family; police
communitarianism, 1, 161, 175
  see also liberal/liberalism
the Concept, 14, 16–18, 20, 24, 31, 40,
  92–3, 109, 152, 154, 156, 181–3
  see also Absolute Idea
conscience, 32–5, 37–8, 44, 52, 82, 129,
  196, 203

Hegel's Philosophy of Right: Essays on Ethics, Politics, and Law, First Edition.
Edited by Thom Brooks.
© 2012 Blackwell Publishing Ltd. Published 2012 by Blackwell Publishing Ltd.

consequentialism, 10–12, 21, 24–5, 28, 30, 35, 37–8
  rule, 13–14, 38–9, 41
  see also deontology; utilitarianism
Cooper, David, 1, 107–8
critical theory, 1, 177
Cruft, Rowan, 66

Dallmayr, Fred, 140
deontology, 10–12, 28, 30, 32, 35, 37
  see also consequentialism; utilitarianism
Deranty, Jean-Philippe, 145, 152, 154
dialectic, 15, 24–6, 30, 33, 35, 46, 80, 87, 108
  see also logic
disobedience, 197, 204
Dries, Manuel, 67
Durst, D. C., 125, 136–7

Eichler, Martin, 67
empty formalism, 3, 43–7, 49, 73–5, 77–8, 90
  see also Kant, Immanuel
estates assembly, 153, 161
Ethical Life, 3, 9–10, 21, 23, 28, 33, 35–9, 55, 66, 124–7, 129, 133, 137, 143
  Sittlichkeit, 54–5, 148–9, 151
  see also Abstract Right; administration of justice; civil society; family; Morality; police

family, 4, 23, 36–7, 45, 124, 126, 129–31, 138, 143–6, 148–55, 159–61, 171, 174
  see also administration of justice; civil society; Ethical Life; police
fascism, 124–5
  see also Nazism; tyranny/tyrant
feminism/feminist, 144–5
  see also gender; sex
Fichte, Johann, 21
Findlay, J. N., 107
Finnis, John, 170, 177
Foucault, Michel, 125, 137

free will, 13–14, 19–20, 22, 44, 132, 147, 188
  see also arbitrary will
Freyenhagen, Fabian, 2–3, 88
friend/friendship, 18–19, 22–3, 63
  see also love
Fries, Jakob Friedrich, 5
Fuller, Lon, 5, 170–1, 196, 207

Galvin, Richard, 89
Geiger, Ido, 91, 95
gender, 144–6, 152, 154, 161, 188
  see also feminism/feminist; sex
German Idealism, 157
  see also Fichte, Johann; Hegel, G. W. F.
Geuss, Raymond, 67
God, 35–6, 81–3, 94, 126, 159, 168–9, 172
Green, Thomas Hill, 117–18
Griffin, James, 94
Guyer, Paul, 95

Habermas, Jürgen, 137
Halper, Edward, 145, 152
Halter, M., 65
Hampe, Michael, 67
Hardimon, Michael, 149
Hart, H. L. A., 168, 205–6
Hegel, G. W. F.
  Encyclopaedia of Philosophical Sciences, 15, 21–2, 41, 96, 122, 178
  Natural Law, 2, 81, 96, 161
  Phenomenology of Spirit, 33, 41, 60, 67–8, 71, 75, 79–80, 96, 122, 184–5, 201
  Philosophy of Nature, 146, 162
  Philosophy of Right (divided into the parts of this book)
    Introduction, 1–3, 5
    Ethics, 9–11, 14, 16, 18, 20–2, 24, 32–3, 39–40, 43–4, 57, 60, 71, 81, 96
    Politics, 103, 107–10, 116, 118, 120, 122, 124, 126, 134, 141, 143, 145, 147, 153, 161–2
    Law, 178, 180, 186, 205, 208
  Science of Logic, 41, 104, 111, 122, 178

Henrich, Dietrich, 69, 87
Herman, Barbara, 40, 49, 53, 55, 57, 64–5,
    68–70
historicism, 3, 129
Hobbes, Thomas, 182, 187, 201
Honderich, Ted, 107
Honneth, Axel, 1, 41
Hooker, Brad, 92
Houlgate, Stephen, 69, 72
Hoy, David Couzens, 90, 93
Hutchings, Kimberly, 3, 140, 163

Ilting, Karl-Heinz, 1
intuitionism, 3, 74, 78, 81, 84, 88, 91–2
Inwood, Michael, 107

Jew/Jewish, 65, 69, 71, 94

Kant, Immanuel, 3, 10, 19, 32–3, 40,
    43–59, 61–70, 73–8, 81–2, 84–95,
    150, 186–7, 189, 202
  Kantian ethics, 40, 90
  see also empty formalism
Knowles, Dudley, 67–70, 177
Korsgaard, Christine, 69, 89–90

legal positivism, 175–6, 181, 205
liberal/liberalism, 25, 59, 125, 134, 137–9,
    147, 161
  see also communitarianism
Locke, John, 186–7
logic, 3, 10, 16–17, 69, 96, 106–9, 114,
    120, 125–8, 136–40, 145, 151, 154,
    161, 183, 185, 189, 203, 206
  see also dialectic
Loudon, Larry, 91
love, 23, 37, 50, 52, 68, 79–80, 144, 148,
    157–8, 198–9
  see also friendship

MacIntyre, Alasdair, 54–5, 68, 70, 179
MacKenzie, J. S., 118
Martin, Wayne, 66
Marxism, 1, 177
McNaughton, David, 91, 93

Mill, John Stuart, 83–5, 87, 94
Mills, Patricia, 145
Model Penal Code, 3, 119
monarch/monarchy, 124, 138, 158–9,
    195, 200–1, 207
Morality, 9, 26–7, 32, 44, 66, 81, 94, 108,
    112, 116, 126, 129, 131, 148–9, 159,
    172, 195–6, 200, 205
  see also Abstract Right; Ethical Life
Moyar, Dean, 2, 40–1
Murphy, Mark, 169
mutual recognition
  see also recognition

Nadler, Jennifer, 207
natural law, 4–5, 69, 94, 105, 167–77, 180,
    183, 185, 200, 203–5
  natural law externalism, 167, 169–71,
    174–7
  natural law internalism, 4, 167, 170–1,
    174–7
nature, philosophy of, 4, 79, 147
Nazism, 12, 65–6, 69
  see also fascism; tyranny/tyrant
Neuhouser, Frederick, 140, 147–9, 151,
    161
Novalis, 158–60
Nussbaum, Martha C., 95

Objective Spirit, 15–16, 20, 22, 24

Pateman, Carole, 144
Pelczynski, Z. A., 1–2, 140
Pettit, Philip, 24–5, 31, 40
Pinkard, Terry, 5, 140, 177
Pippin, Robert, 40, 140
police, 132
  see also administration of justice; civil
    society; Ethical Life; family
Popper, Karl, 146–7
postcolonialism, 135–8, 140
postmodern/postmodernism, 177
poverty, 75–6, 132
Prichard, H. A., 91
Primoratz, Igor, 107

punishment, 1, 3, 26–7, 36, 103–21, 126, 168, 205
  desert, 106–7, 112, 114–16, 119, 188
  expressivism/expressivist, 3
  retribution/retributivism, 3, 26–7, 103–7, 111–12, 114–16, 118–19
  unified theory of, 3, 103–4, 106–7, 118–20

Raatzsch, Richard
Rawls, John, 1, 68–9, 95, 106
recognition, 5, 22–30, 33–4, 37, 39–40, 83, 109, 128, 131, 133–5, 137–8, 185, 189–91, 193, 199–200, 203, 207
  mutual recognition, 5, 21–6, 28, 33, 37, 112, 148, 184–5, 191–2, 195, 202, 204, 206–7
reconciliation, 3, 54, 84, 88, 133, 149, 151
republican/republicanism, 124, 139, 158–9, 200, 207
Riley, Patrick, 90
Ritchie, D. G., 117–18
Robespierre's Inference, 17
Ross, Nathan, 147, 157, 161
Ross, W. D., 92
Rousseau, Jean-Jacques, 187–8, 202

Schlegel, Friedrich, 156–7
Schneewind, J. B., 82–4, 94
Seth, James, 117–18, 122
sex, 144–5, 152–4, 159–60
  sex equality, 151–3, 155, 160
  sexism/sexist, 4, 146, 161
  see also feminism/feminist; gender; love

Shklar, Judith, 1
side constraints, 2, 20–1
Siep, Ludwig, 40
Skirke, Christian, 67
the state, 1, 4, 17, 21, 23, 36, 38, 108, 114, 124–9, 130–5, 137, 139–40, 143, 145–7, 153–5, 157–62, 181–2, 186–9, 191, 206
  organic, 147–51, 156–8, 160–1
Stern, Robert, 2–3, 5, 47, 66–7, 172–3
Stillman, Peter, 107–8, 121
Stone, Alison, 3–4, 161
Stratton-Lake, Philip, 92–3

Taylor, Charles, 1, 140, 149–50, 153, 161
Timmermann, Jens, 64, 67
torture, 69
transcendental idealism, 177
tyranny/tyrant, 180, 190–1, 195

utilitarianism, 11, 29–30, 32, 78, 94, 127
  see also consequentialism; deontology

Verene, D. P., 1

Walsh, W. H., 58
Weinrib, Ernest, 177
Westphal, Kenneth R., 69, 91
Williams, Bernard, 11–13, 40
the will
  see also arbitrary will; free will
Winfield, Richard Dien, 134–7, 141
Wolff, Michael, 148, 150, 161
Wood, Allen, 67, 89–90, 107, 140, 152, 176